THE LITERATURE
OF
SHAKESPEARE'S ENGLAND

From an etching by Wenceslaus Hollar

LONDON FROM THE TOP OF ARUNDEL HOUSE (CIRCA. 1637)

This view is taken looking toward London Bridge, the arches of which are seen on right horizon. Just to the left of the Bridge is the Tower of London. To the left of the Tower are the great houses that lined the northern bank of the Thames. Under caption "London" is St. Paul's Cathedral, at the extreme left is the Hall of the Inner Temple

The Literature
of
SHAKESPEARE'S ENGLAND

By

ESTHER CLOUDMAN DUNN

Professor of English at Smith College

CHARLES SCRIBNER'S SONS

New York • Chicago • Boston • Atlanta • San Francisco • Dallas

FOREWORD

This is not a history of sixteenth century English literature. It has few dates and makes no claim to inclusiveness. I shall be content if the gradual evolution of old ideas into new, the changing values of life in this century of prelude to modern English literature, emerge. Sensitive authors like Wyatt and Spenser and Ralegh, even a genius like Shakespeare, were the alembics into which personal and national experience and the inheritances from a long past were poured. Out of them by way of their poetry and prose, a world different from that past was, I believe, distilled. In this belief and from this point of view I present the literature of Shakespeare's England. It is a view holding many implications for that future world which is our present.

The late Chief Justice Holmes said of the historian of the law: "nor will his task be done until, by the farthest stretch of human imagination, he has seen as with his eyes the birth and growth of society, and by the farthest stretch of reasoning he has understood the philosophy of its being." This ideal is as good for the history of literature as for the history of the law.

My obligations to the work of modern students of the Elizabethan Age are great. In this country such scholars as William Allan Neilson, Tucker Brooke, J. Q. Adams, Karl Young, E. E. Stoll, T. M. Parrott

and Douglas Bush, Theodore Spencer, A. C. Sprague,
Lily B. Campbell and Louis B. Wright have brought
and are bringing to the study of Elizabethan literature
important new methods. In England, Dover Wilson,
W. W. Greg, C. J. Sisson, G. B. Harrison, M. St. C.
Byrne have recently turned up a considerable body of
new material and new angles of judging that far-off
Elizabethan world. U. Ellis-Fermor, M. C. Bradbrook
and C. F. E. Spurgeon have provided a new æsthetic
approach to the Elizabethan dramatists. T. S. Eliot's
independent and provocative essays on the Elizabethans
have challenged my opinions at every turn.

The lists of reading in the appendix are in no sense
a complete bibliography for this book. They are intended as a reliable guide to the most illuminating books
on separate phases of the general field.

E. C. D.

Smith College

CONTENTS

ILLUSTRATIONS

CHAPTER I

Background: Values of Life in Sixteenth Century England

The values of life in sixteenth century England lie beneath the surface. That surface, spectacular and glittering, is easy to present. Who does not know about Ralegh's pearl-shaped ear-rings and Elizabeth's brocades, stiff with jewels? Who has not hungered and surfeited all at one sitting while reading the lists of meats, fishes, sauces, and cakes which the kitchens of some great country estate provided for a visit of the Queen and her hundreds of followers? Yet this colour and extravagance is not the real Elizabethan Age. That reality lies hidden by the obvious things which make the setting. The essentials of thinking and feeling do not assert themselves in any age. In the sixteenth century, they are particularly shy. Before one can attempt to draw them from their hiding, one must reckon with the façade of manners and setting which has distracted the attention of posterity.

The physical symbol of Elizabethan England is a renaissance town with a population variously estimated between 120,000 and 200,000 souls.[1] The city stretched

[1] T. M. Parrott, *William Shakespeare* says that the population of London increased from 100,000 at the beginning of Elizabeth's reign to double that number under James I. J. B. Black in *The*

along the north bank of the Thames. It was a blue Thames in those days, from which shot up a forest of masts from merchantmen lying there at anchor, ships not larger than a modern private yacht. Above this blue water, green gardens sloped down to landing stairs. Another band of green stretched beyond the strip of roofs that made the town. It was the green of the slowly rising Essex hills north of London. This is the skeleton of Elizabethan London. It has been preserved for us in the long panoramic maps of Norden and Visscher. These maps show the square steeple of St. Paul's on its little hill, dominating the centre of the roofline. The Keep of London Tower lifts its four stalwart turrets into the air at the east. London Bridge, a congested huddle of little shops and houses, clutters its way across this blue river to the Surrey side. London was a country town, as the Edinburgh of today is a country town. It was a town with its edges in green fields, yet a town which completely filled the imagination of all England.

Like other renaissance things, Tudor London was an overlay on the Middle Ages. Its mediæval city wall pierced by seven gates was no longer used, yet it stood there. Every land traveller must pass in and out through one of these gates. There were plots of monastic land in London, too, and disused religious buildings. In contrast to these, typical of a new world and a changing social order, were the substantial four-storey houses of

Reign of Elizabeth in the new Oxford History of England series, estimates the population of London at 120,000.

successful merchants strung along the Cheapside-Holborn thoroughfare. The old and the new world stood in friendly physical proximity. The parade of court society, of great names in the making of this new England, was announced by the row of town houses along the Strand, with their lawns and gardens sloping to the river. Here Bacon, Ralegh, Leicester, the Cecils, Essex lived, balancing perilously on the rim of success or failure. Westward of these mansions the gardens and orchards of the Queen's palace of Whitehall took the air spaciously. Beyond them the Thames curved out into the country toward Hampton Court and Richmond and Windsor.

This spot of earth, so crudely preserved to us in a few contemporary maps and some architectural drawings, with its fragrant pear orchards next to stinking open drains, its dark prisons abutting on great mansions, its princes and pickpockets, has had a magical effect not only upon its own world but upon ours. Historians and critics cannot resist describing it. They warm themselves into a frenzy of vividness. In their descriptions, prentices cry, great coaches lumber by and splash the foot passenger. In the taverns superlative wit and superlative sherris sack go together. The fringes of the underworld reveal picturesque crime. The night watchman with his bell, lanthorn and dog plods through the cobbled streets, hustling a belated party home to bed or calling out "All's Well." Young law students, soldiers from the low countries, sailors fresh from being wrecked on Bermuda, poets, potentates, and confidence men, all jostle and curse in the narrow, dirty streets. Out of every barber shop (and there seems to be one at every corner in the modern picture of London) come the notes of an Elizabethan "air" sung to the accompaniment of the public lute. Tailors, booksellers, tobacconists proclaim their wares. Executions or sermons, bearbaitings or plays are equally popular.

Behind these reconstructions of that far-away town, however, lies an unvoiced conviction that we can never catch its essence. What we think it was like is about as near the original as a costume ball. More than any later century, the Elizabethan world withholds from us the solid texture of its everydayness. There is not, for example, nearly enough left in the books and private papers about the life that went on indoors. The humdrum, uneventful sequence which, even then, must have made up the majority of their days is not often recorded. In their letters and books they have not the knack of being dull and commonplace, of letting down and being at the average, as the eighteenth century people had. One cannot imagine a *Pamela* or a *Tom Jones* being written then. They saw life as something either higher or lower than it actually was during the greater part of the time.

The moments which they did record are the unusual moments Their prentices are in a brawl; their honest shoemakers are just on the point of becoming Lord Mayors; their sailors and soldiers are overheard just at the height of their thrilling yarns; their Essexes and

Raleghs and Donnes write letters at a picturesque moment of exaltation or depression. The drab background of the merely ordinary escapes recording. This means that the Elizabethan life which is preserved in written record is falsely stimulating. It works upon the fancy of the modern reader. It tricks him into feeling that with such clear aid he can reconstruct the physical Elizabethan world, that the whole thing is just lying there waiting to be put together. But when he tries this putting together, the result has a false emphasis. Because the evidence is deficient in recording the unexciting side of life, the picture reconstructed from that evidence will be too gay, too spectacular. This is true I think of our modern conception of Elizabethan life. We miss the dullness which certainly did exist.

If we would restore the balance in our view of that age, therefore, we must not rely on their accounts of physical life. We must work on more intangible issues, on what were to them the underlying values. These are the things one finds out by implication, not by direct expression, whether one is studying the past or the present. The pursuit of them uncovers the essential reality. While this is true of all ages it is especially true of the Elizabethan Age and for the reasons I have given. Elizabethan diet or costume or London are relatively unimportant. Over these physical details time has a destroying power which it cannot exercise on the intangible but indestructible ways of their feeling and thinking.

These values of Elizabethan life are the essence of their literature. That is why the study of Elizabethan literature is so rewarding. In its accents and emphases, in that quality which corresponds to personality in an individual, it reveals to a modern reader the very form and pressure of that century. When I speak of Elizabethan literature, I use the word "literature" in the broadest sense. It includes everything that records their thought and feeling, that reveals the things which they sought, that shows the ways in which they felt or wanted to feel when cast among the rapids of human existence. I shall here at the beginning describe some of these underlying values. They can then be tested and scrutinised in the separate divisions of the book.

They were, for instance, concerned about the government and their individual relation to it. They wanted a world in which they could be themselves, work out their ideas, achieve their ambitions, make great men of themselves. The Elizabethans believed that the important thing was to make life full and keen, to have as much of it as possible. They resented the interruption of wars which might come as a result of international rivalry in trade, armament, and possessions. The mediæval system in Europe had, in its own way, been a kind of League of Nations. The differences and divisions between countries had been minimised because of their common dependence upon a central Church. Now all that had gone. The separate nations stood each for itself, seizing new power and new sources of wealth where and when it could. This independence fostered bitter rivalry and ambition.

In order to achieve this ambition, to make England a great nation with the minimum risk from war and internal dissension, the Elizabethans wanted a strong ruler. It is interesting that now in the modern world, people with the same sort of worldly ambition want a strong, central power, to manipulate resources, run public affairs and make the best bargain possible for the individual citizen while he is left free to dare and struggle for his own realisation. The realisations for the Elizabethans were somewhat different from ours but not essentially so. Business and trade were the foundation of an increasingly influential group. Money talked and great, or if not great, spectacular individuals arose in all ranks of society. They were men of capacity and force who knew that life was good and laid hold upon it lovingly and violently. "Personality" was at a premium. The spectacle of man subduing the world to his own ends single-handed, intoxicated the lookers-on. They felt, as we sometimes feel, that it was only a lucky accident that distinguished the great one from themselves. Their own fortune might turn up to the top of the wheel at any moment. These feelings and circumstances have, at long interval and with great divergences, their parallel today.

How man was made physically and psychologically began to be very important. This fearful and wonderful creature who could almost accomplish the impossible, was worthy of analysis. It would not do to ascribe his gifts to God. Rather were they explicable in some combination of liver and brain. They were affected by diet or weather or environment. For man's mental disorders there were prescribed restoratives; for his passionate seizures, clear explanations. The so-called psychological approach to problems of personality·and conduct had already begun.

They blended idealism with crass enjoyment of the material side of life. It would be an overbold critic who would dare to say that the discrepancy between their theory and practice was deliberate. It would be fairer to say that the discordancy was unperceived. Two different strands of thinking ran side by side in the same man because it did not occur to him to relate them to each other or pull them into accord. The Elizabethans were not "integrated." It was the fault of their innocence and youth. Opposing ways of viewing life could exist side by side in the same person because he had no time to gain a perspective upon himself. The "reception" of life was more engrossing than the sorting and constructing of its parts into a consistent whole.

Yet they were clever about the satiric analysis of their society. But the ability to analyse social types is different from the ability to analyse the contradictions within oneself. There is in Elizabethan literature a whole gallery of London types and London follies. Their satire is virulent but not despairing. In fact they were often gloomy about the issues of life and made their gloom vocal in poetry. Yet moving practitioners of this art, men like Essex and Shakespeare, had an eye on the main chance and a zest for the game of succeeding.

In such formative periods as theirs the method of education is constantly being discussed and constantly being altered. The sixteenth century is full of books on the theory of education. The number of schools and the number of children who attended them increased. Handbooks of new general methods of teaching and, specifically, new methods of learning foreign languages were available. Writers on educational theory studied child psychology. They pressed the need for considering each child as a separate problem, requiring a distinctive treatment. They also considered the studies which would fit a child for his struggle toward success in life. School curricula were chosen with a view to the individual's future. They were interested in educating girls as well as boys, and envisaged, though somewhat dimly, a possible career for women.

The Universities were a mixture of conservatism and radicalism. Old ways of thought, solacing the barren cleverness of the dons who had learned how to manipulate them, were in the ascendant. Yet there was a comforting minority in each of the Universities who leavened the lump. They professed daringly that some modern forms of art and literature were good. These as well as the conventionally approved literatures should be studied and enjoyed by the young people under their charge. These innovators in educational ideas had a tremendous following among the students. They sent them out into the world to batter against its follies and make the new time really different, more honestly expressive of its peculiar way of thinking and feeling than the old. Fathers were invariably frightened at this newness of doctrine and its effect upon their sons. But they were unable to stop it. The law school played an important part in the preparation for success in life. One's associates there and the technique one learned were both of value in getting forward on the road to preferment.

The Elizabethan Age was not in the formal sense of the word religious. This is a remarkable fact and one which reveals, by inference, the true nature of their world. The sixteenth century came at the end of a long procession of mediæval centuries where the religious habit was very strong in all classes, and the religious temper of vital importance. Yet the emphasis on religion was much altered in the daily lives of Elizabethan men and women. There were still a good many practising Roman Catholics, though they did not flaunt their allegiance. But the great majority were adherents of the new national church, the English Church of which Elizabeth made herself the head. Most of the people belonged in one or the other of these groups. They considered their religious life important but it did not dominate their existence. Their major exertions both in the material and spiritual realm were still by way of the world.

There was, of course, a vocal minority both among Roman Catholics and extreme dissenters. There were persecutions, investigations, elaborate systems of espionage, executions. Yet the prominence of these in the history of the times is the false prominence which spectacular events in the past always claim. If one judges from them alone one is likely to overestimate the religious fervor of the period. From the Queen downward through the nation, the approach to life was secular, not religious. That does not mean that there was no strong core of spiritual concern, no vivid, if intermittent, devotion to goodness, no keen sense that eternity encloses man's small plot of finite life. In fact the quintessence of life, how and when one could distil a drop of it from the midst of mortal accident and change, was a steady preoccupation of the Elizabethans. They did not, however, come to it chiefly by way of formal religious practice.

The circumstances which fed their imaginations were parallel to the same things by which our own fancies and dreams expand, and they sprang from an equally practical cause. In our world, the invention of the steam engine and the gasoline motor have led to labour-saving machines for households and to time-saving means of travel by motor and airplane. These are practical things, buttressing our material well-being, releasing our energies for further undertakings. Indirectly these practical inventions have expanded our imaginative life, have turned us into beings with a quite different sense of our earth, its variety, its distances. The Elizabethan developments in the art of sailing, the new knowledge of tacking and what it meant to sea travel, were comparable in their effect upon imagination to these modern developments in fast travel by sea, land, and air.

There were, too, the beginnings of new scientific discoveries in the field of mathematics and astronomy which, in their influence upon man's sense of himself in the universe, foreshadow the scientific preoccupations of the next century after Elizabeth, the seventeenth century. A few inquisitive and strong brains among the Elizabethans (Marlowe and Ralegh who were dabblers, Harriot and John Dee who were more serious) were already working upon these new emancipations of mind and universe. These men are interesting as a presage of what was to come but they are exceptional. The discussion of their work is not important in this present connection. This is partly because the knowledge of their discoveries is not yet clear; it is also because their investigations did not colour the fancies of the English world at large. They did not leave the half-humourous, half-worshipful impress upon the common mind that Einstein's work, for instance, has upon ours. But the scientific innovations in navigation and the management of sail immediately affected discovery and travel. And these, in their turn, affected the popular imagination.

The stimulus for this voyaging and discovery was practical. It was the desire to dominate the seas as a nation and thereby to facilitate trade. The travel to Central and South America was made with the idea of annexing territory for England, securing silver mines, building national power beyond the seas. It is reflected in the literature of that time. It stirred the romantic sense of distance and strangeness. It brought the accepted pattern of man and his world into stimulating question by its accounts of different men in a different-looking physical world. It altered one's outlook by its picture of new countries in which a man might grow rich. The voyagers themselves, pitting their skill and spirit against the tumultuous and vast sea, gave increased stature and importance to man and increased the sense of wonder.

In their attitude toward the human race, the Elizabethans were not cursed with a false humanitarianism. They were not sentimental about the incompetent unemployed, the stupid poor. They did not allow themselves for a single moment to indulge the delusion that all men are created equal. No period in history, however, was more sensitive than the Elizabethan to the importance of the remarkable individual. In whatever condition he might be born, he must have freedom to advance and enlarge himself. Consequently the Elizabethan world is full of brilliant self-made men, raised from all ranks of society.

For similar reasons, the thinkers of the sixteenth century were not interested in the communistic form of government. They knew about it, discussed it in theory. More's *Utopia* is only one of many such discussions. But they did not wish to see it practised. They believed there were wide variations among men and that there should be a proportionate variation in their opportu-

nities and accomplishment. They took their greatest joy
in the spectacle of individual effort, neither hampered nor
aided by a too strongly paternal government.

How the day felt to a man who lived in the Elizabethan world was, with a difference in every physical
object, not unlike the feeling of a day now. In London
there was a tremendous sense of movement. Everybody
seemed to be abroad, going somewhere, to the docks or
out southward and northward to the theatre or the fields
where archery was practised or to the taverns for re-
freshment and talk. One might be going to see a new
"motion" or puppet-show on London Bridge, or to St.
Paul's to meet a friend or post an advertisement or
merely to watch the world passing up and down the
centre aisle. The traffic in the narrow streets was slow
and congested. On the main roads leading in to London
from north and south, there were coaches, carriers with
country produce and solitary riders. On the river were
ranks of small boats with vociferous boatmen crying for
fares. They were ready to take one across to the Surrey
side or westward to the country or eastward toward
Greenwich and the docks. Everywhere people were on
the move.

Gregarious and mixed and restless one would have
called London life then. There was, too, a peculiar
sensitivity to rumours, preferably frightening rumours
of invasion or of civil riots or of the death of Queens.
Without the devices of morning and evening news or
"extras," one sensed with remarkable acuteness the

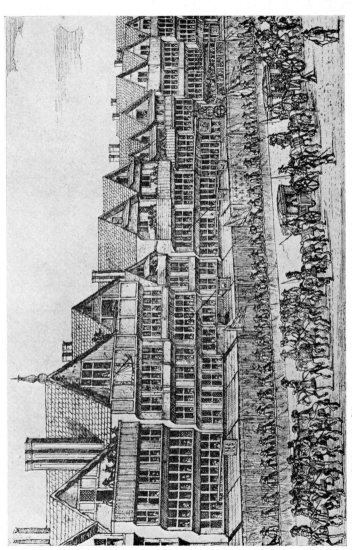

CHEAPSIDE, THE HANDSOMEST STREET IN LONDON

From Puget de la Serre's *Histoire de l'Entrée de la Reyne Mère . . . dans la Grande-Bretaigne*

flurries and scuds of uncertainty which blew across the routine of Elizabethan life. Lout or beggar or signed-off sailor from a recent naval fight, Inns of Court man or newly arrived Cambridge graduate, courtier or actor or master of bear-baiting, Privy Councillor or foreign ambassador or country justice up for the term of court, jostled one another in the ceaseless progress from one thing to the next. Life drove them, enticed them, challenged them, made them miserable or fearful. In whatever form it took, it stirred them so that they could not be still. In such an atmosphere one could reflect only partially upon the meaning of events. One must dovetail one half-digested impression with the next. The resulting view was blurred; it was only a half-focussed design.

All this is reflected in the Elizabethan plays. The life depicted there is always violent and usually public; in the streets, in taverns or theatres or shops, in far-away lands, on the battlefield. If it comes indoors it comes into a palace and echoes publicly in high ante-rooms or great dining-halls, or in the throne-room itself. If the scene is in one's private closet, it is always at high tension. One never loses the sense of a waiting, ill-disposed world standing on the public side of the private door, ready to pounce and tear the private passion to tatters. The reverberations echo through the halls and out into crowded streets. They rumble distantly in foreign courts.

Of course this impression is not the only one. There is also in the plays a reproduction of the life which goes on in sitting-rooms, in moonlit gardens, in kitchens, in dairies. Yet even here the people are not living placidly. Something violent is in the wind. Discord or glory is just about to enter the door. Among citizens and shop-keepers, the modest routine of daily life is constantly in-terrupted by Gargantuan feasts for hundreds of pren-tices or holiday processions or Sunday walks in troops through the mangy grass fields that lay on the edge of town. There are always eating and drinking and music. There is always a guest arriving or departing, or a half-known adventurer talking in tall phrases about some remote part of the world. Forever roused, forever un-satisfied, snatched up and whirled from one thing to the next, feeling a scene or a mood without having time to bring that feeling to the top of the mind and name it, this is the impression that their days give one.

This confused life, felt with merciless intensity, full of caprice, of incalculable ups and downs, of danger and death, was checked at intervals by calculation, by worldly wisdom and intellectual coldness. It gave the authors who tried to reproduce it a turbulent and provocative material. They dealt with it in a great variety of forms of verse and prose. Their plays are full of restlessness and violence. They show great extremes of fortune and feeling. Their satire is ferocious; their realism dis-torted. The lyric poets, probing this intensity, recollect-ing emotion in a fevered lull, turned it out again with a nervous, breathless piling up of image after image. They strove by comparing their intangible feelings to this or that tangible object, to name the unnameable, to stay the exquisite moment and make it lasting. They were not always successful or always intelligent in the methods which they chose. They often stumbled into dullness or absurdity. Second and third-rate people tried to write first-rate literature and were ludicrous in their attempt. But they were born in a time when life was so strong and success seemed so possible that the expression of this feeling in words was irresistible.

There is, allowing for tremendous differences, an essential resemblance in these matters between the Elizabethan world and our own. Working backward from us to them, translating our problems into theirs the modern person enlarges his present by familiarity with a sympathetic period in the past. Elizabethan literature becomes a reflector in which, with vast alterations and variations, of course, one sees more clearly the emphasis and meaning of our own time.

CHAPTER II

The Progress of Poetry across the Century

To discuss poetry which is removed from us by nearly four hundred years, is hard. This is especially true if one puts into a single category the whole range of expression in verse, lyrics, sonnets, songs, and verse tale. Yet the story of this miscellaneous thing, Elizabethan poetry, is moving. It is as adventurous, as high-hearted, as naïvely earnest, as unsure of success or failure as all the other Elizabethan enterprises. The curve of its progress across the century is full of dips and peaks.

In the first place, Englishmen were uncertain about the suitability of English as a language for poetry. Of course Chaucer, more than a century earlier, had written his poetry in English and his music was intermittently in their ears. But there were obstacles in the way of following Chaucer's English metrical scheme. The English vocabulary had changed since his time. There were whole strands of new words in the fabric of English, brightly coloured with the Mediterranean, in its ancient and modern guise. The words, furthermore, did not sound the same. They were differently pronounced. The stock grammatical endings which had supported Chaucer's flexible rhythms were disappearing. The whole cadence of English was different.

Furthermore Englishmen of the sixteenth century did not have the same set of values that the Englishman, Chaucer, had held in the fourteenth century. His ways of regarding secular and religious life had changed with the changes in Church and State. One thing that altered the nature of Elizabethan poetry was the change in the importance of religious feeling. As a centre of lyric expression it was losing power. Secular life on the other hand, as material for poetry, was becoming more important. The new renaissance man explored his private feelings untrammelled by his relation to family, class or Church. What he discovered in this private domain was a rich subject for poetry. The increased freedom for experiment in living brought increased awareness to the individual. The whole range of subjective feeling was opening, furnishing occasion for a kind of secular lyric poetry which had not really thriven in the world since the late Roman Empire. Thus the subject matter for poetry was very different from the subject matter of Chaucer's day. The English language had changed its actual form and necessitated a change in the use of metrical schemes. A new age was ready for a new poetry. To create it was a gigantic task. To the task the Tudor gentleman brought the energy to experiment. He might be a serious poet aspiring toward art. Or he might desire merely to exhibit a fashionable accomplishment, to show that he could handle a sonnet or a sword or a French slop as well as any civilised gentleman from the Continent.

When a project is so new, so self-conscious, so completely a "movement," it is almost like the erection of a new building, Renaissance poetry, upon a sixteenth century plot of ground. It is easy looking back upon it to be too dogmatic about the method by which it was built. One must not forget that it was a gradual process. The infiltration of foreign metres and conventions and their blending with English tradition and experiment cannot be neatly charted. The progress of the sonnet across the century cannot be plotted as on a blue-print plan. The experimenting and borrowing were likely to be modified by the particular moment in the century when a poem was undertaken or by the personality of the poet who undertook it.

The background against which the early Tudor poets wrote was interesting. The Reformation under Henry VIII had not only precipitated a generation of violent dispute but had physically left its marks. Many London religious buildings were in ruins and in Oxford and Cambridge hostels and dormitories (which had earlier been filled with recruits from Church schools) stood idle. It was a time when one might be asked to die for one's opinion and such a time breeds partisans, not philosophers. Thought and emotion ran close and mingled. There was too little security for detached study. Men stumbled through a muddle of mediæval and renaissance ideas. Seneca, Machiavelli, and later Montaigne were brilliant flares in the darkness but were never welded into a single philosophy. There was no clear steady light for the guidance of life. Besides this confusion in abstract thinking, the social world was muddled, too. The old aristocracy of chivalry was dying. Men of obscure birth became rich and powerful. Democracy was on its way to oust aristocracy with all the attendant blessings and scourges which we in modern America know so well. And there was always the menace of foreign wars.

It was this background which the poets of these years, roughly from 1530 to 1550, used. Wyatt and Surrey, as unfairly linked as Auden and Spender in the 1930's, are the best-known names in a group of twenty or more. Their fugitive pieces, penned on the backs of Parliamentary agenda of the day, copied by chance into private commonplace books of friends, were collected and printed in the middle Fifties, some years after most of the poets were dead, by the enterprising printer, Tottel. His *Songs and Sonnets,* familiarly known as *Tottel's Miscellany* appeared in 1559, in the very heart of the century.

At first glance the life, activities and point of view of men like Wyatt are merely representative and typical of the Tudor Court. They are all courtiers. This implies a uniform training, physical, mental and social. They belong to important families, grow up to public duties, are prepared for government at home or diplomacy abroad or military leadership in foreign wars. Their business cannot, by the wildest stretch of the imagination, be poetry. If they do write verses, they do it as a part of their social equipment, as an embroidery upon their leisure. The delights of this leisure, to fall in love, to meditate upon existence, they imprison in a poem which is like a filigreed cage of words and images and patterned sounds. The cage may be a sonnet knowingly adapted from Italian or French, giving to English experience the fillip of Continental style.

If one looks more closely, however, these typical, surface qualities of their poetry disappear. Take Wyatt. His outward life fits the conventional picture of the Tudor courtier. He was born in an influential family, studied at Cambridge, at twenty-three was on an embassy to the Papal Court. He saw Italy on the side, read Petrarch, was resident in that hornet's nest, Calais, succeeded his father in the Privy Council, carried out delicate negotiations with the Emperor Charles, following him from Spain to Nice to Brussels. He interspersed his foreign life with intervals in England where he moved in the society of the Court. His family, close to the Boleyns, was involved in the crest and trough of Anne's fortune. He may have been her lover, before and after her marriage to the King. In any case he was there to pour scented water from a silver ewer over her hands at the Coronation and to go to the Tower for a few months, under no clearly defined suspicion, during her trial. His sister accompanied her to the scaffold. His political astuteness must have been considerable, for he survived the fall of Cromwell, who had been his constant friend, and died in his bed of a fever.

What kind of poetry, then, did Wyatt write? Love sonnets and longer lyrics, with epigrams full of worldly

bitterness over some personal moment, satires and epistles echoing Horace and Persius. There are about a hundred poems of these sorts, of which some thirty are sonnets. Ten of these thirty are reminiscent of poems out
of Petrarch's long garland to Laura. I use the word
"reminiscent" advisedly. Wyatt knew Petrarch, not
only knew but felt the power of the piled-up images and
comparisons with which Petrarch celebrated his love.
He saw how these elaborate devices were made incan-
descent, burned like the paper boats and chariots of
Chinese funerals in the blaze of Petrarch's whole being
for love. As a young Tudor gentleman, passionate for
the success of his country in the arts, sure that a new way
of writing poetry must be grafted upon the old, doubly
sure that Italy and France and Spain had already found
that way, Wyatt practised Petrarchan verse.

But no one can read the ninety-odd poems of Wyatt,
printed by Tottel in 1557, without feeling that they are
more than imitations. They are, also, the passions, confusions and witty reflections of a strong and sensitive
mind working upon actual experience. The borrowing
of style, even the translation of actual lines from a foreign poem, did not keep Wyatt's poetry from being
essentially his own. Along with the use of these foreign
poetical fashions, went a virile independence. Wyatt
naturalised his foreign obligations to Petrarch and
others. He bent them to the service of expressing English life. He learned to run in the armour of Petrarch-
ism. But he wrote it "with a difference." The stock

comparisons, word-patterns, conventional oppositions of ideas, when they were used to carry strong individual feeling, became the inevitable expression of a particular moment. In this highest sense, they became original.

The old spelling and something heavy and uninviting in most texts of Wyatt hide from the reader the fresh detail which reflects his own Tudor world. Look at this list of passages full of lively comparisons:

> With naked foot stalking within my chamber
>
> She sat and sewed: . . .
> She wished my heart the sampler. . . .
>
> Why dost thou stick to salve that thou madst sore
>
> But they that sometime liked my company
> Like lice away from dead bodies they crawl
>
> And knit again with knot that should not slide
>
> Me lyst no longer rotten boughs to clime
>
> Of all my joy this very bark and rind.

This is poetry which records the poet's own experience. His own present presses heavily upon him in such lines as these and he transfers it to paper with whatever figures of comparison he can lay hands on, whether they are his own or borrowed.

Wyatt is, I believe, the most interesting representative of this early group of courtiers. He shows, at its strongest, the way in which imitation of revered models could become the stuff of original lyric poetry. He wore the armour of conventions more valiantly than any of his

contemporaries because he had virility, more strength of
personal feeling. But the difference between him and
them is a matter of degree, not of kind.

After this group, for the first twenty years of Elizabeth's reign, roughly from 1560 to 1580, the output of
English poetry is less interesting. For one thing, the
political and religious confusion of the two brief reigns
between Henry and his great daughter presented no
continuous Court in which a man like Wyatt or Surrey
could live with a feeling of continuity to support him.
In the early reign of Elizabeth men were busier about
public affairs, about settling the kingdom than about
literature. The great men at Court were occupied with
developing public policies at home and abroad. The ad-
justment of power between Church and State took their
energies. They were statesmen rather than poets. Of
course experimenting in verse continued but in general it
did not command such attention as it had in Wyatt's day.

By the middle Seventies, anthologies and collected
books of verse began to appear, bearing such titles as *A
Paradise of Dainty Devices* and *A Gorgeous Gallery of
Gallant Inventions.* Gascoigne printed a collection of
Flowers, tastefully culled from classical and Italian
gardens. Practice in words, in figures, in metre was
going steadily on. First-hand knowledge of Continental
poetry was increasing. For its contribution to what was
coming in the great years just ahead, the period was
important, but the output of poetry was not intrinsically
good. Great imaginative people, who might have been

poets in other times, were engrossed in active life. They
were picking up the pieces of a broken world and putting
them together in a new way. The imagination was stimulated but the convictions were unsettled. The map of
the world was changing under voyages of conquest and
discovery. There was always some kind of war going
on with Spain or in the Low Countries, on the high seas,
in South America. It is fair to assume that the great
people from 1560 to 1580 *lived* their poetry. They were
generals or admirals or foreign diplomats or spies or
politicians. They were remaking their world. What
poetry they wrote was worn as they wore their clothes,
with brilliant self-consciousness, as a fitting light ornament to their serious work.

By the early Eighties, the Elizabethan ship was in
full sail. The pressure of event was still heavy; the
series of crises, national and international, continued;
but the stability of the reign seemed assured. The
Queen was a known quantity, experienced and functioning at the height of her ability. The long upward
struggle of the nation was beginning to tell. The
future looked as if it might ultimately be bright. There
began to be a chance for a slight diversion of energy
from the main concern. If the meaning and beauty of
this England were to be preserved in books, literature
must be put upon a firm basis. Men began to discuss
theories of literature. It was the era of treatises on
poetry, manuals of the art, of which Sidney's *Defense*
is the most brilliant example. Classifications of rhe-

torical figures, anatomies of the physical body of poetry, discussion of metrics went hand in hand with discussion of the ancient philosophy of poetry. The theory of poetry was neatly and falsely compounded from Plato, Aristotle and Horace. It was strained through renaissance Continental criticism. As it finally took form in the English books of criticism, it had a distinctly moral tone.

This moral tone was inevitable. Poetry and the fine arts could only be justified in an ambitious middle-class world (for that is precisely what the Elizabethan world was becoming, even though it was full of titles, social ambitions and the pageantry of an older aristocratic régime) if they served some practical end. Nothing it seemed could be more practical for a young country than the inculcation of moral qualities through the moving music of poetry. Thus the treatises from Sidney up and down harp upon the moral function of poetry in the state. In mediæval popular literature, in the plays, in compilations like *The Fall of Princes,* in the pill beneath the sugar of allegory, this moral point of view was already familiar. Furthermore, according to the Tudor interpreters of the classics, Aristotle was made to support the moral point of view on poetry and Horace had confirmed it in a neat Latin couplet. The idea had the prestige of classical approval. The sterner side of the English renaissance, the forces of the Reformation, the ethical interest of English humanists like More strengthened this pressure for morality in poetry. While the

poetry of the high Elizabethan world at its best, the sonnets, plays, the poems on amorous classical themes do
not strike a modern reader as moral, yet there is present,
especially in the poetry of the plays, a good deal of moralising. But of this more later.

To a modern world like ours which has fallen out of
love with "oratory," the rhetoric with which Elizabethan
poetry is filled is unpalatable. To understand the taste
of the Elizabethan for rhetoric, one has to remember
several things which made their world different from
ours. In the first place their sermons were rhetorical.
Their school curriculum, too, gave a great place to
rhetoric. It had stayed there, defiant of change, from the
time when the mediæval plan of studies was constructed.
It was incorporated into these mediæval curricula from
the Roman world. In that world to be an orator, a
rhetorician, was the key to moving the public and obtaining power. After the fall of the Roman world, rhetoric
persisted, though in different form, in the mediæval pulpit. The people were reached orally. For this oral com-
munication, a style punctuated with rhetoric was effective. The listeners remembered the idea because it was
set in a particular form. The cruxes of argument became
memory gems. Furthermore this patterned style was
acceptable to renaissance taste. The renaissance enjoyed
superficial refinements at the same time that it thrust
ever deeper into the essence of things. For all these reasons the Elizabethan manuals of poetry stressed morality
of content and rhetorical form.

But what of the actual poetry? Sidney's poetry is an unfinished story because he died in 1586 at thirty-two. His sonnets and songs certainly are not pre-eminent for their moral purpose. The rhetorical devices, however, are frequent. His lines recall Petrarch, Ronsard and du Bellay in specific passages which might be called translations save that they are done with originality. They express the reality of personal experience. They celebrate an actual love story and because of their personal feeling, the borrowed devices are made to speak for Sidney from his heart.

But his most signal contribution lay in a piece of prose-poetry, *The Arcadia*, where he struck out occasional passages which foretold that fusing of rhetorical figure and feeling which was to be the very crown of poetry in Ralegh and Shakespeare and Donne. *The Arcadia* has been praised for the curiosities of its imagery. It is, to be sure, often only a curiosity. But in the course of this conventional romance, full of Arcadian vales where "the grass is much too green" and shepherdesses in spun-sugar display Sidney's ingenuity of style, there is matter of a quite different sort. The typical psychology of love, as it had been laid down in behaviour books for hundreds of years, is occasionally supplanted by personal feeling. This emotion is so little acclimated to the world of words that it will not go into straightforward prose. If it can be transferred to paper at all, it must be caught obliquely by a figure, a comparison, a "conceit." It is in passages of this sort, sprinkled

through *The Arcadia,* that one sees an early example of
the "conceited" poetry which was to come at the end of
the century. It is for these occasional successes in saying
the unsayable that Sidney's *Arcadia* deserves to be considered in the story of Elizabethan poetry.

Spenser's place here is an interesting one. He tried all
the things that the lyric poets tried : a sonnet cycle, poems
for occasions, for a marriage, for the death of Sidney.
He wrote hymns and complaints. He also created something new, *The Faerie Queene.* For a man who earned
his living in the field of paid government service, as
secretary to Leicester, to the Lord Lieutenant of Ireland
and as "undertaker" for the settlement of Munster, his
poetical output is surprising. More than any figure encountered thus far in the century he was anxious to be
known as a poet. He supervised the publication of his
works, sought patronage and money for the completion
of his great poetical project, *The Faerie Queene.* In fact,
poetical professionalism had in Spenser an early Elizabethan example. There were plenty of poets who practised drama for a living but in the field of poetry for
reading, non-dramatic stuff, Spenser was something
new.

The gift of poetry toward the end of the sixteenth
century was widespread. There were any number of
amateurs who wrote for the pleasure of it. They cared
for fashion and partly, one must believe, they felt an
inward urgency springing out of the vividness with
which life was lived. There are first-rate bits scattered

all through their second-rate verses. In most cases they wrote for themselves or for their friends, without wish or hope of general publication. There is distinction about this. It seems to make their effort more honest, their poetry more itself. Oftentimes the sense of property, of peculiar right in a poem, was so lightly felt that verses escaped into private circulation with mere initials or no identification. There is in fact a great body of Elizabethan poetry, some of it exquisite, which is anonymous. It makes the last stand for aristocracy in an increasingly vulgar world of middle-class ambition. With Spenser this touch has gone.

The nature and range of Spenser's work illustrate the elements which in varying combinations made up the body of Elizabethan poetry in the last quarter of the century. There is the awareness of precedent among the classics, the sense of English rivalry with the Continent. There is the feeling of national continuity. Chaucer was a revered model. Mediæval allegory contributed to the renaissance pageant. It took on new colours, symbolised new ideas, caught new subtleties of thinking and feeling. Spenser's range of subjects shows clearly these obligations. In the field of metrics he made new combinations of old forms, elaborated existing patterns. He had a precious combination of technical skill in verse, wide knowledge of the practice of metre in several languages, and—saving grace—a musical ear. In a strong and victorious effort to build his own glory and the glory of his country through his verse, he embraced all this variation, subdued it and turned it out as an individual musical setting for his thought and emotion.

In the substance of his poetry, late sixteenth century thought is beautifully reflected. He was happy in selecting *Pageants* as the original title for *The Faerie Queene*. The word *pageants* has just the sense of panorama, beautiful and dissolving views, characteristic of Elizabethan life and art. He can incorporate in a single poem the most disparate elements, gleaned from the four corners of the world of books. They are not discordant because the main structure of his thought is fluid enough to admit many things. Elizabethan art had fluidity. It was growing, taking into itself experiment and swift change, flowing forward with the age, denying standardization. The story in *The Faerie Queene* is not easy to follow. It halts and doubles upon itself. Narrative and lyric go side by side as they do in Elizabethan drama, or in Elizabethan life. Entertainment and instruction alternate as Sidney had insisted they must. In fact Spenser is an excellent illustration of the paradoxical renaissance combination of beauty for itself and morality for England.

Spenser's poetry reflects another new note. Melancholy or disillusion would be too heavy a word for it. It is not so specific as that. At a certain stage in development, whether in an individual or in an age, there comes a sense of overseeing the whole area from which one has come and whither one is going. It was this accompaniment to coming of age which England felt in the Nineties as the long century of arduous climbing was moving to its close. While a good deal of Spenser's melancholy is conventional, yet in his autobiographical poems like *Colin Clout's Come Home Again,* the gap between his ideals for England and what he actually finds in England stirs in him disillusion and bitterness. This same feeling in other Elizabethan poets provides poignant lyrical poetry or biting satire.

This measuring of the discrepancy between the ideal and the actual meant that Elizabethan life became increasingly introspective. Reflection and analysis were forced upon men if they were to estimate their place in time. Medical books began to describe something like psychology. They discussed the physical basis of the passions and moods, explained temperament in terms of bodily chemistry, catalogued individuals. They suggested that psychological analysis, if scientifically practised, with the aid of diet and exercise might readjust a man's soul to his world.

As a result of this an interesting thing happened in poetry. When the doctors and pseudo-scientists of the late Eighties began to explore the soul, they were charting a whole new realm for poetry and the poets began to work in it at once. They became increasingly aware of that sort of experience which lies just on the edge of thought, which is thought sensitised by mood. It was mobile, almost refusing to be caught in words. But it was real. Their own experiences assured them of that. It seemed closer to the core of life than anything they had tried before. The difficulty of expressing it added to the fascination of the attempt. The ingenuity, "wit" as they said, which they had practised in earlier verse was at hand. "Wit" now was practised on the poet's whole range of thought and feeling. It used its cunning to trap that experience which lies beyond the power of full realization. The poets put their intricate rhetorical nets over the winged things that hover on the periphery of mind. They made new poetry, of which John Donne's is only one, though the most familiar, example.

Thus English poetry made its valiant and experimental way across the sixteenth century. It came to something like fruition in the last quarter of that century. Under the altering views of man's private life, under the new scrutiny of human temperament, it took on a new subject matter and a new method. There had been, of course, both old and new in the poetry of Wyatt and that early Tudor group. They were the predecessors of the new developments in later Elizabethan poetry. But toward the end of the century all past English poetry, combining with the keen influence from the classics and foreign renaissance models, was leavened by something new. This leaven, in the best poetry, was potent enough to fuse divergent elements and vivify the past by a generous infusion from the burning present.

I shall in three following chapters, discuss some phases of this flowering of English poetry at the height of the Elizabethan Age. Spenser will be shown as a great epitome of all these tendencies, yet as a poet whose strong

individuality sets him apart from his age at the same
time that he embraces it. The sonneteers, the writers of
story and history in verse, the song writers, Marlowe,
Shakespeare, Sidney, Daniel and Drayton will be the
subject of another chapter. A third chapter will be devoted to the poetry of Ralegh. Written for the most
part without idea of publication, Ralegh's poetry presents little of the "furniture" of formal poetry. It reveals unencumbered the emotions and reactions which
belonged peculiarly to the two decades before and after
the turn of the century. This chapter will also contain
a brief study of the early poetry of Donne for the sake
of enforcing, through another poet, the peculiar flavour
of Ralegh.

CHAPTER III

Poetry in the Nineties

I. NARRATIVE POETRY: MARLOWE, DANIEL AND SHAKE-
SPEARE, WITH SPECIAL ATTENTION TO SHAKESPEARE

The peculiar mixture of circumstances which makes
any age distinguished in poetry will never be defined.
Into that mixture must go the wine of new thinking, or
re-thinking about man's life under new circumstances, in
a new era. There must be, too, and in delicate balance,
both convention and revolt, tradition and experiment.
More necessary than any of these, however, is that flexibility, even that uncertainty about the outward forms of
living, that force the individual steadily to think about
the meaning which underlies these outward forms.

The 1590's in England were just such a mixture of
circumstances. Poets and poetasters, according to their
capacities and in a bewildering variety of forms made
England "a nest of singing birds." Often the poetry was
great; more often it was ephemeral, the ebullient trifle
tossed off in a great or witty moment. Even the trivial
stuff of the song-books and the collections has warmth
and the stamp of authenticity upon it. "This is how life
feels in a great or trivial moment," Elizabethan poetry
seems to say. "These are the nets in which I confine it

for you. They may be pastoral, heroic, pagan or Christian after the custom. Or they may be in a new dialect,
stolen from the everyday world of this present. To catch
the feeling while it is warm, while it is perhaps only half
clear to me, I have ranged through all the ways of writing poetry that I could lay hands on. Rough hands, too,
and working in haste lest the thing I saw and wanted to
catch for you should escape me."

Under these circumstances, it is not surprising that
the Elizabethan poetry of the Nineties is at once imitative
and original. It has the enthusiasm of amateurishness
and experiment. One no sooner defines a type of poem,
as for instance the long narrative poem on Greek mythology or English history, than the type alters into something else. The sonnets of the first years of the Nineties
have become something quite different by 1600. Everything is in flux. New combinations, new re-workings of
new combinations, daring innovation make this decade
in English poetry one of the most various and spirited
in the whole span of English literature.

It is one of the most difficult, too, to classify and
describe. Obviously one must not lean too heavily upon
classification or description. One must live through the
actual poetry. Also one must keep an eye on the year
when a poem was composed, for in the passage of a
single year the poetical fashion may alter. One must not
have preconceived ideas about the category to which a
poem belongs. The understanding of Shakespeare's long
poem, *The Rape of Lucrece,* may depend more upon

comparing it to a Senecan stage play than to another poem which is superficially like it in type. A good deal of what is said generally about the sonnet in the Nineties is not applicable to the greatest sonnet cycle of that decade, Shakespeare's. Again the standard in Shakespeare's sonnets will not fit Donne's, or Ralegh's or even Drayton's later ones. The only thing in fact which is constant in this mass of divergence is the spirit, the energy of poetic feeling and the will to express it, no matter how unconventionally. With this warning, let us look at two long narrative poems by Shakespeare which have been much misunderstood and little read. They are *Venus and Adonis* and *The Rape of Lucrece*. They were written in 1593 and 1594, in the very heart of this difficult decade.

The modern reader must not be deceived by the word "poem" as applied to these two pieces of work. The word may betray him into looking for something different from what is there. Neither of them is a "poem" in the narrow sense of that word. *Venus and Adonis* is nearer to one; for it presents love pictorially and analytically, in a fashion modelled on Ovid's erotic verse stories from Greek mythology. *Venus and Adonis,* however, is not only story-telling according to Ovid. It also contains many things that came into literature between Ovid and the English renaissance. It echoes the insipid prettiness of Sicilian shepherdesses on the flowery hillsides of late Greek pastoral; the rhetorical trifles of the *Greek Anthology;* the oratory of Seneca's plays; the dissection of passion in the manner of Chaucer's *Troilus and Cressida;* and the experiments in licentious living recorded in the books of renaissance Italy.

Probably, too, *Venus and Adonis* carries memories of Shakespeare's schoolboy study of rhetoric. The charts and classifications of figures from his schoolbooks ran along in his mind beside the lively images drawn from actual country and sports; from hunting and horses, from days on English hillsides, grazed over by sheep among whom the small hare ran to put the hounds off the scent. *Venus and Adonis* is a stock-pot of many juices, of scraps from the larders of the centuries. It is classical and mediæval and renaissance by turns.

It is also written for a special person and a special moment. The young Southampton, wealthy, handsome and well-connected, fashionable courtier, book collector, officer in foreign wars, was already a patron of the arts. There are at least fourteen portraits of him. Some of them show him against the background of lovely panelled rooms, with specially bound volumes lying in a window-embrasure. His gloves were notable. In one portrait his cat, sleek and quizzical, looks out from a world where luxury and leisure and sophistication seem to fleet the time elegantly. He collected *erotica* as many a later exquisite has done. *Venus and Adonis* was a deliberate contribution to the Earl's collection of *erotica*.

The poem is a curiously wrought emblem of physical passion, which if Shakespeare had been a goldsmith instead of an author, might have been worked out in precious stones and metal upon the lid of a jewel-box. According to Gabriel Harvey, who observed the reading of the Cambridge undergraduate, the dissection of passionate feeling in *Venus and Adonis* made it a favourite with "the younger sort." This "younger sort" was represented in a contemporary university play as "laying his *Venus and Adonis* under my pillow," thereby to worship and "honour sweet Master Shakespeare." Southampton himself was only nineteen. In fact, without glozing over the sensual details of this poem, one must in fairness say that it seems to have been shocking only to the old generation who peered at and ogled the particular details. But for the young these details were only a part of a glowing, intricate poem, woven of flowers and day and night and the enflaming power of physical beauty. The theme, of course, is sophisticated and' decadent. Venus, accomplished in love, makes overtures to an innocent young boy who loves only the chase and courage and bodily skill. But this theme is the provocation for the finest craftsmanship. The result is a poetic *tour de force,* such as the young Elizabethan gentlemen recognized, admired and even practised for themselves in their own "table-books."

There are, for instance, orations, arguments, pointed with tales from mythology and set in brilliant word-patterns. The piece as a whole has no moral. Yet chinked into the crevices of the story are flashing two-line epigrams which might have delighted Pope and other eighteenth century devisers of wit.

> For misery is trodden on by many,
> And being low never relieved by any.

Shakespeare can describe with elegance. The lark

> From his moist cabinet mounts up on high
> And wakes the morning from whose silver breast
> The sun ariseth in his majesty;
>   Who doth the world so gloriously behold
>   That cedar-tops and hills seem burnished gold.

"Moist cabinet" for a dewy thicket of leaves is elegant but unreal. The pleasure from it lay in its ingenuity. When Venus, following the sounds of the hunt, fears Adonis has been killed, she gives a long rhetorical speech reproving Death. In the midst of her grief learning and rhetoric can produce a couplet like this:

> Love's golden arrow at him should have fled
> And not Death's ebon dart, to strike him dead.

The unreal finish of this speech makes her a figure in a far-away myth. We can believe Shakespeare when he says that she walks without pressing down the lightest flowers beneath her feet. She is a goddess weaving intricate Elizabethan rhetoric, not a woman passionately enamoured.

Yet renaissance materialism is in her, too. But it is curiously and elaborately wrought. Venus's body is a deer park; Adonis the deer. The dead Adonis "lily white," his blood like "purple tears," melts from her sight and in his place a purple and white flower springs up. In fact the modern reader is buffeted between reality and myth, between physical passion and pictorial detail. He does not know how to pass freely from one to the other as the Elizabethan did. There are, indeed, many sharply contrasted elements in the poem. Following closely on a passage of enamelled rhetoric, the reader may find such a realistic line as this

> Like shrill-tongued tapsters answering every call.

This comparison, drawn from a London ale-house, brings noise and the smell of sweat and sawdust to mingle with the marble and coral and lily-whiteness of the poem. The two stanzas where Adonis unfolds the difference between love and lust are suddenly serious in the midst of lightness. They remind one that Southampton not only collected *erotica* but probably read Castiglione and Plato. When Venus in her apostrophe to Death cries out

> If he be dead—O no, it cannot be,
> Seeing his beauty, thou (Death) should strike at it,

one hears that deep renaissance amazement that beauty should be so lovely and yet always so near to destruction.

The young Southampton would like *Venus and Adonis* for other reasons too. He would appreciate its word-play, figures and learned allusions. He would be pleased to see how Ovid and Elizabethan life were deftly mingled, how scenery drawn from tapestry and from life joined without visible seam. Besides, he would enjoy receiving a poem of a sort already fashionable. He may have read Marlowe's *Hero and Leander* as early as 1592. Drayton's *Endimion and Phœbe* was printed in 1593. Lodge's *Glaucus and Scilla* was well known and Nashe was circulating in manuscript an erotic poem, *The Choice of Valentines*. This poem presumably was dedicated and presented in manuscript to Southampton for the delectation of the Earl and his friends. It was not printed. Altogether the fashion in this sort of poem was, one can see from these titles, widespread.

On the whole and purely on the merits of the piece, Marlowe's *Hero and Leander* has stood the test of time better than *Venus and Adonis*. As a story it is more satisfactory. Rhymed couplet gives any continuous tale a better chance to unfold than the stanzaic form of *Venus and Adonis*. The theme, too, is less repugnant. Both Hero and Leander are young, beautiful and in love. In this variegated tale the mediæval touches such as Venus's church in which the lovers meet and Hero's "solitary" tower, placed

> Upon a rock and underneath a hill
> Far from the town

fit happily, side by side with the rhymed catalogues of mythological figures. The digression on Mercury and the shepherdess blends mythology with pastoral. The tale also has a witty application for Marlowe's fellow authors and scholars. It explains by way of an ancient feud among the gods why scholars live in poverty and fools are rich.

> And to this day is every scholar poor:
> Gross gold from them runs headlong to the boor

. . . .

> And still enrich the lofty servile clown,
> Who with encroaching guile keeps learning down.

Another charm is that the main story flows so easily that it can be taken for granted at intervals, pushed aside while some briefer story is islanded in it.

Not only does it tell a better "story" than *Venus and Adonis* but it uses newer, more original methods. Marlowe's descriptions often are only full enough to evoke the picture in the imagination of the reader instead of offering him a long list of details. He describes Hero, for instance, in terms of her effect:

> But far above the loveliest, Hero shin'd
> And stole away th' enchanted gazer's mind;
> For like sea nymph's inveigling harmony
> So was her beauty to the standers by.

This stimulates the reader's imagination; it does not confine it. Then, too, the epigrams of *Hero and Leander* are more enlightened than those of *Venus and Adonis*. They penetrate deeply. Take, for instance,

> Like untun'd golden strings all women are,
> Which long time lie untouched, will harshly jar

or

> Ah simple Hero, learn thyself to cherish!
> Lone women, like to empty houses, perish.

There is disillusioned wit, psychological fact, here. On the whole, one does not find it in the proverbial couplets of *Venus and Adonis*.

To explain this superiority of Marlowe over Shakespeare at this time, one remembers that Marlowe, if he wrote *Hero and Leander* about 1590, was at the top of his career. His experiment in conveying life to paper was successful. He was more experienced than Shakespeare. Marlowe's worldliness, too, is more mature than Shakespeare's, more sour and realistic. He does not have to protest loudly that he has it. The argument in *Hero and Leander* against virginity and the analysis of actual passion are cogent and sophisticated. To record the feeling behind certain situations Marlowe dares to grasp at any figure of speech whether it is authorised in poetry's book of rules or not. He sometimes achieves a homeliness and immediacy of effect which reminds one that a new way of writing poetry already exists, side by side with the old. Leander separated from Hero is described thus:

> Home when he came, he seem's not to be there,
> But, like exiled air thrust from his sphere,
> Set in a foreign place.

This is a new kind of description of feeling, impressionistic and vivid. Another instance is the passage describing Hero when she has a moment of passionate confusion.

> . . . Like a planet, moving several ways
> At one self instant, she, poor soul, assays,
> Loving, not to love at all.

In general one may say that the first two Sestiads of *Hero and Leander,* the only ones which Marlowe completed, while they draw the thread of their tapestry from the great reels of late Greek and mediæval story, while they weave their figures with an eye on renaissance taste in *erotica,* do also add something new to the pattern, give more than this pattern calls for. Into the elaborations of richness and colour, poetry in the concentrated sense of that word thrusts its vivifying strands. With sudden luminosity it enlivens the design. Life as Marlowe by now so sharply knew it, trespasses in the rose-strewn chamber of classic-mediæval dalliance. It might have become unmanageable, might have broken the design, if Marlowe had written further sestiads. The poem might have stepped out of its niche and become something quite different and new. One wonders whether this predicament was foreseen by Marlowe, whether it made him leave the poem as a fragment.

This new quality in *Hero and Leander* was found in other poets, too. It lived side by side with the older method. The external and merely descriptive poetry which fills much of *Venus and Adonis* and *Hero and Leander,* for instance, belongs in the same decade which produced the curt allusiveness, the witty brevity of half-articulate passion in Donne and Ralegh. How is one to relate these two very different phases of poetry in the Nineties? The simple explanation that Donne is a reaction from the over-elaborateness, over-explicitness of this earlier poetry will not do. It is not true. It is perhaps nearer the truth to say that men like Marlowe and Shakespeare, who wrote *Hero and Leander* or *Venus and Adonis,* were also capable of harder, briefer poetry, drawn more immediately from life. In the mythological pieces, they were revealing chiefly one side of themselves, picturing the ancient world where life was not seen in the round. Perhaps the Elizabethans wilfully did not vitalise the ancient world. They kept it for a decoration, an overlay upon the full realities of life as they knew life. With no sense of incongruity therefore, they mingled ancient figures with modern dress. Quite naturally Venus tilts Adonis's hat awry or Hero appears without her gloves. The Greek myths had no clearly realised world of their own but lived to enliven an Elizabethan tale.

In the emotions of love as in the costumes, pieces like *Hero and Leander* reflect neither the Greek nor the Elizabethan idea of passion. To be sure there was plenty of amorous intrigue in the English Court. But it was deeper than the passion in these mythological poems, haunting the lovers with afterthought. But these long, erotic poems by Marlowe and Shakespeare were devised on a pattern outside life. Marlowe would not have wished to transfer the values of love in *Hero and Leander* to love in *Tamburlaine,* even less to love in *Faustus.* But in these fantastic earlier poems, love was handled as it might have been in a world divorced from experience. It was shorn of the deep emotions, the upheavals, attractions and repulsions which accompanied it in Elizabeth's English world. In the very thought of Italy and Greece, perhaps, there was release from a realistic set of values and in its place there was binding enchantment to another less rigorous, more fanciful world.

By a critical mischance, Shakespeare's *Rape of Lucrece* which appeared in 1594, again dedicated to Southampton and printed by Field, has been placed in a false category. It is not merely another erotic poem on a classical theme. It is not merely Shakespeare's amend to that portion of the public who found *Venus and Adonis* too sensual and were to be soothed by a moral Roman tale of a faithful wife "whose death was witness of her spotless life." Most of the complaints against *Venus and Adonis* came long after *Lucrece* was written and published. They were at least five years after the event, when the lines of seventeenth century Puritanism were being more sharply drawn.

Harvey's superficial comment about *Venus and Adonis* pleasing the "younger sort" and Lucrece "the wiser sort" was made several years after the publication of these poems, in his marginal note in the Speght *Chaucer,* 1598. In this same year, another commentator on the literary scene, Francis Meres in his *Wit's Treasury* goes as far in the other direction. He makes no distinction between *Venus and Adonis* and *Lucrece*. They are both proofs that "the sweet, witty soul of Ovid lives in mellifluous and honey-tongued Shakespeare." The truth of the matter seems to be this. Shakespeare was trying a poem in a different category from *Venus* when he published in the next year his *Lucrece*, "this pamphlet" as he calls it. Probably he was not appeasing any outraged moralists. He was working in a different vein, in one offering larger opportunity for more serious work and in a field more nearly related to drama where he had already had a success.

Drayton knew what general category this new poem by Shakespeare was in. Although it was not in the form of a stage tragedy, he knew that it belonged in the general classification, moving story. In the Elizabethan mind the chasm between tragedy in stage dialogue and tragedy in a narrative poem was not deep. Drayton's *Matilda*, published in the same year as *Lucrece*, has these illuminating lines:

> Lucrece of whom proud Rome hath boasted long
> Lately revived to live another age
> And here arrived to tell of Tarquin's wrong
> Acting her passions on our stately stage.

The reference is probably to Shakespeare's *Lucrece* in which the long soliloquies and rhetorical speeches might in the language of the day be called "passions." No *bona fide* play on *Lucrece* at the time is known. Would

Drayton, furthermore, have referred to the literal Elizabethan stage as stately? But whether this passage refers to Shakespeare's narrative poem on Lucrece is not important. What is significant is that it might have done; that from the Elizabethan point of view, a violent story punctuated by rhetorical speeches was equally at home either in the form of a narrative poem or in the dialogue of the actual stage. In fact, I have contended elsewhere that the only way to appraise fairly the effectiveness of many Elizabethan stage tragedies is to see them as awkwardly metamorphosed narrative poems, conveying the story by dialogue alone, grafting the long rhetorical speeches into the stage performance.

For a poem like *Lucrece,* Shakespeare had many precedents. Daniel's *Complaint of Rosamond,* published two years earlier, may have been the immediate stimulus. That poem tells the story of the guilty love of Rosamond for Henry II. Rosamond enters the poem as a ghost. She might as well be entering a Senecan play.

> Out from the horror of infernal deeps
> My poor afflicted ghost comes here to plain it:
> Attended with my shame that never sleeps
> The spot wherewith my kind and youth did stain it.

Kyd's Senecan play, *The Spanish Tragedy,* begins with just such a ghost's speech. So do the closet Senecan plays which Sir William Alexander and Lady Mary Pembroke and Daniel himself produced in the Nineties. In other words with Shakespeare's *Lucrece* one stumbles again across that Elizabethan truth that the story was the important thing, not whether it was in the form of a narrative poem or a stage play. But the fashionable vogue among the Elizabethan public for stage performances and the skill of authors in catering to this fashion emphasised the dramatic rendering of story so much that the narrative rendering of story became a minor art. But let us watch Daniel and Shakespeare practise this minor art.

To respond to Daniel's *Complaint of Rosamond* one has to divest himself of modern standards of story-telling. Daniel's poem belongs with the "cautionary tales" of the *Mirror for Magistrates* and poems of more ancient lineage still. It is told by the ghost of a lady who allowed herself to become the mistress of Henry II. From the "horror of infernal deeps" she comes to recount her story, to "complain" her woes, to admonish any mortals who will lend ear to turn from their wickedness before it is too late. She rehearses the steps of her temptation and fall. She recalls, word for word, the long speech of the court lady, "A seeming Matron, yet a sinful monster," who persuaded her to become the King's mistress. In terror of the jealous queen Henry had imprisoned Rosamond in a palace entered only through labyrinthine halls. Her ghost, recalling that event, bursts into a "well-languaged" apostrophe to Jealousy, the cause of all her love. How Henry encountered the dead Rosamond's body being borne to its grave, her ghost remembers and thereupon recites its long lament. In this way, by the account of crucial moments in skillful rhetoric, the whole story is told. But the method, acceptable and pleasant to the Elizabethans, leaves us unmoved. Yet this sort of story, as it was found, for instance, in Brooke's long poem of *Romeus and Juliet,* when it is turned into the lyrical stage tragedy of *Romeo and Juliet* still enchants us.

The reasons for the difference in effectiveness of the two methods of story-telling are not hard to find. Take, for instance, the passage in *Rosamond* where King Henry, admiring the beauty of his lady's corpse, swings into rhetoric:

> Ah now methinks I see death dallying, seeks
> To entertain itself in love's sweet place:
> Decayed roses of discoloured cheeks
> Do yet retain dear notes of former grace:
> And ugly death sits fair within her face;
>   Sweet remnants resting of vermilion red,
>   That death itself doubts whether she be dead.

We read this unmoved. The whole tale has not come sufficiently near us to warm this rhetoric into life. Yet when Shakespeare makes Romeo in Juliet's tomb express the same idea in the same kind of rhetoric, the mounting emotion of the whole play carries the lines into effective contact with our feelings. Romeo cries:

> Death that hath sucked the honey of thy breath
> Hath had no power yet upon thy beauty.
> Thou art not conquered; Beauty's ensign yet
> Is crimson in thy lips and in thy cheeks

.   .   .   .

> Shall I believe
> That unsubstantial Death is amorous, . . .

The situations are parallel. Both Henry and Romeo use
the convention of soliloquy and the trappings of rhetoric.
The figures of speech are almost identical, sanctioned by
long approval. This is a regular device in the recount-
ing of sad stories. We respond to it in one case but not
in the other. The reason lies in the fact that for one
ancient and honoured Elizabethan method of story-telling we have lost the taste, to another we are still susceptible.

Of course the difference in effect between *Rosamond*
and *Romeo and Juliet* in this small detail, is not merely
a difference between narrative poem and stage play.
There is a more telling difference, the difference between
the artistic ability of Daniel and Shakespeare. Happily
we can take the measure of this difference by comparing
Shakespeare and Daniel when they are both writing narrative poetry. We can turn from *Rosamond,* which
Shakespeare certainly used, to his own *Lucrece,* which
recounts in narrative set with rhetorical speeches the sad
story of another lovely lady.

The Rape of Lucrece in some 1850 lines tells a story as
old as Ovid and Livy, handled too by Shakespeare's
great forebear, Chaucer. Shakespeare in his dedication
to the Earl of Southampton calls it a "pamphlet." This
is a sufficiently nondescript category. For the modern
reader it is useful to think of it as a narrative poem, very

closely approaching the form of dramatic poems which
Seneca, nearly sixteen centuries earlier, had the temerity
to call plays, when they were declaimed for his master,
Nero. Or, coming to Shakespeare's own time, it is not
unlike, in general technique, Marlowe's early lyrical
drama, *Tamburlaine.* To say this is, of course, to over-
state the case. *The Rape of Lucrece* is not a play. Yet it
hovers on the borderline between the narrative and the
dramatic method of telling a story. Because it is such a
borderline piece, it is peculiarly helpful to the modern
reader. It furnishes a concrete instance of the fact that
ancient and famous stories altered their contours or de-
formed them in the Elizabethan Age so that they could be
put upon the stage.

With just a slight effort, Shakespeare could have
pushed *The Rape of Lucrece* into a "lamentable tragedy
of a chaste Roman lady, with the revenge of Collatine
upon the wicked Tarquin." It is significant that just at
the time he produced this "pamphlet" he was working on
the revision of a play on Roman history, full of rage and
brutality and revenge. That play, *Titus Andronicus,* is
hardly more of a play from the modern point of view
than *Lucrece.* Both pieces of work carry the burden of a
violent story. Tucked into the interstices of these stories
are rhetorical passages of incitement to violence and reflection upon it. Such passages bulk large. In the
"pamphlet" Shakespeare puts the preliminary stages of
the action in a prose "Argument" of twenty-six lines.
There is in this "Argument" the stuff of some excellent

stage scenes. How effectively Shakespeare might have dramatised the following sentence:

The principal men of the army meeting one evening at the tent of Sextus Tarquinius . . . in their discourse after supper everyone commended the virtues of his own wife.

Because Shakespeare is creating a dramatic poem and not a poetic drama, he passes this material over. He opens his story at the point where Tarquin, already having seen the beautiful Lucrece and having listened to her husband extolling her faithfulness and chastity, suddenly is possessed to visit her alone and win her.

> From the besieged Ardea all in post,
> Borne by the trustless wings of false desire,
> Lust-breathed Tarquin leaves the Roman host
> And to Collatium bears the lightless fire.

Shakespeare plunges *in medias res* as relentlessly as all the great story-tellers, Homer, Vergil and the rest.

Once within the confines of his story, he uses the double facilities of narrative and dramatic technique. At first Tarquin and Lucrece are opposed with the sharp simplicity of a symbolic morality play. They are types of good and evil, about to engage in mortal strife:

> This earthly saint, adored by this devil.

But after supper when, as decorous-seeming guest, Tarquin has gone to bed for the night, he debates with himself in the privacy of his room. He subtly weighs motives and analyses emotion in speeches packed with rhetoric. This debate reveals a living person, not a typical villain. He is, in fact, a potential subject for a moving play around a conflict in character. He debates with himself the meaning of honour, as Falstaff is to do with such dramatic effectiveness on the battlefield of Shrewsbury. He reflects in witty rhetoric upon the complexity of his position:

> And for himself himself he must forsake.

At the hour of midnight when Tarquin is about to set forth for Lucrece's bed-chamber, Shakespeare creates by poetry the same kind of frightening atmosphere which the blank boards and hard daylight of the Elizabethan stage forced him to use in place of lighting or setting in *Hamlet* or *Macbeth*.

> No comfortable star did lend his light
> No noise but owls and wolves' death-boding cries.

This sort of thing is conventional. But as Tarquin sets forth along the dark, drafty passages of the palace, the setting gets more realistic:

> As each unwilling portal yields him way
> Through little vents and crannies of the place
> The wind wars with his torch to make him stay,
> And blows the smoke of it into his face.

Whether the method is story or play, little things have a symbolic significance at dreadful moments. For example, to light his torch for the journey from his room to hers,

His falchion on a flint he softly smiteth
That from the cold stone sparks of fire do fly
Whereat a waxen torch forthwith he lighteth
Which must be lode-star to his lustful eye ;
   'As from this cold flint I enforced this fire
   So Lucrece must I force to my desire.'

On his way to her chamber he finds a glove of Lucrece's
which has been dropped with a needle in it. He picks it
up from the rushes on the floor and the needle pricks
him as a kind of warning. It seems to say:

   . . . . . . This glove to wanton tricks
   Is not inured ; return again in haste ;
   Thou see'st our mistress' ornaments are chaste.

In the plays, too, this kind of symbolic implication from
little events at great moments, is made again and again.
It is one way in which the universal meaning of the particular story is enforced. In *Lucrece* Shakespeare does
it awkwardly with prentice skill and conscious effort.
Yet sometimes even in *Lucrece* the device is effective.
The reason for noticing it at all lies in the fact that it
is a device common to the dramatic rendering of events,
whether in "poem" or "play."

So too the debate which features the struggle between
good and evil in Tarquin's soul is not different in kind
though different in intensity from the soliloquies which
portray character in the plays. The same kind of thing
occurs in *Richard III, Richard II, Henry IV, Hamlet,*

Macbeth, Antony and Cleopatra, The Tempest. The
débat which presents both sides of an issue is as old as
story. Ovid used it. The mediæval story-tellers in lays,
ballads and romances used it. It was useful, too, in the
dramatic poems of Seneca. This practice, therefore, was
there in his sources ready for Shakespeare when as a
dramatist he undertook to transfer secular story to the
stage. Because this rhetorical debating of motives had
so long been familiar in story form, it was undoubtedly
less awkward on the stage for the Elizabethan audience
than for the modern. At any rate it turns up in *Lucrece,*
longer, more consciously rhetorical perhaps but funda-
mentally not different from the soliloquies upon the
stage.

There is also a good deal of dialogue in this "pamphlet." Lucrece pleading with Tarquin speaks (uninter-
ruptedly, to be sure) for ten stanzas. He replies in one.
She continues for two when he interrupts her again. Her
conversation with her maid the next morning is much
more broken up and nearer to stage dialogue. Speeches
of two characters in conversation sometimes exist
within a single stanza. Another element in the poem
which belongs equally to drama is the description of
gestures and behaviour. Shakespeare visualises the
action that would accompany the words and offers potential "stage business" and "stage direction." Lucrece
hesitating about how to begin the note which shall summon her husband home, is mentally seen by Shakespeare
doing her part upon the stage:

Her maid is gone and she prepares to write,
First hovering o'er the paper with her quill:
Conceit and grief an eager combat fight;
What wit sets down is blotted straight with will.

The groom who is to bear the letter to her husband, has
no lines but there is enough "business" suggested to give
him upon the stage a spirited minor part:

The homely villain court'sies to her low,
And, blushing on her, with a steadfast eye
Receives the scroll without a yea or no,
And forth with bashful innocence doth hie.
But they whose guilt within their bosoms lie
    Imagine every eye beholds their blame;
    For Lucrece thought he blush'd to see her shame.

The situation, innocent on his side, significant and terrible on hers, is prolonged for two more stanzas of description. On the stage it would make a moving scene.
It is the germ of such a scene as Juliet's with her nurse,
or Hamlet's with the gravediggers, or Cleopatra's with
the countryman. Lucrece's groom of course is not humourous. Yet he is awkward and lumbering, and would
need only a slight push to be made the humourous point
to a pathetic moment.

The motivation of Tarquin's character is clumsy. In
the first third of the poem he is too sensitive a fellow, too
deeply enamoured. Then suddenly for the sake of the
story he becomes the crude, scheming villain. This kind
of inconsistent motivation is found in the plays, too,
whenever story is stronger than probability or whenever

a sensational scene is needed. Another point in common
between *Lucrece* and the plays is the way in which individualised characterisation alternates with characterisation of type. After a highly individualised scene between
Lucrece and Tarquin, Shakespeare shifts and makes
them like two figures in a tapestry:

> He thence departs a heavy convertite;
> She there remains a hopeless castaway.

For the modern reader this abrupt change is ludicrous.
Yet one must believe that both methods of characterisation held pleasure for the Elizabethan.

The end of the poem like the end of many Elizabethan
plays carries the story beyond what the modern audiences would call "the final curtain." After Lucrece has
confessed, charged her husband to revenge her upon Tarquin, after the embroidered grief in the speeches by her
father and Collatine, we should cry for an end. But
Shakespeare carries the story on. Neither he nor his
public could forego the tidying up of the events. This
fact, at least from the modern point of view, ruins the
end of many of his plays.

The part of the "pamphlet" which is essentially
"poetry" and not even potential drama comes in Lucrece's
twenty-seven stanzas of lament with which she greets
the day after the departure of Tarquin. Yet even here
one remembers the apostrophe of Juliet to her wedding
night; thirty-one lines of conventional wedding song by
Juliet alone on the stage at the opening of II, ii. There

is, too, the lyric duet to the dawn by Juliet and Romeo in
III, v. The feelings in *Romeo and Juliet* and in *Lucrece*
are entirely different. Yet the emotional need for self-
expression in rhetoric is common to both. Even in the
play Shakespeare halts the action while Juliet apostro-
phises night:

> Come, gentle night, come, loving, black-browed night
> Give me my Romeo and when he shall die
> Take him and cut him out in little stars
> And he will make the face of heaven so fine
> That all the world will be in love with night.

The play is stopped again later while Juliet and Romeo
in antiphonal lines fear and cajole the dawn that will
separate them. What this means is that the rhetoric of
apostrophe, of set invocation for set occasions, though
essentially not dramatic material, is used with equal assurance in a poem like *Lucrece* and a play like *Romeo and
Juliet*.

Lucrece's apostrophes to Night, to Opportunity, to
Time (that cruel Time that let Tarquin into her bed-
chamber) occupy the centre of the poem. The rhetoric in
these apostrophes is sometimes merely dexterous, not
moving. Take the following. Time's glory is, among
other things,

> To fill with wormholes stately monuments,
> To feed oblivion with decay of things,
> To blot old books and alter their contents,
> To pluck the quills from ancient ravens' wings,
> To dry the old oak's sap and cherish spring.

The figures here are good enough but not notable. Yet a few lines further on, Lucrece's apostrophe to Time as

> Thou ceaseless lackey to eternity,

is Shakespeare, the poet, at his best.

In these passages, the reader moves from the presentation of factual life in figures to the presentation of ideas behind factual experience. "Thou ceaseless lackey to eternity" is not different in kind from the figures that precede and follow it. In the idea it evokes, however, it is at the other pole. It is a brief abstract from living; it gives the meaning of a whole phase of life. Yet it comes in here in the poem with no trumpets. It is not even the climax of the poetical discussion of Time. Did Shakespeare know it was better than the rest? Is he, half consciously, beginning to appropriate to his highly personal uses the rhetoric which his literary world offered him ready-made? He seems here to be equally content, as in the earlier plays, either with merely ingenious figures of speech or with this other creative use of figures which belongs to poetry of the first order. When Lucrece and her maid stand weeping, he likens their tear-stained faces to

> . . . conduits coral cisterns filling

The image is forced and obscure. But when Lucrece, sad and in black, meets her husband after all that has passed, the figure Shakespeare uses to describe them is exquisite:

Both stood, like old acquaintance in a trance
Met far from home, wondering each other's chance.

In twenty-five stanzas Lucrece beguiles the time between her note to Collatine and his return by studying a "well-painted piece" of the Fall of Troy. The form of painting whether tapestry or painted cloth and the possible identification of the actual piece of work, have been the subject of much inquiry. Also critics have wondered whether it might be possible to gather from the description whether Shakespeare knew something about the art of painting. Nothing very definite or satisfactory has come of these inquiries. In the many stanzas of description, Shakespeare's repeated point is that the presentation is life-like. It is full of "pencill'd pensiveness" and "colour'd sorrow." Ever since the days of Achilles' shield and the carved bowl of Theocritus' shepherd, the meticulous description of a curiously wrought object has been a *tour de force* of the poet's art. Daniel's *Rosamond* describes a casket on which are wrought scenes from Greek mythology appropriate to persuade Rosamond to yield to Henry II. Shakespeare is giving the same kind of performance in the description of the painting of Troy. He makes it pertinent to Lucrece's situation. She finds Hecuba's face as full of grief as her own and Simon *Sinon* as plausible a villain as Tarquin who ruined her:

. . . as Priam him did cherish,
So did I Tarquin: so my Troy did perish.

With such diversions and digressions this amphibious

creature, *Lucrece,* creeps to its end. In the course of its
1850 lines, Shakespeare has met all the requirements he
contracted for. He has told a story drawn from the enchanted land of Roman mythical history. He has provided the appropriate accompaniments of rhetoric, débat,
descriptions of wall paintings, apostrophe and lament.
While he has been telling it, however, he has added to the
story an element not called for in the specifications. The
skeleton for a Senecan play has appeared with the curses
and invocations to revenge. Because the potential dramatist here is Shakespeare, the dramatic formula has taken
on life. At times both Tarquin and Lucrece give promise
of the tragic figures of the great period yet to come. At
times the narrative stanzas yield dialogue and stage set-
ing. To be sure the story falls half-way between a tale
in a book and an action on the stage. But this indecision
between these two habitations did not worry the Elizabethans. They themselves hardly thought beyond the
great simple category "story"; though they were coming
to have a decided preference for the fashion of telling it
by way of the stage.

II. THE INHERITANCE OF ELIZABETHAN LOVE POETRY
AND THE SONNET CYCLES OF SIDNEY, DANIEL,
SHAKESPEARE AND DRAYTON

When one comes to love lyrics in the Nineties and especially to that most popular form of love lyric, the sonnet, one finds the same mixture of poetical precedent and

TAPESTRY FROM
CHÂTEAU
D'AULHAC
(15TH CENT.)

'Figuring a battle un-
der the Walls of Troy
. . . with the Trojan
Women above look-
ing on from the
Walls.'

Such a tapestry as
this, a mediæval con-
ception of a classical
scene, may, according
to Sir Sidney Colvin,
have been in Shake-
speare's mind when
he wrote *The Rape
of Lucrece*

experiment which one finds in *Lucrece*. In the sonnets the development from tradition toward originality is shown in the change from formal love-making into a personal love story. There is a great change, too, from the kind of sonnet that opened the decade and a quite different kind in the middle and end of the Nineties. Furthermore the passion of love which differs so markedly in different individuals makes the variability of the sonnets even more bewildering. Before one comes to the great love sonneteers of this decade, however, one must review the inheritance of the Elizabethan sonneteer from earlier love poetry. It was a rich, ancient and varied heritage.

In the first place, the English poets then had ready for their use a hundred conventional ways of making love. They inherited these from civilisations, ancient, mediæval and renaissance, from a range of love poetry extending over nearly two thousand years. The business of expressing the experience of love in words has always been difficult, whether it was in pagan or Christian, Athenian or Roman, feudal or renaissance times. Till Catullus and Ovid, practically no poet except Sappho hit upon the plan of direct reporting, saying in words exactly what being in love felt like. It was far easier and more usual to describe the imaginations and ideals which the emotion of love set up in the brain and fancy of the lover. These ideals and fancies differed widely in their expression according to the difference in social setting; whether it was the island of Lesbos, Athens, imperial

Rome, the shores of the Black Sea, or mediæval castles and courts of love—or the high citadels of renaissance Italian cities. From this magnificent range of love poetry the Elizabethan love poet might draw.

Of all this variety of feeling and expression about love, the mediæval tradition had perhaps the greatest influence on the Elizabethans, though they did not accept it without many modifications. What were some of the qualities of mediæval love-making? With the Middle Ages there had come a ritual of devotion paid from afar to some beautiful and important lady. A new chivalrous behaviour toward the lady became necessary in a world that believed one mortal woman had been the Mother of God. Laws were formulated prescribing the whole duty of the lover to his lady. These laws were tested and discussed in the mediæval courts of love before a tribunal of lords and ladies. Thus mediæval love-making became a ritual. It conventionalised the private passion of love and generalised its personal caprices. The lover, moving through these intricate conventions, released his inward feeling, as a worshipper in the ritual of the Mass releases and makes constructive his inward religious ecstasy. Oftentimes, as in the Mass, the ritual was performed without the feeling. Thus a great deal of merely external love poetry sprang up.

When, however, the feeling of love was immediate and real, a great dilemma accompanied the experience of physical love. According to the Christian doctrine all earthly passions including love are ultimately an impediment to the soul. They stand in the way of its growing and single-hearted devotion to God. The holiest men and women became celibates. Earthly love withdrew one's mind from heavenly love. How was one to balance one's conduct between keeping love and foregoing it? Mediæval love poetry did not meet this dilemma squarely. It remained both sensuous and ideal. Early renaissance love poetry, in Dante, in Petrarch, in the French sonneteers, inherited this dilemma. For instance in Dante earthly love in its early stages set up such a frenzy of intense being, so clarified his perception of life, that it became for him the first step in a career of holy love. Petrarch was not so successful in metamorphosing his love for Laura into holiness. The worship and the sensuality alternate in his sonnets. Out of this conflict, it is true, come some of his most moving lines. This discussion of mediæval love and the confused attitude toward it leads one to an interesting conclusion. It is that after the advent of Christianity the experience of earthly love was both heightened and degraded. It might be a sin or something very near a sin. Yet it might be an experience whose apotheosis was very heaven.

The renaissance love poets inherited this idea but they modified it. Re-reading and often mis-reading Plato's ideas about love, they found in him a possible reconcilement between earthly and holy love. Plato was made to say that earthly love is the first stage in a progress toward heavenly love. This doctrine allowed one to love and yet be holy. With ingenious blending from one philosopher

and another, with a mystical o'er-leaping of the final
barriers of logic, Bembo, Ficino and a whole group of
renaissance Italian theorisers brought about a plausible
argument for love and holiness as one and the same
thing. For thoughtful Englishmen like Spenser, however, the reconcilement was not easy. His first two
Hymns on Love and *Beauty* are full of this Platonism.
Yet looking back at them, Spenser felt that they encouraged the young who were already "too vehemently carried with that kind of affection." Therefore he brought
out two more *Hymns,* this time addressed to Heavenly
Love and Beauty. Here Christ and God take the place
of Cupid and Venus.

Of course, it is not easy to name the precise ingredients
which made up the renaissance idea of love or to trace
the stages of its evolution. But the mediæval, Christian
idea and its blending with Plato formed an important
element. One must recognize this if one is to understand
the conflicting emphases of much Elizabethan love
poetry.

Another ingredient was the love poetry of Ovid. Ovid
was not new in the renaissance. He had in one way and
another been in constant view during the Middle Ages.
The sharpness and strength of the mediæval view of life,
however, had always subordinated Ovid to its own needs
rhetorical, metrical or passionate. But now in this amorphous renaissance world which was building itself slowly
up into a new order Ovid assumed more power. His
Metamorphoses still belonged to a land of tangled story

and delightful magic. But the *Amores,* the *Ars Amatoria*
and the *Heroides,* written in a pagan world innocent of
chivalry and high romance, innocent of the worship of
all women for the·Virgin's sake, spoke the very accents
of physical passion. This passion was not ennobled, not
idealised. Its sensual and psychical history were accurately reported. The Elizabethan writers of love lyrics
knew Ovid as well as they knew Petrarch. Yet something
in their Christian inheritance and in their racial tradition
weighed down their valiant attempts to report the phenomenon of love realistically. They did it more thought-
fully than Ovid. Ovid's analysis of passion, what stimulates it and retards it, how and why and when one suffers
from it, was deepened and altered in the Elizabethan's
psychology of lust and love. Yet Ovid's influence is
strong, even though it is modified. Its realistic view of
earthly love fitted in with the new scientific view of man's
life which was beginning in England at the end of the
sixteenth century.

Out of this embarrassment of riches, these alien elements, a host of Elizabethan sonneteers in the 1590's
made sonnet cycles about love. The poems were trivial
or earnest, academic or strongly felt. The poets might be
merely practising their rhetoric or they might be easing
a very real smart. The thing that differentiates the good
sonnets from the bad is the energy, the reality of feeling.
To utilise this old convention and assimilate Petrarchan
lines out of an elder Italy and, at the same time, to convey immediate reality, this was the problem. Let us look

at some famous Elizabethan sonnets and see how they solve the problem.

Take, for instance, Sidney's cycle, *Astrophel and Stella*. It was very famous. The sonnets were written presumably between 1580-83 and circulated in manuscript for ten years. They then appeared in careless and unauthorised editions in 1591 and 1592. Finally in the definitive edition in folio of Sidney's works, edited by his literary sister, Mary, Countess of Pembroke, in 1598, they achieved authoritative form nearly twenty years after their writing. Sidney of course did not begin the practice of sonnets. That had happened in the Thirties and Forties in the hands of Tudor courtiers under Henry VIII, as I have written in another chapter of this book. Neither was he the first one to revive the tradition. But the prestige of this young nobleman, his acceptance of leadership in the revival of English letters gave his poetry prominence. When that poetry was as intrinsically good, too, as his sonnet cycle certainly is, its influence was assured.

The Elizabethans, both "private friends" and general public, usually imagined a love story behind any set of love sonnets. Besides, the Elizabethan world was not versed in allegory for nothing. It knew how to read flesh and blood into such shadows as Diana and Delia. It saw specific calendar dates behind Primavera. It identified an actual country-house in an Eastern county of England when it read

Toward Aurora's Court a nymph doth dwell.

The authors of these cycles took the public's muckraking for granted. They often half-revealed and half-concealed the real facts deliberately, as if this method had what we should now call "advertising value." Giles Fletcher in his "Preface to the Reader," for his cycle to *Lycia* in 1593 wittily summarizes this situation:

If thou muse what my Licia is : take her to be some Diana, at the least chaste ; or some Minerva ; no Venus—fairer far. It may be she is learning's image, or some heavenly•wonder, which the precisest may not dislike. Perhaps under that name I have shadowed Discipline. It may be I mean that kind courtesy which I found at the patroness of these poems ; it may be some college. It may be my conceit, and portend nothing. . . .

In the case of Sidney's *Astrophel and Stella,* an actual love story seems certain. Because of it, certain ways of viewing life and writing about it characterise the sonnets. Sidney seems to have fallen in love with Penelope Devereux, daughter of the first Earl of Essex. Sidney was in "society" and so was she. In the train of the Court, he met her at her father's country-house in 1575 when he was twenty-one and she thirteen. He proposed himself as her suitor for marriage in 1576. In 1577, her mother, newly widowed, married Sidney's uncle. They may, for some reason, have retarded Sidney's suit. In any case Penelope married Lord Rich in 1581. A good number of the sonnets seem to have been written after her marriage and there are puns upon her married name. It is as if, once definitely beyond his possession, she became even

dearer. Sidney himself married in 1583 and died abroad
in 1586. One realises of course that the episode behind
the sonnets is but the ghost of an episode. Nothing can
be proved. Yet the actual circumstance and the social
setting of Sidney and this lady seem to have left the impress of reality upon the conventions and Petrarchan
borrowings of the cycle.

For instance, Sidney opens his *Astrophel and Stella*
with the conventional affirmation that his love is so
strong that it does not need mythology and old romance
to supplement its invention. This is the regular conventional opening. But the simplicity and directness of his
lines fool the reader into believing that the protest is
honest, that it springs from Sidney's own feeling. We
know he borrowed freely from Petrarch and the French
sonneteers. Yet in the opening sonnet he declares that
decorations from old books for his new and present love
seem unfitting. They are an actual impediment;

And other's feet still seemed but strangers in my way.

If he is hoaxing us, we yield ourselves willingly. He
flings out against the love poets who practise Euphuism;

Enam'ling with pied flowers their thoughts of gold.

He complains that they

. . . with strange similes enrich each line
Of herbs or beasts which Ind or Afric hold.

Yet no one is more cunning in this "enam'ling" of lines
than Sidney, himself. Other poets, he says, who lack the

inspiration of his Stella, must resort to mechanical means
to fill their lines:

> You that do dictionary's method bring
> Into your rhymes running in rattling rows;
> You that poor Petrarch's long-deceased woes
> With newborn sighs and denizened wit do sing.

Yet even while he is commiserating this artificiality, he
is practising alliteration (in the second line) and many
of his own sonnets echo "Petrarch's long-deceased
woes."

Yet *Astrophel and Stella* gives the effect of real poetry
about real happenings. The impress of yesterday's event
seems again and again to overlay an old pattern. For instance, in a formal entertainment for the French Embassy of 1581 Sidney has ridden well in the lists. As he
reflects upon the event, he likes to think that his skill
arose from his knowledge that Stella was there to watch
him. He turned this feeling into a sonnet. Even if the
original framework of that sonnet is in Petrarch, the
poem has the validity of feeling aroused by a specific set
of actual events. More intense and ruthless is the sonnet
in which he talks politely about foreign affairs in France,
in the Orient, in Ireland with this or that court acquaintance; yet all the while his love for Stella dwarfs the importance of foreign wars and international parleys. This
sonnet springs, by all tests of feeling, from the actual
moment. It begins "Whether the Turkish new moon,"
etc.

There is another way in which Sidney's cycle shows

the impress of the moment. It reflects the English attitude
about physical love. They refused in theory to accept
love as an ultimate thing in life. They contended rather
that it is a beautiful and perilous distraction from more
serious things. This attitude is reflected again and again
in *Astrophel and Stella*. The idea sometimes appears in
Platonic costume:

> True that true beauty virtue is indeed
>   Whereof this beauty can be but a shade
>
> .   .   .   .
>
> True that on earth we are but pilgrims made,
>   And should in soul up to our country move;
>   True, and yet true that I must Stella love.

His friends realising the career that should be ahead of
this gifted young man, try to deflect him from preoccupation with love. He summarises their argument:

Your words, my friend, (right healthful caustics) blame
  My young mind marred, whom love doth windlass so
  That mine own writings like bad servants show
  My wit's quick in vain thoughts, in virtue lame;

.   .   .   .

                    to my birth I owe
Nobler desires lest else that friendly foe,
Great expectation, wear a train of shame.

This is all very English, very serious, and what is to our
purpose here, out of his own life. The lines that record
these feelings are not conventional sonneteering. In the
last two sonnets he turns, *faute de mieux* one remembers

since Stella apparently was never in love with him, from earthly to heavenly love. They are two exquisite sonnets. One begins "Thou blind man's mark" and the other "Leave me, O Love." They contribute to the long war between earthly and heavenly love which reached back into the past beyond Petrarch, to the very bounds of the pagan world. Yet they illustrate how an old convention and a new reality of personal experience can be fused.

The wit and world-play in *Astrophel and Stella* are clever. He can riddle fiercely on the word "Rich" which was Stella's married name. He can build up the whole difficult scaffolding for a sonnet on the fact that his lady said No! No! and that two negatives make an affirmative. He has the nonchalance and sureness of touch of the aristocrat. He writes knowingly of this event and that to which "society" will understand the reference. He writes as an amateur, for his own set. R. M. Alden was not wrong when he applied to a certain quality in Sidney's cycle the phrase *vers de société*. The stiff sonnet form is lightly handled. There is something conversational in the broken lines and the tone of talk.

> For grammar says—oh, this, dear Stella, weigh—
> For grammar says,—to grammar who says nay?—
> That in one speech two negatives affirm.

On the whole the *Astrophel and Stella* cycle is a page out of Elizabethan "society." The amenities of the Seventies and early Eighties at Elizabeth's Court are here reflected in the love poetry of her most perfect courtier. "Most perfect" but not necessarily most spectacular or most interesting. Comparing these sonnets to those of Shakespeare which were written in the middle of the next decade or to those of Drayton which belong in the late Nineties and 1600's, one finds Sidney's acceptance of love simple and whole-hearted. But it has not that teasing power to disintegrate a man which it has in Shakespeare or Donne. It is not so intricate, so cruelly tangled in its effect. There are many reasons for this difference. The Eighties were not so reflective and self-conscious, so mercilessly analytical as the Nineties. Besides, Sidney belonged to the aristocracy. His great worldly position must have saved him from the distracting effect of uncertainty. Shakespeare and Drayton were not so assured. Their assault upon life was single-handed. For them, individual success or failure was all. By being, perforce, more watchful of the human scene, they perhaps became more aware of the perilous power of caprice in winning or losing. At any rate, love in *Astrophel and Stella* is strong and unhappy but not torturing. It does not pirouette into eternity or chaos, nor quibble with the very centre of feeling. It does not decompose the soul that entertains it.

Daniel's sonnet sequence to *Delia* furnishes an historical bridge between Sidney's *Astrophel* and Shakespeare's cycle. Daniel lived at Wilton for a time, as a tutor and literary adviser to Sidney's sister, the Countess of Pembroke. He was learned and competent. He did

most things well. His cycle, published in part sur-
reptitiously in 1591, amended by him in 1592 with a
dedicatory letter to his patroness, and enlarged in the
edition of 1594, throws an interesting light on the difficulty of appraising a man rightly in his own time. The
Elizabethans thought highly of Daniel's sonneteering.

> Sweet honey-dropping Daniel doth wage
> War with the proudest big Italian
> That melts his heart in sugr'd sonnetting.

It was thus that the Cambridge play, *Return from Par-
nassus,* described him. "Sugr'd" as an adjective for the
sonnet was a favourite. Meres applied it to Shakespeare's
sonnets. But the "sug'ring" yields a very different sort
of sparkle in the poems of these two, Daniel and Shakespeare.

If Shakespeare read Daniel's *Delia,* and there are
many fairly conclusive evidences that he did, what would
he find? To that question we, removed by three and a
half centuries, will not venture an answer. It is safe to
say that he thought better of the sonnets than any modern reader possibly can do. They are meticulously correct in form. The obvious allusions are ingeniously
made. The lover cries out to Youth, to Time, to the
lady's lute. His classical knowledge is nimble: he mocks
Leander, Hyacinth, and the figures of the *Iliad.* He calls
on Petrarch and his Laura. Yet there is no "lift" about
Daniel's sonnets. They never come off the ground. They
crawl, weighted down with abstract words, dutiful. To

see a personal passion, real or imagined, beneath them is impossible. The belief that Delia is Daniel's literary patroness, one to whom he feels duty and gratitude, one who would appreciate his skill in this literary game of sonneteering, grows as one reads. Their academic perfection and their frigidity exactly fit the case. Daniel has distinct powers as critic, historian, teller of tragical tales. He talks well in verse. But the love sonnet does not call for talking. Yet the success of *Delia* proves how contemporary judgment is limited by contemporary fashions. We condescend to the Elizabethan "fashions" in sonneteering and praise only the poets who transcend them. But for the Elizabethans themselves the perfect response to contemporary demand in itself gave a pleasure which we are unable to re-create.

What did Shakespeare do in his own cycle with the materials for sonnet-making? How much concession did he make to the Petrarchan tradition? How far do his ideas coincide with Ovid on love? How nearly does his poetry come to his own feeling? Such questions are easier to answer and more satisfactory when answered than questions about the precise autobiographical incident which lies behind this poetry. All the sonnets of this period were supposed to have some autobiography behind them. Surely these of Shakespeare do have. The cycle is addressed to a man. It has no fancy name. Some at least of the sonnets were known in manuscript for eleven or twelve years before an edition was brought out in 1609 with a dedication to Mr. W. H. signed by the printer Thorpe. Who Mr. W. H. was, precisely what Shakespeare's relationship to him was, it is impossible to determine.

Yet, as in the cycle of Sidney, the closeness of an actual situation is felt at every turn. The man is young, beautiful, gifted. Shakespeare is older and his inferior socially. He advises him to marry. If he does this he will defy time, change and death by transmitting his qualities to children. A lovely wanton is involved. She tricks Shakespeare and the friend, and tangles the relationship between them. One feels there is an actual story behind these sonnets. One falls upon the very accents of an hour ago, yet the precise situation which aroused them is gone forever. Wordsworth and Browning were both right about Shakespeare's *Sonnets.* Shakespeare did unlock his heart in the *Sonnets,* yet so elusively, with such chariness of actual incident that the story will never be clearly deciphered.

But to these other more abiding questions it is possible to give answers. In the first place, the Petrarchan convention appears in Shakespeare's *Sonnets.* But obviously it is adapted. As in all the things Shakespeare did, he followed the fashion in these sonnets. Yet he created within that fashion something new. The first hundred and twenty-six sonnets being addressed to a beautiful young man find no place for the same kind of languishings and cruelties that are in the regular cycles. The rhetoric, the figures, the ingenuities and extravagances are all there but the situation is different. It is still a situation of love but the exhortation is that the beloved object shall marry and have children and so preserve his loveliness through posterity. In the course of this change in the essential relationship, the whole conventional sonnet style comes alive. One feels, even in the midst of apostrophes and alliteration, a little like an intruder when reading Shakespeare's *Sonnets*.

Into the course of this passionate story many subjects and many kinds of treatment come. For instance, Shakespeare here and there says a good deal about poetry, its present and future, its futilities and successes. Another point which occupies him is the difference between love and lust. Also his personal moods come in. He pities himself and flings out in bitter disillusion about life. Specific happenings are glanced at. He writes a sonnet to accompany the gift of a notebook. It was probably one of those "table-books" which fashionable young men like Hamlet and John Donne took to the play to record good lines in. Sometimes he finds it hard to say what he means. The idea seems only half-worked out and left unfinished in the sonnet because of the press of living and earning his living. He is not disturbed by the intermingling of second-rate with first-rate poetry. In fact the whole series must be taken realistically, for the piecemeal, uneven thing that it is. Then its supreme beauties may be honestly distinguished and its trivialities will be engaging just because they are so frankly unimportant.

If one proceeds thus honestly one finds, for instance, that the first eleven sonnets are more ingenious than

poetical. They are the precise and meticulous meeting of
an obligation. This obligation was to embroider appropriate sentiments into verse for an important person.
The result is not great poetry. There is so much conventional idolatry of Shakespeare's *Sonnets* that it is necessary to speak out sharply, to clear the air of empty praise
and look at what lies before one on the printed page.
The theme of these opening sonnets is that one so beautiful, so important, so endowed with gifts should marry
and have children so that this precious heritage may be
preserved. As a minor accompaniment to this main
theme, Shakespeare uses the idea of change, decay, the
devouring of a thing by mere time. Flowers die, suns set,
seasons pass, and the end of all these beauties is not beautiful. The setting sun "reeleth from the day." Something precious is wasted if this young man, having the
power to transmit his gifts to another generation, instead
makes "worms thine heir." The ingenuity which can say
the same thing over and over in different images during
the first eleven sonnets is great. But ingenuity is not
enough to make poetry. Shakespeare describes the feeling of futility and decay; but he does not reproduce that
feeling.

Archibald MacLeish, writing of the situation in poetry
today, makes this necessary distinction between actual
poetry and lines which have only the external form of
poetry. "Poetry," he says, "is not ornament, is not flowers, is not the pumping up of language with metaphors
. . . is not a charm to make the mind forget, is not a

paint, an enamel, a veneer. Poetry . . . is revelation, is
discovery. . . . Its quality is to illuminate from within,
not to describe from without. Its language is not com-
munication but experience." Thus a playwright, poet
and critic of the 1930's prescribes a formula for poetry
which applies to Shakespeare's *Sonnets*. One can go
through them using this modern formula and by it one
can separate the elegant gesture, the mould for poetry in
some sonnets from the living presence of poetry in others.
For instance, Sonnets XII, XIII, and XIV are still harp-
ing on the same idea as the first eleven. There is the same
kind of imagery, too. Yet in these sonnets this imagery is
not mere ornament; it is the living feeling. In XII, for
instance, there are the usual images. The violet, the summer's green, the figure of Time with his scythe are all
used. Yet in this case the sonnet needs them in order to
be the feeling of terror that is at the heart of change.
They create the desperation of finite man faced by
infinity.

> And nothing 'gainst Time's scythe can make defence
> Save breed, to brave him when he takes thee hence.

Shakespeare says a good deal about his own idea of
poetry in the course of the *Sonnets*. He is writing to a
person who is not merely beautiful but has brains, learning, an interest in the arts. Furthermore this man to
whom he writes is a possible rival in a passionate affair
with a dark lady, and knows the vicissitudes of existence
in a man's world. Shakespeare, therefore, in the midst

of his devotion stops to talk to this friend about the artistic expression of subjects in which they are both interested and especially about poetry. Spenser, Sidney, Essex, all of them in fact, were as concerned about the future of English poetry as the young literary people of England and America are today. They felt, and rightly we think, looking back through the perspective of years, that English poetry after Chaucer had declined. Nothing that they had yet done in the sixteenth century was intrinsically great, yet the actual production had the stirrings of immortality in it. The conscious effort of poets, the talk about poetry, the essays written upon it all were moving toward the realisation of this greatness. Just then in the Nineties Spenser's poetical publications began to show them what English poetry already was achieving. The plays were, of course, the last place where they looked for "poetry," in the exalted sense in which they used that word. We, looking back, see that in the plays more than anywhere else Elizabethan poetry reached its heights. But they, thinking more conventionally, looked at *Lucrece* and *Hero and Leander* and at the published sonnet cycles and there found something like great poetry.

Shakespeare and his friend were interested in this contemporary experiment with poetry. They may have had access in manuscript form to the poetry of Donne and Ralegh in the Nineties. Certainly in a sonnet like XXXII, written probably between 1593 and 1596, Shakespeare gives expression to the change and development in poetry

which was then going on. He thinks that perhaps these
sonnets of his will soon be eclipsed by a new and more
moving kind of poetry, for the Muse is growing "with
this growing age." It is a time which is likely to produce
a better, more true poetic style. In LXXVI he is harp-
ing on the same idea:

> Why with the time do I not glance aside
> To new-found methods and to compounds strange?

Some rival poet writing in praise of his own patron and
friend, steals his thunder and stops his mouth.

> Was it the proud full sail of his [rival's] great verse,
> Bound for the prize of all too precious you,
> That did my ripe thought in my brain inhearse,
> Making their tomb the womb wherein they grew?
> (LXXXVI.)

He wonders about the diction and figures of speech of
these rival poets:

> . . . yet when they have devised
> What strained touches rhetoric can lend,
> Thou truly fair wert truly sympathized
> In true plain words by thy true-telling friend;
>   And their gross painting might be better used
>   Where cheeks need blood; in thee it is abused.
> (LXXXII)

To be sure there is personal rancour mixed with this
literary criticism. Yet the question of plain as against
decorated style is raised.

Of course it was not merely a matter of plain as against decorated style that produced the rift between the "old" and the "new" poetry. It was a matter of having deeper things to say, things felt rather than clearly known, things about which one could not rhyme elaborately and prettily. One needed a new unused set of images, chosen because they were pertinent not because they were beautiful or usual. Oftentimes the thing one had to say was so tenuous, so difficult to realise that one could approach it only by a subtle comparison, a half-articulated metaphor. This sort of material in this sort of poetic image comes very close to being what has been called, since Dryden first applied the word, "metaphysical." While Shakespeare is certainly not a "metaphysical" in the strictest sense of this word, yet several times in the course of his sonnet cycle both the material and expression almost deserve that label.

For instance, in Sonnets XLIII to XLVI he writes on a paradoxical idea, that nearness to the beloved comes through absence and memory. He discusses by the aid of figures of speech the relationship of the physical being to the psychical being. He compares the actual sight of the beloved with the imaginary sight of the beloved in absence. He uses simple words. Yet because his idea is difficult to understand, the words are difficult to follow. He uses an elaborate image in XLVI. It is an image not out of conventional poetry but out of the law courts. It is a device for trapping and presenting to the reader a

subtle idea. In CXVIII he compares the moods of appre-
hension and testing that accompany love, to certain medical processes:

> As, to prevent our maladies unseen
> We sicken to shun sickness when we purge,
> Even so, being full of your ne'er-cloying sweetness
> To better sauces did I frame my feeding
>
> .   .   .   .
>
>   But thence I learn, and find the lesson true,
>   Drugs poison him that so fell sick of you.

The meaning is intricate; the riddle is difficult to de-
cipher. The comparison is certainly not "pretty" or
"poetical." Yet we can work out the idea far enough to
know that Shakespeare has felt the involutions of passionate experience and has tried, only half successfully
one must admit, to convey them. The psychology of lust,
the pursuit of it and the after-effects are defined in
CXXIX in all their ugliness and folly. In this case it is
the idea that is unconventional for a sonnet cycle. The
style is plain and lucid enough. It is even wittily brief:

> All this the world well knows: yet none knows well
> To shun the heaven that leads men to this hell.

It is almost wit in Pope's sense of that word.

Often in such passages as this, the poetry of Shakespeare's *Sonnets* is close to his own experience and the
unconventionality of his style expresses this unconventional material. It places him distinctly in the group of
experimenters, of arduous young men who struggled to

make art imprison life as it is, warm and confused, ugly and maimed. Out of their struggles they were forging a new, more lucid medium for expression.

Yet even so, this sort of thing in Shakespare's *Sonnets* is not most characteristic of them. On the whole, they had their contemporary success and probably a good deal of their success with posterity because they possessed those obvious and universal qualities which make poetry "popular." They are full of commonplaces about life, wittily worded. They express the common feelings of all time about love. Sometimes the expression is not any more personal or penetrating than the expression of a popular love lyric. They ring the changes on absence and separation, on self-depreciation by comparison with the beloved, on jealousy, on love and life being one and life being useless without love. To illustrate this, take

How like a winter hath my absence been   (XCVII)

or

So are you to my thoughts as food to life   (LXXV)

or, in disgust with the round of existence,

Tired with all these, from these I would be gone
Save that to die I leave my love alone.   (LXVI)

These are all commonplaces of the experience of being in love. He declares that to talk about love is to say the same inadequate thing over and over, that love itself cannot be expressed:

> "Fair kind and true," is all my argument;
> Fair kind and true varying to other words;
> And in this change is my invention spent.   (CV)

Shakespeare's reflections upon these conventional feelings show a beautiful use of conventional figures and diction, yet that use *is* conventional.

Some of the sonnets are obscure not by intention nor from the difficulty of expressing the feeling but because they were probably hastily written and not worked over. After all, one remembers that the *Sonnets* were in manuscript for ten or twelve years "among his private friends." They were not revised by Shakespeare for publication as were *Venus and Adonis* and *Lucrece*. They have the incompleteness of material from one's private notebooks. The meaning, for instance, of the exchange of hearts in XXII is not clear. In XXIV the elaborate image which compares a picture in a shop window to the picture of his love which is in his bosom's shop is obscure. The sonnets which contain these figures do not seem to be finished. They need, in the plain prose of editorial criticism, to be "worked over." In XXVI he confesses his failure to convey his meaning. He asks his friend to read the poems and make allowance for the defects of their expression,

> Till whatsoever star that guides my moving
> Points on me graciously with fair aspect
> And puts apparel on my tatter'd loving.

Sometimes the obscurity of expression is the result of

compression. He feels deeply and inarticulately and
flings a few words after his feeling but does not quite
catch it.

> O, let me suffer, being at your beck,
> The imprison'd absence of your liberty.   (LVIII)

One thinks one knows what this means. It sets up the
right feeling in the reader. But it should not be scrutinised too closely, else the meaning becomes uncertain and
the expression unsatisfactory. It is intuition, not gram-
mar that gives these two lines clarity.

All in all, in the *Sonnets* as in his other work, Shakespeare plays the game of the particular type of poem he
is writing according to the contemporary rules. There
is a good deal of the Petrarchan tradition, of Ovid on
love, of Platonism (explicitly in LIII for instance), of
ringing the beautiful changes on Time and Mutability
and Death. There is under the convention that necessary
feeling that the convention shrouds an actual affair.
Again and again we are on the heels of a particular moment in Shakespeare's life. There is metrical ingenuity
and word riddling. In fact, he meets all the specifications
of his contract for a sonnet cycle. He goes much further,
however. He shows himself to be one of the greatest of
those daring creatures of the Nineties who peered into
forbidden depths and took life without preconceived
ideas. He reflects upon a poignant private experience.
Its very form and pressure warm the beautiful convention of the Elizabethan sonnet.

How lightly the sonnet passed. If it did survive, it continued only by taking on the colour of life as it really was, by speaking of other and more immediate things than pearls and roses, than tempests from the lady's frowns or supplications to the moon or sleep. This is shown in the great sonneteers of the Nineties, Sidney, Spenser, Shakespeare. Increasingly, if a poet kept to this form, he was more and more inclined to throw away tradition and pour into the sonnet mould his present honest feelings.

This deepening of the sonnet as the century drew to an end is shown with especial clarity in Drayton, whose sonnet-writing career extends for twenty years from 1594 to 1614. In its course it runs from convention to stark realism. The first edition of his sonnets, *Idea's Mirror,* 1594, prints fifty-one sonnets. The young Drayton, then twenty-eight, claims that these poems "long have slept in sable night." Printing does not rouse them. They are as smooth as one could wish. They play according to the rules, satirize the sonnet, dream upon old books, compare the lover's heart to an anvil. But they are not poetry. Very little of the real Drayton emerges. In XIV he is strongly vexed at the lady. But the anger is screened behind a long description of the sun's daily journey across the sky. As a whole the 1594 *Idea's Mirror* is dull. In the second augmented edition of 1599, however, a new Drayton, growing acid under the pressure of life and the lack of success with the old Queen, betrays himself. When he feels passion, he teaches the sonnet, as in

XIII, to record it. When love takes too great a toll, he wittily rebukes it as in XXIV.

By the fourth edition, in 1605, he is a man of forty-two, whose footing in this new Jacobean seventeenth century is none too sure. He has tried for favours and not received them. His small fame has not grown. He has read Nashe and the realistic satirists. He still writes sonnets but into their metrical confines he dares to put realistic images, conveying the macabre side of life. L of the 1605 volume, for instance, compares his lady's advances and retreats toward him to the experiments made by surgeons on a condemned criminal. It is not pretty but it is moving. The surgeons

> First make incision on each mastering vein
> Then staunch the bleeding, then transpierce the corse
> And with their balms recure the wounds again
> Then poison and with physic him restore,
>
> Not that they fear the hopeless man to kill
> But their experience to increase the more.
> Even so my mistress works upon my ill,
>   By curing me and killing me each hour
>   Only to show her beauty's sovereign power.

From the point of view of style, this sonnet is well wrought. But it is more than that. It is also the witty expression of his little agony. There was nothing so biting and realistic as this in the 1594 edition. Of course, Drayton is eleven years older.[1]

[1] The reference to the fall of Essex in the next sonnet enables one to be quite sure that No. L was written after 1601.

The change in the general flavour of his sonnets across these twenty years, shows as in a mirror the progress of English poetry. It has developed from discipleship, respect for great models and imitation of them, into maturity. The lessons in metrics and diction have been learned. English poetry now no longer goes in leading strings but speaks out boldly and with originality about the depths and heights of living. After the opening of the seventeenth century, the sonnet cycle waned. When the form survived in single sonnets or small groups, it survived only because the life and air of reality were allowed to circulate through the quatrains and couplets and to make room for the impress of a changing world. Drayton's later sonnets are full of hard, everyday words. They are often close to satire, surfeited or disillusioned with love. They are not bad company for the poetry of Donne whom, through the young Sir Henry Goodyere, Drayton must have known or known about.

III. THE "SONG BOOKS" AND DRAYTON'S "POLYOLBION"

Behind the major poetry of the Nineties whether it is the ambitious narrative poem or the sonnet cycle, behind the work of clearly outlined individuals like Spenser, Sidney, Shakespeare, Ralegh, or Drayton, there is a chorus of minor song. Often it is unclaimed by a particular singer. Often it is mediocre. In the actual Elizabethan world of course there was constant singing; either of madrigals, which were part songs unaccompanied, or of "airs" sung to the accompaniment of lute or virginal. Sometimes the words to accompany this music are famous, often they are good, but more often still they are undistinguished. Sometimes they are only an after-thought, subordinated to the music. The words and music were put together in *Song Books*. They also were included in those heterogeneous verse collections which were called *Miscellanies*.

In the outstanding case of Thomas Campion's *Book of Airs,* both words and poetry were composed carefully by a man who reverenced his art. "What epigrams are in poetry," says Campion in the preface to the 1601 *Book of Airs,* "the same are airs in music: then in their chief perfection when they are short and well seasoned." In the 1613 preface, he is still working consciously and reverently on these trifles: "I have chiefly aimed to couple my words and notes lovingly together, which will be much for him to do that hath not powers over both."

As a reflection of music in actual life, songs find their way into the Elizabethan novels and plays. Greene's songs in his romances are often the lovely reward for pages of boredom. Dekker and Heywood build songs into their plays. Shakespeare used them, too. In his early plays the songs are likely to be merely a diversion, a melodious interruption of the more serious dramatic interest. Then as he grows more artistically economical in his plays, the songs are not merely isolated things. They serve as overtones from the mood of a character who has just been speaking. They interpret through atmospheric effect the heart of a dramatic situation. In a late play like *The Tempest,* the songs echo the quintessential meaning of the play as a whole.

In general, however, the verses for these songs are not good poetry. They are not penetrating enough to be interesting or moving. They are too light, too pretty, too merely pictorial. They give too obvious a picture of an obvious mood like gaiety or sadness. Sometimes they play a trifling game of double meaning:

> Ah dear heart, why do you rise?
> The light that shines comes from your eyes.
> The day breaks not, it is my heart,
> To think that you and I must part.
> O stay, or else my joys will die
> And perish in their infancy.

This goes prettily when set to music. Yet verses of this sort are only a melodious background for the real poetry of the Elizabethans.

The circumstances of their singing, in great halls after dinner, in a lady's antechamber, in a barber shop; the easy procuring of street musicians, hailed in on the spur of the moment to make a party, these are the things which throw a glamour over the Elizabethan songs. Such circumstances, still vivid in the perspective of centuries, give to the *Song Books* the warmth of personal presence. The company that sang from them has only just said "good night" and gone through the door. Because warmth and immediacy still belong to these trifles, we hold onto them. They become a passport to the living interpretation of the greater poems of the same period. Because of our jolly companionship with these minor fellows, we find great poets and the conventions of their verse less formidable.

One sees, too, by reading these countless verse trifles that verse was an everyday means of writing. The Elizabethans were not pontifical about it. Anybody could practise verse and a good many nobodies did. It could be used, for instance, to record history or the topography and antiquities of Britain in a work like Drayton's *Polyolbion*.

This *Poly-Olbion*, the "many blessed" England, begun in 1598 and continued to great bulk with maps, was printed in part in 1613 and completed in 1622. It offers a verse catalogue in alexandrines of the rivers, woods and wonders of the English counties. Drayton's long descriptive title shows how handily Pegasus trots in harness. This title reads: "A chorographical description of all the tracts, rivers, mountains, forests and other parts of this renowned isle of Great Britain with intermixture of the most remarkable stories, antiquities, wonders . . . digested into a poem." Poetry was a sturdy affair when it was capable of drawing such loads. True, the *Polyolbion* has no flights. Yet if one has a taste for detailed description of English country and for the leisurely itemising of a view, with a façade of legends about the marriage of streams thrown in for good measure, then the *Polyolbion* is an experience. A Warwickshire deer-park looked like this:

. . . Both sorts of seasoned deer,
Here walks the stately red, the freckled fallow there
The bucks and lusty stags amongst the rascals strewed,
As sometimes gallant spirits amongst the multitude.

As the hermit walks through the country,

Each little village yields his short and homely fare;
To gather windfall'n sticks his great'st and only care
Which every aged tree still yielded to his fire.

One can find one's own favourite corner of Sussex or
Westmoreland in the *Polyolbion* and look at it through
Drayton's Elizabethan eyes. The *Polyolbion* is a griev-
ously neglected book. Our modern world is too impatient to savour the quiet details of an unhurried journey
through England on Drayton's smooth-riding alexandrines.

A general view of the poetry of the Nineties is not
unsuitably concluded by an account of *Polyolbion,* this
rhymed gazetteer of England. To be sure it is a pedestrian affair. It is, too, at the opposite pole from the
lightning-like revelation of great poetry in some of the
sonnets and the long narratives. But it shows how natural, for a tremendous range of occasions, writing in
metre was. It removes this whole era of poetry from the
danger of being too reverently regarded. It reflects a
period when poetry, heavy with tradition, was yet daringly original; when it was a part of life, as it has never
been since; when it came home, magnificently or prettily,
to the infinitely various business and bosoms of men.

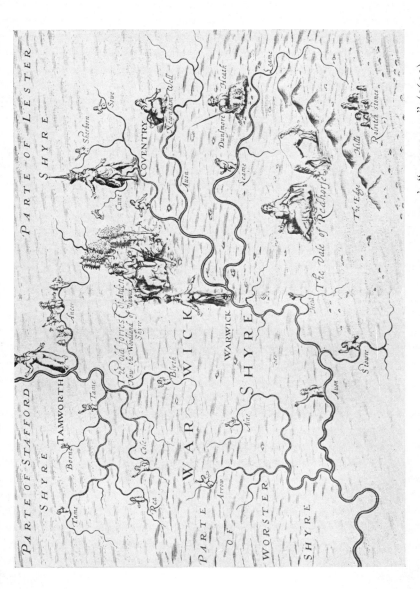

PICTORIAL MAP OF WARWICKSHIRE MADE TO ILLUSTRATE DRAYTON'S "POLYOLBION" (1613)

This map engraved by William Hole pictures Shakespeare's and Drayton's native county as it was during their life-time

CHAPTER IV

Edmund Spenser

On first acquaintance Spenser's poetry has the remoteness of a fairy tale and the unreality of a tapestry. Happily this aloofness of his poetry is offset by a vivid knowledge of his life. One can make him walk beside the Cam; lounge in the embrasure of some window in the great hall of Essex House in London; pass over the drawbridge into the towered fortress of Dublin Castle where he lived for two years as secretary to Lord Grey. One can see him inspecting the ploughed lands on his 3000 acreage in Munster; or looking out for the decent housing of his six English tenant farmers; or tempting a wandering Irish minstrel into the hall at Kilcolman Castle to sing an Irish ballad to the accompaniment of some outlandish instrument.

His actual acquaintance with the authors and critics of his day is also easy to trace. One can reconstruct, on actual evidence of their acquaintance, long conversations on the function and method of poetry with Sir Philip Sidney and Sir Edward Dyer in London. Spenser described these conversations in his letters from London to Gabriel Harvey, the Cambridge don who had influenced him during his undergraduate days. The material of these conversations is not very interesting. What makes them real is their reflection of the intense interest which these young men felt in matters of art. Poetry was, in frequent moods, more important to them than daily bread or success. Spenser recalls in a letter of October, 1579, two lines "which I translated you *ex tempore* in bed, the last time we lay together in Westminster." Precious young fools, arguing hotly and inconclusively about art. Through this heat of argument, even though it is preserved in the heavy prose of letters and prefaces, this young man comes alive and entices us to look at his poetry.

The key to this poetry lies, I believe, in a right understanding of the man. Just as it would be impossible to appraise fairly the public achievement of two such different men as Stanley Baldwin and Ramsay MacDonald without taking into account the fundamental attitude of each, so it is footless to compare Spenser and Ralegh or Spenser and Shakespeare without a clear-cut preliminary idea of the different bases upon which their lives were built. Spenser was a public official who made reports on Ireland, compiled statistics, studied the theory of government in French authorities like Bodin. He was also a poet who wrote letters about poetry and criticism. These two major interests provide a rich material from which to reconstruct his point of view. That point of view is always conservative. Spenser is an orderly, careful, serious man with an accurate knowledge of the history of whatever activity he is engaged upon, and a capacity for turning the light of that history upon his present undertaking. He lived in a changing world, was aware of it and did not enjoy it any more than the conservative person today enjoys it. But like the constructive conservatives now, he worked carefully and constantly at the problem of the best adaptation of the old to the new, and by his method created stability in the midst of flux.

In school he came under the influence of one of the most progressive educators of his day, Richard Mulcaster, master of the Merchant Taylor's School in London. In Mulcaster's book, *Positions,* on the theory and practice of education, the curriculum exists for the student and the student is not daily offered up to the system. It is an epitome of all that was finest in the mingling of tradition and experiment in the renaissance. It was to this man that the schoolboy, Spenser, presented himself every week-day morning at seven. He pursued the long day's round of study in classics, renaissance Continental authors, and English diction and style, with two hours out for luncheon, until five o'clock.

It was a famous school in the best sense of that word. The integrity and independence of Mulcaster, his sound learning and intelligent experimentation, drew the attention of important people. Busy men like the Dean of St. Paul's and the distinguished translator, Miles Coverdale, found time to be public examiners at the Merchant Taylor's. The question of the English language and how it could be shaped and smoothed into a fitting instrument for the voice of this new England was one of Mulcaster's chief concerns. Unquestionably Spenser's interest in the English language and the problem of metre began there. He worked hard, won prizes and went up to Cambridge. He found Cambridge in a state of healthy revolt from tradition, inclining to follow those leaders of modern thought who would "substitute for mediæval formalism the natural light of reason." In religion, too, the University stood on the side of Puritanism against the traditional Church.

It was at Cambridge that the magnitude of this man began to emerge. He took a conservative point of view about new ideas and revolutions. Gabriel Harvey, with his belligerent pedantry and his fashionable, self-centred classicism, undertook to impose his ideas upon the young Spenser. Spenser swam out gallantly from under them. Gently he took the measure of Harvey, kept him as a friend, but defied his point of view. Harvey's position on classical metre as a model for English metre was ludicrous but logical. The classics were the great masters. English poetry, anxious for reformation and new life, must imitate them even in metrical patterns. But Spenser opposed Harvey. He argued that the English nation and the English language must find their own metres. The English past had much to offer, though it was not to be followed slavishly. This past contained Chaucer; it contained the mediæval romances with their blend of realism and symbolism, their combination of faith and fact.

Spenser's greatness is in no way more evident than in

his use of the English mediæval tradition. He was great
enough to love new things, to wish to follow them, yet at
the same time to hold onto England's native past, to
effect a transition. He suspected abruptness. Ben Jonson, in 1619, twenty years after Spenser's death, criti-
cised his language and metre. But Jonson was the very
opposite of Spenser. He judged and wrote according to
the standard of the classics, as he understood it. Unhappily, with a few brilliant exceptions, he wrote according
to a standard which meant nothing to the English public.
Spenser, on the other hand, knew that he was a part of all
the English tradition that lay behind him. The pageantry and symbolism of the mediæval Church; its blending
of didacticism and sensuous beauty; the chivalric literature which rested upon it; that *double-entendre,* mediæval allegory; all these were things to which Spenser had
the key, which he wisely and honestly never threw
away. He was not embarrassed by the inconsistency
of retaining them side by side with new and different
ideas and methods. From them all he made something
vital.

The preface to his first public success in 1579, *The
Shepheard's Calendar,* illustrates this blending of old
and new. It was written by E. K., presumably Edward
Kirke, a friend of Spenser's at Cambridge. E. K. shared
with Spenser a vital interest in the future of English
poetry. The argument of the Preface presents Spenser's
point of view. He maintains that fitness of material re-
gardless of its source has been Spenser's only concern in

writing *The Shepheard's Calendar*. Consequently the
poem draws from every period. Each thing is selected
for its appropriateness in the part of the poem where it is
used. E. K. names the strands from which the fabric is
made. In the first place, the poem is allegorical. It aims
"to unfold great matter of argument covertly." E. K.
admits that he has not all the keys to the allegory but a
few are clear. Colin is Spenser, Hobbinol is Harvey, and
so on. Allegory had begun to creep into pure pastoral as
early as Vergil's *Eclogues*. Spenser has, therefore, an
ancient precedent for using it in his own poem. E. K. reminds the reader of the long past of pastoral poetry. It
began with Theocritus. It came down across the early
renaissance via Mantuan in Italy and Marot in France
to "this our new Poet, a bird whose principals be scarce
grown out but yet as that in time shall be able to keep
wing with the best."

When one turns to the sources of Spenser's poem, one
finds that E. K.'s long list of predecessors was honest.
The Shepheard's Calendar, while it contains much original matter, is patched all over with rich colours out of
the pastoral poets. They gave both general ideas and the
originals of many specific passages. Besides these, the
Calendar has adaptations of mediæval débats and illustrative fables. The theme ranges from the private emotion of love to public concerns and on beyond to more
abstract ideas. The "moral" pastorals are "mixed with
satiric bitterness." In fact one can hardly find a better
example of the mingling of ancient, mediæval and mod-

ern, which made up renaissance literature. Chaucer and
the author of *Piers Ploughman* are never out of Spenser's mind. In some of the pastorals he revives the accen-
tual alliterative verse. The extraordinary thing, at least
to a modern reader, is the poem's vitality in the midst of
so much borrowing. It transcends this mass of tradition
and becomes an original poem with the stamp of Spenser's own world.

For all its borrowed glory, *The Shepheard's Calendar*
is full of English country, English flowers, English
songs, and, on its more serious side, English affairs, political and ecclesiastical. E. K. in his dedicatory letter to
Harvey had carefully divided the eclogues into "plain-
tive," "recreative" and "moral." Love, friendship, and
the philosophy of conduct, private and public, are the
things Spenser writes about. Decked though his platter
is with foreign garnishes, the *pièce de résistance* is sturdy
English. It may be Leicester or Elizabeth or Bishop
Grindal whom he discusses or it may be a more abstract
theme, the quintessence of life as a thoughtful English
poet understood it. Modern art tries to discard tradition
and convention which may stand between the artist and
the piece of life he is re-creating upon canvas or paper.
But the renaissance artist loved his inherited parapher-
nalia, cherished and adapted it. He was so close to the
piece of life he was transforming into art that he had no
fear of the garnish obscuring the main dish.

To see how lightly Spenser used tradition, one has only
to look at the language of *The Shepheard's Calendar*.

Ben Jonson, much less independent than Spenser, was horrified by the archaisms which Spenser introduced throughout his poetry. "He writ no language" was Jonson's succinct judgment. In a practical sense, Ben Jonson was probably right. In order to launch *The Shepheard's Calendar* fairly, even upon its own public, it was necessary to provide a glossary "for the exposition of old words and harder phrases." E. K. provided this glossary:

as I knew many excellent and proper devices both in words and matter would pass in the speedy course of reading either as unknown or as not marked, and that in this kind as in other we might be equal to the learned of other nations, I thought good to take the pains upon me.

But any poetry, even if it is as beautiful as that of Burns, which is written in a real or artificial dialect (for this latter phrase fairly describes Spenser's language) scares off readers. Jonson's objections were perhaps justified. Although *The Shepheard's Calendar* gave Spenser reputation, one wonders what percentage of a random Globe Theatre audience, for instance, had read it. His public of the future, too, has been limited, chiefly because of the difficult language.

Spenser chose this archaic language with complete independence of tradition. It reflected the staunch originality of his thought. In the first place, as E. K. points out, Spenser had read the great English authors of the late Middle Ages. Walking in the sun of this great poetry "needs he mought [must] be sunburned."

Though Spenser had been burned by the light of Chaucer and Langland, he acknowledged it in his own practice more openly than most Elizabethan poets. This shows how free from contemporary fashion Spenser was. It is true that Chaucer was usually salaamed to by Elizabethan writers. But they paid their lip-service graciously and passed on to the poets whom they really wanted to quote and imitate. These were the Greeks, though they were handled superficially, and the Romans who were plundered more heartily. Then skipping the vast bulk and beauty of mediæval literature, the Elizabethans were likely to take up the line again with Petrarch and follow through the whole gamut of renaissance writers in Italy and France and, to a lesser extent, in Spain. It is in his difference from this usual emphasis that Spenser shows his independence.

On the whole he is liberal. He wished to retain the past, not to break with it but to bring it into conformity with his own changing world. His liberal point of view was remarkable in that age of violent partisanship. His attitude toward religion shows this liberality. He would have liked to see the edifice of the Church remain, renovated and purified, fusing with itself newer and stronger ideas, growing, in other words, with the expanding renaissance world. I believe that the religious position of the young Sir Thomas More, fifty years earlier, was not unlike Spenser's. If a schism, a violent break and the consequent creation of new dogmatism had not occurred, More in his day, and Spenser in his, would have been reformed Catholics. Spenser had the English mediæval Church still in his heart. He felt its long influence more often than he would admit. He loved the English past, its literature both ecclesiastical and chivalric, its great poets and its values of life. He had been "sunburned" under its blazing glory.

Spenser also had a new flexibility of mind, born of new angles in thinking. He knew the renaissance world, Italian or French or English. He was familiar with new standards, political, ecclesiastical and moral. He shared the vigour and positive energy of the renaissance. He had a youthful passion to remould life and make it richer. This vigour and independence are shown specifically in his choice of a new-old kind of English for his first public attempt in poetry, *The Shepheard's Calendar*. He could have hid safely behind the argument that shepherds speak "old and obsolete" words. Hence archaic English was suitable to a pastoral poem like the *Calendar*. He grants this, but he defends his archaism on broader grounds. To be sure, Cicero had argued that a language needed to be freshened by conscious revival of obsolete words, and Cicero was a tower of strength to lean upon. E. K. cites Cicero but leaves him on one side and goes on to the very core of the matter :

One special praise of many which are due to this poet [is] that he hath laboured to restore as to their rightful heritage such good and natural English words as have been long time out of use and clean disherited. Which is the only cause that our mother tongue which truly of itself is both full enough for prose and stately enough for verse, hath long time been counted most bare and barren of both.

This, says E. K. in effect, is a logical argument. The only barriers will be raised by persons for whom Spenser has no regard, the unthinking conservatives, the stupid enemies of sound change.

In this question of language, then, one sees Spenser's whole artistic point of view. In taste he is closer to the past of the Middle Ages and especially the English Middle Ages than to the pagan past of Greece and Rome. One has only to think of Spenser and Ben Jonson for a moment to see how Spenser draws imaginatively upon the mediæval past and Jonson upon the classical past. This is a matter of temperament. Yet Spenser, in contrast to Jonson, had the willingness to familiarise himself with and love the destroyers of the old order that he loved. He studied pagan philosophy and classical criticism and the renaissance exponents of them. He not only read the literature of his own world but he sympathised with the impulse beneath it. He was ready to reconsider the meaning of life in the light of newly discovered thought. These new ideas and new methods might renovate his own world. It was a strong thing intellectually to admit this, if one's natural sympathies were still with the Middle Ages. It was more difficult than to repudiate the Middle Ages, and try to join on to a pagan Mediterranean tradition, essentially alien and intractable. Yet Spenser did this. For it alone he is greater than Jonson and many other Elizabethans.

When one has really grasped the nature of Spenser, one finds it possible to go forward sympathetically in his company. His spiritual adventures are less easy to discern than some of Ralegh's and Donne's but they are very great. In fact before one attacks the problem of *The Faerie Queene* one must remember to compare it not with Ralegh's *Poems* or Donne's *Songs and Sonnets*. These were literature to be circulated among one's friends, not for the public ear or press. To make a fair comparison between *The Faerie Queene* and the works of Ralegh and Donne, one would have to measure against Spenser's poem the serious productions of these two. One would have to consider Ralegh's *History of the World*. To this book research yielded material, philosophy and morality lent lights and shadows, and conscious style encompassed both in a beautiful design. The fairest comparison in Donne would be his *Sermons*. In these learning and first-hand experience, scholarship and imagination fused in a spacious and moving style. Of course *The History of the World* and the *Sermons* are not poetry. But if one may be daring, even *The Faerie Queene* is not always poetry. Its metrical pattern is hardly more elaborate than the prose pattern of Ralegh and Donne. Its poetry, if by that one means lyric insight, is only occasional, just as the exalted moments in Ralegh's *History* and Donne's *Sermons* are occasional.

For the sake of argument, then, we may approach *The Faerie Queene* not as poetry in that meaning of the word which we associate with certain brief lyrics, but as a huge slow piece of construction, a "work," in fact. *The Faerie Queene* is one of the Leviathans of Elizabethan literature. It must be considered with them, not with the iridescent, darting creatures that leap from the deeps of personal emotion, take the blinding sun of realisation for a moment and are gone.

How shall we take the measure of this great beast? In the first place it had an appropriately long gestation. As early as the spring of 1580, *The Faerie Queene* was already begun and Harvey did not like it. It was in this spring that Spenser, perhaps dashed at not getting the commission abroad which he had expected, went to Ireland as secretary to Lord Grey, the Lord Deputy. This life in Ireland is important. It furnished the background from which in his spare hours Spenser continued *The Faerie Queene*. Dublin Castle with its moat and drawbridge had been recently renovated by Sir Henry Sidney, so that once within its walls an Englishman might live as became him and forget the misery of exile in this bare ferocious country. Uprisings, deceits, cruelties existed as they always do wherever a spirited but undeveloped little country like Ireland is fought over by the great powers. In the midst of these conditions Spenser was to live practically all of the next nineteen years until his death in the winter of '98-'99. The raids, the butcheries, public executions, displays of traitors' heads above the gates of the Castle, the reports of surprise attacks in remote fens and bogs, all these things made Dublin an outpost of empire before Britain was an empire.

They produced the usual effect upon the people living
there. Englishmen became more English than ever,
more domineering, more cruel than they would naturally
be at home. The veer and flaw of international situations, the curve upward and downward of Spain and
France in their relation to England, of Catholicism versus the new English Church, of treaties made and broken,
of trickery in trade and shipping, all these daily instabil-
ities in England rumbled ominously in the ears of English exiles in Ireland. Spenser saw wholesale atrocities
committed in the name of patriotism. His life must have
been frequently in peril. His sense of the volatility of
English policy must have embittered him as he watched
it from across the Irish Sea. This must be taken into
account in appraising Spenser's attitude toward government in general and toward the specific government of
Ireland in particular.

The influence of these things upon *The Faerie Queene*
is not direct but it is certainly there. When Spenser took
up his pen to move further through the long Cantos and
Books of *The Faerie Queene,* his mind was not only
upon England as it then was. He thought, too, about the
meaning of conduct, private and public, the philosophic
concepts which lay behind this chaos of day-to-day political and private life. His distance from the centre of
activity turned his exiled mind to the general laws which
governed current events. In this sense of the word, Spenser's *Faerie Queene* is unblushingly moral. Spenser admits it in the letter to Ralegh which accompanied the

printing of the first three Books in 1590. The purpose
of the poem is "to fashion a gentleman" and so on. The
passage is well known. Equally well known is the fact
that Spenser did not follow this scheme even in the six
Books (and fragments perhaps of a seventh) that he
finished. More important than this definite moral scheme,
however, is the depth of moral and philosophic reflection
which permeates *The Faerie Queene*. It sprang out of
intense immediate experience. It was part and parcel of
Spenser's life and thought.

It was a part, too, of daily conversation in Dublin.
The small group of Englishmen out there were standing
together against an alien tradition which they controlled
but did not understand. This fact unified them and they
came to know one another intimately. When they met
for leisure they talked about ideas. Lodowick Bryskett
was a member of this group. He had held important
posts in Ireland for many years. He had lived abroad
for three years, part of that time with young Sir Philip
Sidney. He became secretary of the Council for Munster in '82. Spenser acted as his clerk there for the last
ten years of his life. Bryskett in his spare time was a
man of letters. He read Cinthio and probably all the best
Continental authors.

In 1589 he brought out *A Discourse of Civil Life
Containing the Ethic Part of Moral Philosophy*. It was
the fashion then to write about philosophical problems
in the form of dialogue and to give this dialogue a realistic setting in an actual house or castle, with actual per-

sons taking part. Bryskett's introduction describes such
a setting. It was at his cottage near Dublin that a group
of friends were gathered, including Edmund Spenser.
This particular group upon an actual day may not have
gathered there. But if Bryskett's setting is a fiction, it is
based upon real occasions when the English officials, free
for the moment from the exactions of their posts, met.
They exchanged ideas, discussed the latest books and
queried the principles which lay behind their permissions
and refusals, snap judgments and decisions of the moment by which they administered the English government of Ireland.

The talk upon this particular meeting at Bryskett's
"cottage" turned to one of these general subjects. Bryskett had long desired to question Spenser, "knowing him
to be not only perfect in the Greek tongue but also very
well read in philosophy, both moral and natural." The
company set upon him, asking him to expound "the great
benefits which men obtain by the knowledge of moral
philosophy . . . whereby virtues are to be distinguished
from vices." Spenser was already known to his friends
as a man proficient in these matters, though at least another year would pass before any of *The Faerie Queene*
was in print. Spenser declined to produce an *extempore*
lecture on the subject. He said that he had a work under
way, *The Faerie Queene,* covering just these matters:
"to represent" as Bryskett reports him, "all the moral
virtues, assigning to every virtue a knight to be the
patron and defender of the same." This passage of Brys-

kett's is significant for *The Faerie Queene* from several points of view. It shows that the work which Harvey had seen in 1580 was still a chief concern after Spenser had been nine years in Ireland. It shows, also, that Spenser was known to his friend as an authority on moral conduct. That phrase "moral conduct" need not have a chilling effect upon the modern reader. This moralising, as one can see from the discussion in Bryskett's cottage, was only the other end of the violent, risky and passionate life which they led.

Of course, Spenser would have been interested in the philosophy of conduct if he had never had anything to do with government. In him, perhaps, more than in any other figure of his time the mediæval concern with morality and the renaissance concern with the conduct of life met and fused. To be sure the ends to be obtained by good mediæval conduct and good renaissance conduct were poles apart. In one, the end was purification and eternal bliss; in the other, the end was worldly success and power, and the capacity to take off from beautiful physical objects into a realm of æsthetic enjoyment. For the attainment of either goal, there must be theories of behaviour. Books that discussed these theories and led to a better understanding of them were important.

The way of presenting such discussion in books was altering. Most renaissance authors tried to escape from the mediæval methods of expounding theory, including allegory. But Spenser kept the old machinery for his new ends. As early as 1579, he had confided to his friend

E. K. the titles of several works in hand; "his Dreams, his Legends, his Court of Cupid." Although none of these appeared, the titles show how strongly the mediæval framework for literature was impressed upon Spenser's mind. It was a framework generally allegorical where the literal figures and setting symbolised an abstract meaning.

Yet Spenser knew as well as we do now that allegory was already considered by some Elizabethan readers old-fashioned. In the letter to Ralegh, which was really Spenser's defense of *The Faerie Queene,* he gives the key to the allegory. He has certain reservations about its success with the reading public:

To some I know this method will seem displeasant which had rather have good discipline delivered plainly in way of precepts or sermoned at large, as they use, than thus cloudily enwrapped in allegorical devices.

Allegory, however, in this new Elizabethan world was capable of serving the new mood. He is thinking this when he concludes his letter about *The Faerie Queene* with the phrase,

from thence gathering the whole intention of the *conceit.*

The whole design is a colossal "conceit" or "imagining," weaving itself across hundreds of pages. It describes what is not seen through images which are seen. It can, not too fantastically perhaps, be compared to those flashing assumptions that one thing is not that thing but another vastly different, which characterise "conceited"

Elizabethan poets like Donne. By preposterous assumption in both cases, the deep crevasses of human emotion are illumined and the essence of life is captured by a flank attack.

One persistent question arises frequently as the modern reader turns the pages of *The Faerie Queene*. How clearly did the meaning underlying these intricate pages come home to the Elizabethan reader? Was he so much cleverer than we at decoding the message? Could he so much more easily read on two levels at once, taking in the chivalrous deeds and at the same time reading, under this surface, Spenser's meaning?

In that Faerie Queene I mean Glory in my general intention and in my particular I conceive the most excellent and glorious person of our sovereign the Queen and her kingdom in fairyland. . . . So in the person of Prince Arthur I set forth Magnificence.

It is true that for the full understanding of *The Faerie Queene,* one must not neglect the allegory. It was an important part of Spenser's construction. But to understand it requires detailed study. One must be willing to build surmises about the meaning and qualify or alter those surmises in the light of new discoveries. Another reason for the confusing effect of *The Faerie Queene* is that Spenser did not follow his original scheme. While the work was in progress he was reading here and there in philosophy and fiction. The new ideas and images from this reading clouded his first intention. His sensitive response to the life and literature around him overloaded his mind and indirectly overloaded and confused his poetry. There was, too, enough of the antiquary about him to make him love unusual details, old histories and symbols, for themselves. He could not resist putting them in. It would be fairer to say that he did not even think of resisting. His model was still the mediæval romance, which with aristocratic leisure told all, incorporating details for themselves as a mediæval cathedral bears the beautiful inconsequence of minute carving upon its soaring structure. Sometimes, as a veil for criticism of contemporary England, allegory was decidedly useful. Forgetting Chastity and Glory and Magnificence, Spenser could slip the shadow of a particular court figure, Burleigh or Mary of Scotland or Essex behind this or that knight or lady. It cloaked his adverse comment on contemporary affairs and saved him from the charge of treason or slander. In various ways, then, allegory served the pleasure and convenience of the new renaissance word. The severity of its original instruction was relaxed. On the whole, we may conclude that the modern reader of *The Faerie Queene,* who but glimpses the allegory and avoids rigorous pursuit of it, is only imitating a good many Elizabethan readers.

A contemporary estimate of how the public read allegory is found, as H. S. V. Jones points out, in Sir John Harrington's Preface to his English translation of *Orlando Furioso.* The advantages of allegory are, Harrington says, "to be able with one kind of meat and one dish . . . to feed diverse tastes." He then divides the readers of allegory into three kinds, in the first of which many modern readers will be comforted to find themselves. First "weaker capacities will feed themselves with the pleasantness of the history and sweetness of the verse." Second, "some that have stronger stomachs will . . . take a further taste of the moral sense." "A third sort, more high conceited than they, will digest the allegory." One may encounter this Leviathan, then, as one will, lightly and intermittently, as he turns his iridescent sides in an occasional flash of sunlight, or with annotation in hand. Either method of reading *The Faerie Queene* has its Elizabethan precedent.

The end of the sixteenth century and the early seventeenth were marked by the confusion of thought which arises when new philosophies, new questionings of old assumptions are abroad. There were, for instance, changes in the values of life following the acceptance of the Copernican theory of the solar system. Spenser was no philosopher but like the rest he felt the discord between life as it might be and as it was. New theories of the sun and stars unnerved him. Man's place in the Universe shifted from day to day, it seemed. Some contended that the Golden Age, far in the past, was best and the world was in slow process of decay. Others argued for progress and built staunchly upon the future. The issues were raised, combatted or supported in the books which Spenser read. They were fought over in conversation. The unhappy thing, at least to the modern reader's way of thinking, is that Spenser did not express

his confusion in the midst of this change in such short
lyrics as Ralegh kept for his private notebooks or Donne
for his private friends. Always it seems, even when
Spenser is most privately himself, remembering friendship, suffering again the agony of personal defeat, or
facing with his little wisp of ego the merciless expanses
of eternity, he expresses himself through some formal
device, allegorical or symbolic. This is no doubt partly
because he wrote always with the consciousness of a
public. Ralegh and Donne, in their most intimate poetry,
never envisaged a public. One wonders if Spenser ever
tossed off a poem, only partly succeeding in putting on
the page the unhappy tumult within him, yet easing his
private convulsion by the attempt. It is hard to imagine
that he did. But if one will overlook the formal
dress, one can find in his poetry the same questionings
which became brief lyrics in the hands of contemporary
poets.

Under the guise of change, Mutability, and the mys-
teries wrought by time, under the wistful belief that
some past time was man's golden time and the present
a poor remnant of that past, Spenser speaks his feelings.
In the sixth Canto of the third Book, before 1590, he
devotes several stanzas to the problem of change and the
power of time. Why is it that perfection is not allowed
to remain but that everything alters? He traces the
progress of creation from

> An huge eternal Chaos which supplies
> The substances of nature's fruitful progenies.

He dwells upon the idea that the substance of all things is indestructible though the form in which it appears may alter:

> That substance is eterne and bideth so,
> Ne when the life decays, and form does fade,
> Doth it consume and into nothing go,
> But changed is, and often altered to and fro.

But this idea of permanence under change is not very comforting to a mortal who has come to love the particular form so well that its alteration has, for him, the same effect as its destruction:

> For forms are variable and decay,
> By course of kind and by occasion;
> And that fair flower of beauty fades away
> As doth the lily fresh before the sunny ray.

The enemy, then, to this beloved permanence and perfection seems to be Time. Time is the villain of the piece, "the great enemy," "wicked," "the troubler."

In this passage Spenser is dealing with a phenomenon which was peculiarly moving in his day. Because of Copernicus and for other less explicit reasons, the whole question of the meaning of man's life was raised. The late Elizabethan Age suffered from the wearing necessity of thinking newly and from the beginning about the universe. It did not achieve lucidity or even the brave acceptance of a sceptical position. It left this for the seventeenth century to accomplish. But the muddle of thinking and belief through which it struggled is responsible for much good. It made poetry, for instance, for Spenser and Donne and Hamlet.

Spenser gave full expression to these disturbing ideas in the so-called Mutability Cantos. They were not printed in his life-time but appeared first in 1609 with a new folio edition of the six Books of *The Faerie Queene*. That they belong to *The Faerie Queene* is not certain, for they are quite independent of the principal characters and events. The enterprising publisher who brought them out with a later edition of *The Faerie Queene* says that they "appear to be parcel of some following Book of *The Faerie Queene*." Modern scholars have found reason for placing their writing anywhere from 1579 to the last years of Spenser's life. The fact that they mention two hills in Ireland near Spenser's Castle of Kilcolman, the Mole and the Arlo, proves nothing. He knew Ireland probably as early as 1576. The description betrays no intimate knowledge of a particular place there. The later date for this curious fragment seems the probable one. Spenser's private confusions are formalised. The scene is a court judgment. It echoes the dispute of Gods and Titans as set forth in Ovid. It seems to reflect ideas from two thousand years of thinking, from Parmenides and Heraclitus, Empedocles of Agrigentum, Plato, Lucretius, Ovid, not to mention the Old Testament conception of the Universe as God's creation. Spenser's contemporaries such as the Dutch scholar Lipsius, and Giordano Bruno, the Italian who had spent nearly two years in England in 1583-85, dealt with some phase

of this same problem of Mutability. Change and permanence, the power of Time, entered into every special problem. It could not be dismissed.

The question to be decided in these two isolated Cantos, numbered Canto VI and Canto VII, and the two stanzas of the "imperfite" Canto VIII, is whether "Proud Change" is the sovereign of both gods and men. In Canto VII Mutability or "bold alteration," mounts to the moon and tries to force her from her throne. The Elizabethan poets just then, not by accident one conjectures, since the new astronomy was so spectacular, wrote a good deal about the heavens. Spenser contributes to this kind of poetry in Canto VI of Mutability. He describes Cynthia upon her throne:

> Her sitting on an ivory throne she found
>   Drawn of two steeds, the one black, the other white
>   Environed with ten thousand stars around,
>   That duly her attended day and night:
>   And by her side there ran her page that hight
>   *Vesper,* whom we the Evening-star intend:
>   That with his torch still twinkling like twilight
>   Her lightened all the way where she would wend,
> And joy to weary wand'ring travellers did lend.

The trial of Mutability's claim for sovereignty over men and gods was finally set in Ireland. To her defence before the tribunal of Nature, she summons witnesses. On the description of these witnesses Spenser lavishes his art of pageantry. First the Earth and her tenants are cited, beasts and men:

From youth to eld, from wealth to poverty
From good to bad, from bad to worst of all.
Ne do their bodies only flit and fly
But eke their minds (which they immortal call)
Shall change and vary thoughts as new occasions fall.

In the last two lines, I think, Spenser puts his sense of
the instability of his own world.

The Seasons are summoned and the Months. To each
Spenser gives its attributes and provides a poetical script
which would be suitable for an Elizabethan mask. Day
and Night, the Hours, Life and Death, all appear as witnesses for Change. Jove attempts to present on the other
side the argument that the gods control time and change.
Mutability replies that to postulate some unseen power
of stability behind change is easy enough. But who shall
believe these postulates which cannot be proved?

       . . . The things
Which we see not how they are moved and swayed
Ye may attribute to yourselves as Kings,
And say they by our secret power are made.
But what we see not who shall us persuade?

With this question, the new era of doubt which will
proceed scientifically from knowns to unknowns or will
not proceed at all, is ushered in. Spenser, to judge from
his opinion in these unfinished stanzas, could not face
the issues created by this new point of view. He alternates between daring scientific enquiry and relieved re-
treat to faith and the traditional idea of God. The two
stanzas of Canto VIII illustrate the two sides of his

dilemma. In the first, Mutability has won him to her side in all except the rule of Heaven. Mutability is queen of earthly life as he knows it. Her miserable shifts make him cry out to be through with earthly life:

> Which makes me loath this state of life so fickle
> And love of things so vain to cast away:
> Whose flowering pride, so fading and so fickle,
> Short *Time* shall soon cut down with his consuming sickle.

The Elizabethan feeling of mingled love and loathing in the presence of material beauty, the pursuit of this world and the disgust at its transiency, are reflected here. Enough of the mediæval emphasis on life still persisted to make the Elizabethans uneasy in the presence of worldliness. The second of the two stanzas lulls Spenser in the all-embracing arms of conventional religious belief. There is no more argument. In its place is the comforting assertion of faith:

> For all that moveth doth in *Change* delight
> But thenceforth all shall rest eternally
> With Him that is the God of Sabboath hight
> O that Great Sabboath God, grant me that Sabboath's sight.

If in the end he flies to cover in religious faith, yet the tormenting confusion in his heart never ceases.

After one has a sense of Spenser as a man, one finds the collection of small poems printed in 1591, revealing. *The Complaints,* printed in 1590-91 by William Ponsonby and containing nine poems is not a great book. But it is a very Elizabethan book. The story of its compi-

lation, the personal flavour of the dedications, with that "you know what" reference just behind the lines make *The Complaints* too rich in the flavour of that high world to be passed by. After the success of the first three Books of *The Faerie Queene,* it seems likely that Spenser had the idea of many professional writers, to utilize his public while it was keen and produce another book. His papers and old notebooks were ransacked and out came nine poems, old and new, ranging possibly from things composed while he was at Cambridge as a student to pieces of contemporary satire. Translations from the classics and French, imitations, all were gathered together behind the decorative woodcuts of William Ponsonby's title-pages. Ponsonby takes full responsibility for collecting and printing. His prefatory letter to the "Gentle Reader" would disarm the criticism which might have arisen if Spenser himself had seemed to take the poems seriously enough to collect them. Ponsonby recounts his assiduity in gathering together these fugitive pieces "dispersed abroad in sundry lands and not easy to be come by—some having been diversely embezzelled and purloined from him since his departure over sea." They make a homogeneous collection he says, "being all complaints and meditations of the world's vanity, very grave and profitable."

Let us take up this quarto and flick over the pages. The first one in the collection is called *The Ruins of Time.* It is a workmanlike poem. Spenser knows the standard types of poems, visions and stanzas on the

power of poetry to give lasting fame to its subject. Reading them one thinks how many neat, spiritless verses Horace spawned with his "Monumentum exegi aere perrenius." Among the poems is a fling at Burleigh who did not appreciate warriors and poets as Walsingham had before him. There is an elegy for the death of Sidney, originally intended for another volume. Spenser pays, in a dedication, his duty to the Countess of Pembroke. The whole thing is thoroughly workmanlike and nothing more. Spenser's eye is on the world and on his study. He is competent in learning and versification and careful for his reputation. But *The Ruins of Time* is uninspired. It has nothing to say to later worlds.

Mother Hubbard's Tale is of the same sort. It is a beast fable with satire of types in rhymed couplet, all very competent. This piece of work in its first draught seems to have belonged to those exciting years in London just after Cambridge, when Spenser was in the service of Leicester. The state of English politics just at that time seems to be reflected in *Mother Hubbard*. It contains a thinly veiled warning to Leicester that Elizabeth' proposed marriage to the Duc d'Alençon will bring him no good. We know that Sidney had the same point of view at this time; for he wrote a letter of protest to the Queen, for which in 1579-80 he was banished from the Court. The outspoken advice of these young men must have embarrassed Leicester. Even when *Mother Hubbard* was finally printed in 1591, though the offending passage was revised and Leicester was dead, it seems to have caused the suppression of the volume. Beside the references to politics, there is a famous passage on the slow torture of depending for preferment, or "suing" as it was called, upon the caprices of the Court. It reflects personal annoyance and concludes with the wish that "suing" be the punishment of Spenser's enemies. "That curse God send unto mine enemy."

The volume of *Complaints* continues with an adaptation from Vergil, addressed to Leicester and beseeching forgiveness for some now unknown offense; a translation from du Bellay, another via Marot from Petrarch, containing neat stanzas to describe emblems, those curiosities of renaissance literature. In all these pieces, Spenser plays the learned game of renaissance versifiers. In one poem, *Muiopotmos or the Fate of the Butterfly,* he makes a spirited original on an old model. It is the story of a chivalrous encounter between a butterfly in full panoply and a spider. It takes place in a beautiful garden. The airy invention of mock-epic is here. The batteries of gods stand behind the gossamer knight and his foe. There is time by the way for turning the flowers in the garden into pretty catalogue-verses. There is a moral complaining of the briefness of joy:

> But what on earth can long abide in state?
> Or who can him assure of happy day?

Turning the tall, double-columned pages of his green cloth Spenser to the *Muiopotmos,* John Keats must have "let the fancy roam" in this poem. He took from it two lines for the title page of his first published work:

What more felicity can fall to creature
Than to enjoy delight with liberty.

Upon these stanzas of Spenser's, contrived out of thistledown, Elizabethan readers with a gift for allegorical meanings laid a heavy hand. References to a contemporary love affair or political situation may lie just back of the lines. At any rate, Spenser feared this unwelcome sort of interpretation; for in his dedicatory letter to the Lady Elizabeth Carey, he asks her "of all things therein according to your wonted grace to make a mild construction."

The *Complaints,* then, is a fitting book for an Elizabethan window embrasure. Brought together out of Spenser's papers, at the height of his career, it represents the literary background from which the competent professional poet "took off." Allegory ranges through the poems in old and new guises. Satire impales Court policy and individuals. The dedications include names of ladies in Court society with whom Spenser seems to have had some real connection. "Warmed over" to make another book to follow the first three of *The Faerie Queene,* it is interesting as an index of Elizabethan taste but it is not great poetry.

From Ponsonby's press in the same year as the *Complaints,* came a slender book, which Spenser calls "this

pamphlet." It is an elegy of nearly six hundred lines upon
the death of a young woman, Douglas Howard, daughter of Henry Lord Howard and wife of Arthur Gorges,
the friend and companion in adventure of Sir Walter
Ralegh. It must have been through Ralegh that Spenser
came to write the poem. Gorges had married Douglas at
thirteen, though her father contested the marriage before the Star Chamber and said Gorges had committed
theft in wedding her. She bore a daughter, Ambrosia,
and died after a long illness in 1590 at nineteen. The
material for a violent and beautiful tale might lie behind
these few facts. It is too bad that Spenser steered so far
away from the possibility. He held safely to the pattern
laid down for a poem on the death of a lady, any lady,
good, beautiful, resigned and lamented. It is merely as
this that the young Douglas Howard appears in *Daphnaida.* The poem, to the modern taste, is uneven. Some
of the conventions seem so far-fetched as to be ludicrous.
Gorges, under the name Alcyon, appears in the guise of
the distracted lover, wearing black and in disarray. This
was the way that Romeo and Hamlet reflected their inward tumult. But they showed more spirit than do these
obedient stanzas of Spenser. Douglas, alias Daphnaida,
appears as a white lionness. The lion had been in the
armorial bearing of the Howards. Her bereft husband
describes how he tamed her :

> Yet I her fram'd and won so to my bent,
> That she became so meek and mild of cheer,
> As the least lamb in all my flock that went.

It will do no good to summon the ghosts of Greek
pastoral lament, or Chaucer's *Book of the Duchess* as
precedent for this blended symbolism. Spenser is too
cold and the tradition too conscious to give these lines
any poetry. The lady's deathbed address, as reported by
Alcyon, is puritanical and priggish. Nature laments for
Daphnaida's death as it had from the days of Moschus's
lament for Bion:

> Let birds be silent on the naked spray.

One wonders whether this line had sunk deep into the
well of Keats' mind, and came out transmuted in the
lines from *La Belle Dame*:

> The sedge is wither'd from the lake
> And no birds sing.

Sometimes the conventional lament in *Daphnaida*
moves with haunting music:

> She fell away in her first age's spring
> Whils't yet her leaf was green, and fresh her rind,
> And whil'st her branch fresh blossoms forth did bring,
> She fell away against all course of kind:
> For age to die is right, but youth is wrong;
> She fell away like fruit blown down with wind:
> Weep, shepherd, weep, to make my undersong.

There is, too, a good example of that pictorial detail
which rouses the visual and tactual sense through
words:

How happy was I when I saw her lead
The shepherd's daughters dancing in a round,
How trimly would she trace and softly tread
The tender grass with rosy garland crowned.

One remembers Botticelli's Primavera. Coming upon
these delights in the midst of frigid failures, one wonders whether a modern judgment of either success or
failure in a poem like *Daphnaida* has any value. We may
understand with our intellect what were the delights of
this poem to an Elizabethan reader. Yet emotionally this
understanding does not enable us to read a "pamphlet"
like *Daphnaida* with more than a ghost of the response
which it must have aroused in its own day. It seems
probable that the appeal of any poetry except the greatest
dies with its age.

Another "occasional" piece, the *Astrophel,* written on
the death of Sidney, belongs in the same general category. It was printed in 1595 with a collection of poems
on Sidney by various authors. For some reason Spenser
was slow in paying his tribute to this important young
man, who had died in '86 and had taken with him the
hopes and ambitions of the earlier Elizabethan world.
Friends took Spenser to task for delaying to lay his
wreath upon Sidney's grave. When he came to make it
in *Astrophel,* he produced a stiff thing. Compared with
his dedicatory poem to Sidney at the opening of *Shepheard's Calendar* in the long-ago days of '79, *Astrophel*
is cold. One wonders whether the paling of Sidney's
image in Spenser's mind may not be the result of the

rapidly changing life then. He had gone through a crowd of changing events, allegiances, and transitions in the ten Irish years since 1580 when he knew Sidney best. By 1590, Sidney belonged to a past remoter than the number of intervening years would indicate. He was an "early" Elizabethan compared with the disillusioned men of the middle and late Nineties. Ralegh was still of Spenser's world, struggling with it. But Sidney was a beautiful ghost who belonged to a simpler, more heroic past.

In the 1595 volume, along with *Astrophel* and laments for Sidney by several other authors, Spenser published a different sort of poem, *Colin Clout's Come Home Again.* Although it follows the pastoral convention, the personal quality transfuses the convention. It is intimate autobiography, really, under a thin pastoral veil. The real world lies just below its surface. *Colin Clout,* in fact, opens a window upon Elizabethan London. It shows the voyage from Ireland, the Court, the London poets, the ladies who gather there, the Queen, and more than these, the idealism and disillusion commingled. Spenser meant the poem to be immediate and real. He dedicated it to Ralegh as if from his castle in Ireland immediately after his return from London. Most scholars now think that this dedication is not to be taken literally. *Colin Clout,* however, is full of those comments which Spenser might have made after he was safely back on his Irish estate, turning the whole London experience over in his mind. Whether he finished it in London or in Ireland is unimportant.

In the dedicatory letter to Ralegh, he speaks of "the meanness of the style" in *Colin Clout*. It is true that he has given up the archaism which he used in the earlier pastoral. He forgoes rhetorical figures, too. Instead he writes about life as it actually appeared to a man at the height of his powers, seeing Elizabeth's Court at its most vigorous moment. This fact gives *Colin Clout* an importance historically beyond its poetic worth. Yet even for itself it is stronger than the poems we have just been describing because it expresses the immediate concerns of Spenser himself. His fame wavered just on the crest in 1590. After ten years in Ireland, his maturity artistically and politically was achieved. He came back to London in company with Ralegh, who knew his way in the world. Three Books of *The Faerie Queene* were on the eve of publication. The journey was big with implications. The reflections of this important moment in his life are preserved in *Colin Clout*. No wonder it feels differently from the poems which were cut to a conventional pattern and were little more than that.

The imagery is homely, often clumsy. Fantasy and realism of detail appear in friendly mingling. The ship, for instance, in which he set sail for England is worth pausing over. In a world which depended for its riches and stability upon ships, the actual vessels must have been surrounded with fancy in the minds of the people. Voyagers like Drake, reporters of sea fights like Ralegh, found no time for description of the ships themselves in their succinct accounts. But Spenser says what many

Elizabethans must have felt about the mystery of ships:

> For as we stood there waiting on the strand
> Behold a huge great vessel to us came
> Dancing upon the waters back to land
> As if it scorned the danger of the same,
> Yet was it but a wooden frame and frail
> Glued together with some subtle matter,
> Yet had it arms and wings and head and tail
> And life to move itself upon the water.
> Strange thing how bold and swift the monster was,
> That neither cared for wind, nor hail, nor rain,
> Nor swelling waves but thorough [sic] them did pass
> So proudly that she made them roar again.

Often his imagery is country-ish and intimate. For instance, the Queen's looks are like the morning sun

> Forth looking through the windows of the East:
> When first the fleecy cattle have begun
> Upon the pearled grass to make their feast.

To be sure, it is a convention to speak this way. But conventional landscape and real landscape as Spenser had seen it may be identical. Spenser loves the pictures he makes and the flowery detail:

> And long while after I am dead and rotten
> Among the shepherds' daughters dancing round,
> My lays made of her shall not be forgotten
> But sung by them with flowery girlonds crowned.

Colin Clout, of course, caters to the peculiar tastes of the Elizabethan time. Disguised under riddling names

are twelve poets whom he heard of at Court and twelve
Court ladies. He says nothing very striking about them.
Yet solving the problem of who these poets and ladies
were would be sure to give pleasure to his readers. The
real core of the poem for us is his reflection on the parade
of Court life, its idealism and its rottenness. He sees
and describes both. The idealised side of the picture is
not original; it is Castiglione's *Courtier* adroitly versi-
fied. When he describes the rottenness, however, the
lines grow putrid under the strength of personal revulsion. Love, too, presents the same opposites. There is
the so-called Platonic love. There is also something they
call love at Court, which is very different. Spenser is
satiric about those sonnet cycles and protesting lovers
whose emotion, like as not, springs from ambition and
political manœuvring:

> For all the walls and windows there are writ
> All full of love and love and love my dear,
> And all their talk and study is of it.
>
> .   .   .   .
>
> Ne anyone himself doth ought esteem
> Unless he swim in love up to the ears.

Because of the reality of this ill temper, and because of
the immediacy and honesty of Spenser's comment
throughout the poem, a modern reader turns again and
again to *Colin Clout*.

The *Prothalamion* (published in 1596) was for a
double marriage at Essex House of the daughters of

Courtesy Folger Shakespeare Library

RIVER PALACES — SOMERSET HOUSE

It is this sort of great house with gardens leading to river-stairs that Spenser describes in the *Prothalamion*

Somerset, Earl of Worcester. In its ten intricate stanzas, Spenser adapts well-known legends of the marriage of rivers, of royal swans bestowed by gods and kings to sail upon them. The gardens of Essex House reached down to the River Stairs. The two girls, as swans, journey along the Lee and Thames to these River Stairs. There the bridegrooms and the host greet them and conduct them to the marriage ceremony. One willingly yields to this pleasant fantasy, especially when the actual appearance of London, the Tower and the Temple as seen from the river, are woven into it. It is like a familiar scene embroidered in needlepoint:

> There where they came, whereas those bricky Towers
> The which on Thames broad aged back do ride
> There now the studious lawyers have their bowers
> There whilom wont the Templar Knights to bide
> Till they decayed through pride.

Spenser's decorated way of writing poetry is effective in a subject like this which handles life from a distance. One also responds to this style in a poem conceived along great lines like *The Faerie Queene*. It is fortunate therefore, that the bulk of Spenser's poetry is of a sort which can support this elaborate style, that it is occupied with the orchestration of life on a great scale, handled with reverence and from a distance.

The *Epithalamion,* a poem for his own marriage, was "a song made in lieu of many ornaments." It was printed in 1595 together with his sonnet cycle, the *Amoretti.* In it Spenser manipulates the strands of classical and ren-

aissance tradition, along with scenes from an Elizabethan village on a wedding day. There appear in the
company of Venus, Hebe, Hymen and Aurora, English
boys shouting, young men ringing bells, merchants'
daughters. There are birds among the dewy leaves and
at night the frogs croaking "make us to wish their chok-
ing." The bold mingling of traditional ornament and
realistic setting is successful because Spenser is not
aware of the boldness. He does not think of the incongruity. His affection and joy melt all diversities into a
unified tribute to his bride. Even at the altar, the painted
angels come to life and

> Forget their service and about her fly,
> Oft peeping in her face.

The *Epithalamion* is a piece of work into which Spenser
braids the resources of his learning, his skill in metrics.
He weaves all together into a wreath to crown a simple
and "decent" affection. For the psychology of passion,
its terrible alchemy, transmuting caprice and mood into
mountainous tumult, lending accident the significance of
Fate, crossing and recrossing the nerves of the lover,
Spenser cares nothing. He passes through this intricate
porch of song to an affectionate and fruitful married
life. His lady possesses all the qualities of a good wife.
But as an individual, as a person whose dear perversities
and caprices have ensnared Edmund Spenser, she does
not exist.

The *Amoretti,* printed with the *Epithalamion* in 1595,

are usually supposed to celebrate the progress of his own
love affair with the lady he married and to have been
written between 1591 and 1594. If this is true, one must
remember that they are the reflections of a man of forty.
He is humorous, mature. His feet are on the ground.
He laughs at the absurdities and extravagances of his
feelings. Yet the experience, for all its couching in the
sonnet conventions, is immediate. He writes of things
that happen and how he feels on a particular day. The
labour on *The Faerie Queene* is often mentioned. In
Sonnet XXXIII he cannot work because his love is so
intense. In LXXX he has finished the first six Books:

> After so long a race as I have run
>   Through Faeryland, which those six books compile,
>   give leave to rest me being half fordone
>   and gather to myself new breath awhile.

Compared with this great work, his sonnets for his lady
are of lesser importance:

> But let her praises yet be low and mean
>   fit for the handmaid of the *Faery Queene*.

In XLVI it rains and he must stay longer than he had
planned at his lady's house. In LXXV they walk together by the sea. The sonnets end in separation and
unhappiness.

To celebrate this love affair, Spenser has all the poetical material, traditional and new, at his command. He
knows the French and Italian sonneteers. He is original
in combining the quatrains and couplets in a new

metrical mould. As a whole, the resulting poems are distinct in feeling from other Elizabethan sonnet cycles. They speak with maturity, with seasoned compromise about life. The combination of homely everydayness and decoration in hands less skillful than Spenser's would be a failure. In his, even, the total effect is somehow disappointing. One resents Spenser's coming to earth so abruptly, and to his private present. He narrows his scope, circumscribes the field too much, deprives us of the full sense of his design.

One feels on surer ground again in the Anacreontics printed between the *Amoretti* and the *Epithalamion* in the 1595 volume. Translated out of Marot and Ronsard, with obligations in general feeling to the Alexandrine world, these trifles say very little that is profound. But because the material is remote, the decoration is welcome. We are not confused between the warmth of a private love story and the cool ornaments of learning. We take such a stanza as the following lightly for what it is:

> I saw in secret to my Dame,
>   How little Cupid humbly came:
>   and said to her All hail, my mother.
> But when he saw me laugh, for shame
> His face with bashful blood did flame,
>   not knowing Venus from the other.
> Then never blush Cupid (quoth I)
>   for many have err'd in this beauty.

Spenser wrote his best love poetry in the *Four Hymns*

printed in 1596. The dedication to two titled ladies implies some interesting things. The first two poems, he seems to say, were too occupied with earthly love. He has made amends by printing them with two more recent "Hymns" on heavenly love. Whatever is fiction or fact in the circumstances of Spenser's four hymns is less important than the *Hymns* themselves. They contain ideas from Plato by way of the Italian followers of Plato. There are additions from Giordano Bruno who had been in England in Sidney's set from 1583 to 1585. With these ideas Spenser combines mediæval concepts of love, of cosmic order and æsthetic principle. He put all this in poetry whose involutions and decorations are necessary to the nuances and combinations of ideas. It is perhaps not exaggerated to say that Spenser was more deeply moved by the philosophy and æsthetic of love as he found it in the learning of the past, than by the love story of his own life. At least, the *Hymns* are greater poetry than the *Amoretti*.

On the whole, then, it will not do to dismiss the greatness of Spenser with such phrases as that he was "the poets' poet" or that philosophy and ethics were the chief burden of his work. Yet, in a certain sense, these things are true. He wrought curiously and elaborately a theme whose greatness was no whit diminished by the fact that his poetry leaned upon learning and proposed to build anew from past and present a world of its own.

CHAPTER V

Ralegh and the "New" Poetry

Against the background of English poetry at the end of the sixteenth century Sir Walter Ralegh fits protestingly but that is as it should be. No time is adequate to explain a great individual. He moves against the general background, breathes the general air but never entirely belongs to his particular world. In this sense poets are "not for an age but for all time"—all time and no one time, for they will somehow catch the accents of eternity. The chemical solution which we call the age may develop shadings in a poet's work but as a whole it is independent of that solution. Ralegh's poetry has many Elizabethan qualities. He wrote from new centres of interest as had Wyatt and Spenser. He was like them in that his approach to the meaning of life was secular rather than religious. He was characteristic of his age, too, in that he experimented with the phenomena of his own experience and abstracted from it with his brain and his feelings the material for poetry. He watched himself think and feel and generalised from his little world to The World. He would have done this in any time but it was particularly easy to do it in the late Elizabethan time.

For reasons in the social and political evolution of the age which we have commented upon, poetry then was moral and rhetorical. So, too, was Ralegh's poetry. His personal attitude to life was moral in the largest sense of that word. What is life, what is man, what is the meaning of his terrible or beautiful or stumbling pilgrimage across time? After he does this thing, why does he feel that way? Where lies the truth between this momentary exaltation and that sharp depression? What stays when all seems to go, when each thing changes into some other thing while one is looking at it? These were the questions he was always asking himself in his poetry and they are essentially moral questions.

To express in words this kind of questioning is very difficult. The Elizabethan word-patterning, however, the puns, alliteration, balance of phrases, all that they called "rhetoric," was well adapted to undertake this difficulty. Elizabethan "rhetoric" objectifies feeling into word schemes, catches intuitions in a figure, furnishes structure by word designs. Through the visual arrangements of words the reader can see the questing, half-formulated ideas as if they were stayed in midflight for a moment by the word-patterns. Often, not always, the rhetorical devices which Ralegh used in his poems accomplished precisely this effect for his ideas. His poetry, too, was adapted to the atmosphere of the late Elizabethan world. England was coming of age and ready for that reflective scrutiny in which success and failure are seen as two parts of one whole. Ralegh's private reflection, highly individual as it was, accorded with this general attitude.

The material out of which his poetry came, his life, has strong outlines. Because of the tenacity and drive which his personality had he seems always to have been present to the imaginations of men from his day to ours. He was a soldier, a sailor, a conceiver of magnificent projects in the New World, a courtier something "out of suits with fortune and men's eyes," a prisoner in the grand style, going at last to a spectacular and gallant death. Everybody knows that. It is almost enough to know only that. For in the interstices of that story hang implications of the other side of his nature; of deception, ambition, greed, monstrous caprice, rashness, long calculation and sudden impulse. The impact of vastly divergent experience upon the sensitized thinking apparatus inside him, made his poetry.

The courtier's tradition in that day included skill in the various forms of verse-writing. Partly to acquiesce in this accomplishment, but chiefly, one must believe, out of sheer compulsion to ease himself of tumultuous thought and feeling, Ralegh wrote at various times what, for lack of a better name, I shall call lyric poetry. The verses which existed only in his own manuscript for private reading were copied by friends. Sometimes the originals must have been borrowed and not returned. They drifted away on the currents of London's social world and were lost. All through the seventeenth century they were copied into gentlemen's commonplace books.

Only four exist in Ralegh's own hand. These four have a grim reason for their preservation. They were found at Hatfield House in the last third of the nineteenth century among the papers of Cecil who had played an important part in Ralegh's trial and death in 1618. One wonders whether some petty official had found them in the mean little quarters in the Tower from which the prisoner had gone to his death in Palace Yard. Not noting their trivial content he might have sent them as possible traitrous remains to Cecil's files.

Often, of course, his poems did get into print almost as soon as he wrote them but without his intention. The sense of private ownership was so slight that compilers just took them willy-nilly for anthologies and song books. Five appear with musical accompaniment between 1588 and 1612 in famous collections by musicians like Byrd, Ferrabosco and Gibbons. Anthologies of poetry for reading, like the *Phoenix Nest, The Passionate Pilgrim, England's Helicon* included some of them. They are usually anonymous. Their assignment to Ralegh frequently rests on the printing of his name with the poem in some middle or late seventeenth century collection. At this later date his fame had grown and the interest was keener in the whole question of authorship. Yet haphazard as the Elizabethan method of publishing was, it made Ralegh's poetry well known. As early as 1589 (and that is early in the annals of the great Elizabethan poetry) Puttenham in his *Art of Poetry* refers to the "crew of courtly poets, noblemen and gentlemen of her majesty's own servants . . . [who] have written excellently well, as it would appear if their doings could be found out and made public with the rest." Among the "crew" was Ralegh. Only two of his poems (and only one of these a love poem) were in print when Puttenham wrote that "for dittie [a short poem usually set to music] and amorous ode [also usually for musical setting] I find Sir Walter Ralegh's vein most lofty, insolent and passionate." *Insolent* in the Elizabethan sense of *swelling, exulting,* will seem very apposite as the essence of his poetry emerges. *Passionate* is used again and again in descriptions of him with a meaning which his poetry defines and colours.

Out of the nature of his activities and his essential self then came this poetry, tossed off in private, capriciously and carelessly given to the world. It is largely subjective but the circumstances of its creation have given this subjectiveness a peculiar quality. His work is never fully articulate; it never completely conveys its thought and feeling. More than in most poetry there is a residue of meaning outside the lines, an ambiguity unresolved, an accent not clearly heard. Ralegh's poetry is never really detached from the umbilical cord of himself, from that chaotic, becoming thing which we call a man living. Reading Ralegh's poems, therefore, is very like seeing Ralegh as a living man. If one is interested, one has the patience to piece him together, bit by bit, as one sees him under the light of this moment or that. But the articulation of his personality is never finished. He is always becoming and in one's progressive contact with him there is always something transient.

This is at once the reason why his poetry is not first rate and yet why it has so intimate a hold upon the reader's imagination. Because of this feeling about his poetry, legend, even in his lifetime, created precise circumstances for the writing of certain poems; in his Bible in the Gate House the night before he was beheaded, in prison to his wife the night before he expected to die, to the Queen at a particular moment of tangled personal and political aspiration, to Marlowe when he wrote too prettily of love, to a lady-in-waiting when his astuteness made him foreswear his passion and he slipped his sharp summary of the situation into her pocket. His poetry is the extension of moods that pass through him, and pass over the paper at the same time.

The length of his poems reflects the circumstances of creation. With one exception, they are all short; couplet, quatrain, epigram, a verse pattern repeated in successive stanzas, with a slightly different refrain. He has little to do with the sonnet as if its extended intricacy were too taxing to his mood and method. He gets into the full-dress of this form in dedicatory verses for Spenser's *Faerie Queene*, for Gorges' translation of Lucan's *Pharsalia*. But these are public occasions and must be met by the public face, which for Ralegh means the sonnet form. The ten books which he is supposed to have written of a long poem, *Cynthia*, to the Queen are lost. The Eleventh Book in its unfinished state (among those papers which found their way into Cecil's files) is written mostly in four-line groups, with an occasional five or three, when the pulse went a little stronger or a little more intensively in a rhyming triplet. What this brevity and irregularity of verse-grouping argues is the impulsiveness of a man feeling and thinking in bursts.

The subject matter of his poetry arises out of the same peculiar personal conditions. It is concerned with those feelings which come upon him in the pressure of a full and important life. It is the private residue of his public days. It marks the point where the life of action stops for a moment and one faces oneself, appraises events and sorts out their meaning. Love in all its protean shapes occupies him; false love, lust, how one is to subdue love to life. The power of time, transiency, change, these are three aspects of a phenomenon to which he is peculiarly sensitive. There is, too, the awareness of discrepancy between what is and what might be in government, in men's dealings with one another. Consequent upon this awareness comes the impulse to avoid things as they are, to turn from them into happy seclusion.

But this, one says, is what all lyric poetry is about. Granted. Yet in Ralegh the idea is expressed with a considerable difference. Five of his poems were printed in music books during his life-time. The way in which things are said in these five poems is worth scrutinizing and the way in which the words were to be sung. One must discard the modern idea of words in relation to music and must consider instead the nature of Elizabethan music and singing. Elizabethan music for singing was, it has been said, "a kind of prose music," that is, it had something of the patience and steadiness of exposition. It repeated, elaborated, expounded a theme, reinforced the essential meaning by ornamental variations. It displayed the idea and then enhanced it.

In Ralegh's five poems printed for a musical setting, the words were worth this setting. Take "A Farewell to False Love" which appeared in William Byrd's *Psalms, Sonnets and Songs* in 1588. It is a poem of five stanzas, each stanza with six lines, four of alternate rhyme and a concluding rhymed couplet. It is a rain of missiles, of comparative figures, one pell-mell after the other, as if by flinging at the notion in his mind this shower of likenesses he would at last bring it to ground:

> A quenchless fire, a nurse of trembling fear,
> A path that leads to peril and mishap,
> A true retreat of sorrow and despair
> An idle boy that sleeps in pleasure's lap
> A deep distrust of that which certain seems
> A hope of that which reason doubtful deems.

There is rage and fury here. First-hand feeling produces figures that are immediate. There is a sense of actual experience behind this rhetoric and wit. Take the lines

> A deep distrust of that which certain seems
> A hope of that which reason doubtful deems.

There is not only the balance of opposing ideas in *certain* and *doubtful, distrust* and *hope*. There is not only ingenuity of alliteration, *d*eep *d*istrust . . . *d*oubtful *d*eems. But, more important, these rhetorical devices enhance the meaning.

This complicated stanza with its rhetorical pattern will be even clearer when set to the music in a part-song by several voices. Musical repetition will bring out the implication of the phrasing. The music will lengthen the briefness of each image till the lines, overcrowded with thought and feeling, will, by these musical devices of holding and repeating the word patterns, at last convey their burden to the slowly opening mind of the listener. Musical division within the stanza is therefore the very element necessary for impressing the intricacy of thought.

That music was thought suitable for enhancing words is shown by the inclusion in Barley's music book in 1596 of a *tour de force,* probably by Ralegh, in verbal arrangement. Here is the way the first stanza looks upon the page:

Your face	Your tongue	Your wit
So fair	So sweet	So sharp
First bent	Then drew	So hit
Mine eye	Mine ear	My heart

The visual design is in this trifle the chief source of delight. It is a maze, an arrangement of pieces in a design with physical balance and spatial quality. That its intricacy was stronger than its spiritual implication is

evident by the titles under which it appeared in some
seventeenth century books. It is called "The Lover's
Maze," is printed in a collection entitled *Fancies and
Fantastickes,* and in another compilation, *Recreation
for Ingenious Head Pieces.* As a poem it has no value.
The important thing, however, is that its arrangement
upon the page could be transferred to musical sequence
without losing its effectiveness. It shows how sharply
the Elizabethan musical setting for words differed
from ours.

In general Ralegh is clever at utilising intricate patterns of words and figures of speech to convey the
deepest meanings. He chose for one poem, for instance,
a kind of parable-riddle on man's withdrawal from the
world. He used the physical attributes of the hermit,
his staff, his gown, his meagre fare, his bed, his gate.
The symbols of an old religious pattern were galvanized
into new meaning to convey disillusion. Although this
particular figure of the hermit was common among poets,
Ralegh in his use of it gives the image poignancy and immediacy, as if personal experience had made the convention real. "My staff," he says, "of *broken hope* whereon
I'll stay." This is a brave overstatement, a *reductio ad
absurdum.* One cannot rest upon a broken stick. Through
his figure the heaviness of disillusion after confidence is
made terribly clear. His bed is made "Of late repentance
linked with long desire." He puts repentance and desire
side by side and binds their bitter divergence together by
two alliterative adjectives, *late* and *long.* How life can

end at the caprice of love or fortune he shows in a riddling couplet at the end:

> And at my gate Despair shall linger still
> To let in death when Love and Fortune will.

Another symbolic idea, that man's life is like a play in a theatre, is so common all through Elizabethan literature that it would seem impossible for a poet to give it originality. The prominence of the theatre, of course, in the physical life of the time made the symbol very pertinent. The brave swagger of man, playing a part before the public for a little time; then the inevitable exit, after a good or ill reception; in these ways the theatre was very like life. Ralegh's comparison of life to an actor occurs in the poem beginning "What is our Life? a play of passion." It is a series of six couplets in rhyming pairs. The symbolism is given point and emotional force by this rhyming. The repetition of the same sound at the end of the second of two lines brings a unity of feeling. The difference in the meaning of the second rhymed word, its note of something new and dissonant, gives poignancy to the whole. These qualities are particularly effective in the last couplet:

> Thus march we playing to our latest rest,
> Only we die in earnest, that's no jest.

Some people suspect the sincerity of feeling when poetry is written in calculated form, when it calls upon wit to imprison feeling in a pattern. That feeling is more itself because it shines through a design, they do not know. But the Elizabethans did know this. In the first place they were accustomed to verbal intricacy. Word patterns and symbolism were already a tradition in English poetry before the sixteenth century. In the hands of men like Ralegh who put these patterns to new uses, verbal wit enriched the feeling of Elizabethan lyrical poetry. Moreover their way of setting words to music, as I have shown, further clarified and impressed this wit upon the listener.

But the best of Ralegh's poems are still to be reckoned with; the well-known ones like *Give me my scallop-shell of quiet* and *The Lie,* Ralegh's *Reply* to Marlowe's *Come Live with me and Be my Love,* and *Even such is Time.* How can one speak of them lightly, enticingly, without dissecting them or pinning them down with heavy critical phrases? For in Ralegh's poetry more than in most, these sins must not be committed. The immediacy of what he confided to paper, his unawareness that a future public would scrutinize it, make a heavy approach to it rather ridiculous.

Perhaps the best way of introducing a poem like *Give me my scallop-shell of quiet* is to show how it gathers into itself all the stuff of poetry which tradition laid in Ralegh's hand. In the first place, it is one of those frequent allegorical-riddling poems. It utilises the attributes of the mediæval pilgrim and the imagery of mediæval heaven. Yet out of this stock in his lumber-room he constructs a poem so new that, correctly or not, it was assigned to a particular day and hour in Ralegh's life. It was said to have been written somewhere between November 17, 1603, when he was condemned to death and December 6 when he was released. It was printed anonymously the next year as *The Passionate Man's Pilgrimage*. It is "passionate" in the Elizabethan sense, subject to the "affections," embracing a content both intellectual and intuitive. Yet it is a poem full of "wit." Ralegh puns with reverence. Christ "the unblotted lawyer, true proceeder," the antithesis of worldly legal corruption, "hath angels but no fees." In the courts of heaven there is "No conscience molten into gold." Humour and seriousness are found here in rare combination. Not only is the old furniture of symbolic wit and punning used as if it were new but into the midst of this allegorical story of man's pilgrimage from earth to heaven, Ralegh without incongruity puts realism:

> Just at the stroke when my veins start and spread,
> Set on my soul an everlasting head.

Within its small compass the poem embraces the figures of a past ideology, the rhetoric which his own time liked and the realism of a particular physical moment. It is tradition and experiment, convention and revolt in moving and true combination as two halves of an honest whole.

When Marlowe wrote his song *Come Live with me and be my Love,* he challenged to a wit-combat the verse writers. Donne, Herrick and Ralegh all replied. Ralegh's

poem, beginning "If all the world and love were young"
is a sophisticated reply. He had found Marlowe's poem
purely pictorial, naming lovely objects but innocent of
thought and passion. Ralegh's reply might be called the
answer of the "courtly" group to popular Elizabethan
poetry. He summons to contradict Marlowe's pleasant
picture of love among the shepherds, the figures of
Truth, Time, Change, and Decay. He reproves Marlowe for his prettiness. Youth moves to age, love to the
end of love, joy to the end of joy. His disillusion is
made palatable and saved from wistfulness by his brief
and dexterous use of verbal wit:

> In folly ripe, in reason rotten

or

> A honey tongue, a heart of gall
> Is Fancy's spring, but Sorrow's fall.

The implication in the sharp, brief phrases brings rhetoric to the service of lament and gives it objectivity and
form.

Other poems, *Farewell to the Court* and the eight-
line epitaph *Even Such is Time,* seem more autobiographical. They fit well into particular moments of disaster in Ralegh's own life. But their burden is the same.
They are the sensitive study of the feelings which accompany disappointment and unhappy change. The refrain
of the *Farewell,* thrice repeated, is

> Of all which past, the sorrow only stays.

The same line turns up in that Eleventh Book of *Cynthia* which was found after Ralegh's death in Cecil's files. Apparently Ralegh liked the line.

If one moves from subjective and personal poetry to satire of contemporary abuses in poems like *The Lie,* one finds society's sins impaled. There is a sweeping defiance of things as they are in a neat design of words:

> Say to the Church it shows
> What's good and doth no good
>
> .   .   .
>
> Tell wit how much it wrangles
> In tickle points of niceness,
> Tell wisdom she entangles
> Herself in over wiseness.

Thus with incisive judgment and concentrated phrases he ranges over the manifold aspects of the time and reveals them. Under the wit Ralegh is always probing to the centre of that fundamental problem in life, the relationship between the manifestations of man's spirit and the essence of that spirit. *The Lie* concludes with the couplet:

> Stab at thee he that will,
> No stab thy soul can kill.

There is a small group of poems devoted to differentiation between psychological states, as between lust and love. In these he uses metaphor very adroitly. Thus Desire

. . . while it seeks our hearts to have
Meanwhile there Reason makes his grave.

· · ·

So fond Desire when it attains,
The life expires, the woe remains.

One is reminded in such poems as this that the Elizabethan Age produced several books on the "passions of the mind," the humour of melancholy, and the relationship of mind and temperament to the body. Elizabethan rhetoric was a fitting and becoming habit for these matters.

Ralegh wrote four poems for special occasions, three for books by his friends and one for the death of Sidney. The verses for Gascoine's *Steel Glass* and the poem on the death of Sidney are not distinguished, but the sonnets for *The Faerie Queene* are a different matter. Spenser was his friend. They had met in Ireland in the late Eighties and through Ralegh Spenser had come to Court in London and arranged for printing the first three books of *The Faerie Queene*. Spenser recorded this in *Colin Clout* and dedicated the poem to Ralegh. Meanwhile the first three books of Spenser's great poem had appeared with his appended letter to Ralegh. Ralegh wrote two dedicatory sonnets which head the list in a long procession of poetical compliments printed with *The Faerie Queene*. The second of the two is unimportant. But the first, "Methought I saw the grave where Laura lay," is great.

This sonnet carries a heavy freight of learning. For instance, Petrarch weeps because he is surpassed. Homer's spirit trembles and grieves at the power of this new poet, this "celestial thief." Yet Ralegh runs lightly with this burden of reference from the past. He contrives within the confines of this sonnet to make *The Faerie Queene* walk down the galleries of Time, drawing irresistibly to her the graces of love and virtue, insolently and surely detaching them from great poets of the past and adding them to her splendour. Allegory which is so adroit in Ralegh's hand is in this sonnet quickened into a magnificent and sweeping compliment. Of a different pitch are Ralegh's verses for his cousin Gorges' translation of Lucan's *Pharsalia.* The poem written in or near 1614 when the book was published has no distinction of form or feeling. But it has this engaging quality. It shows Ralegh identifying Lucan's independence of Nero's tyranny with his own spirit in prison as an enemy of the government. Thus his reaction even in this minor trifle is still predominantly personal.

This chapter has been entitled "Ralegh and the New Poetry." What has there been in the various phases of his work that is essentially "new"? The "newness," I think, depends not upon an absolutely fresh element but lies in an increasing use of poetry as a container for individual experience. Ralegh was a poet only in the interstices of his active life. Because there was no idea of appearing as a professional poet before a public, he wrote without the restrictions and standards which a profes-

sional performance in that day imposed. One sees, therefore, in his poetry the emphasis which men in their
private hearts gave to experience. More than anything
else this emphasis may be defined as a desire to observe
honestly the workings of themselves and their world,
to see things as they were and to see all of things. Ralegh
and men like him wished not to be categorical about life,
but to embrace contradiction, confusion or caprice if
these qualities actually made up experience. Perhaps
this is merely saying that poetry became more introspective, but I think it is saying more than that. The introspection was, as far as might be, not sentimental but
scientific. Poetry like Ralegh's probed the phases of living with a relentless scalpel.

The result of this probing was the discovery of a
material very difficult to convey, a material which perhaps could never be perfectly conveyed and made objective in words. This is what one feels again and again in
Ralegh. The meaning of a whole poem is still inside
him, still "becoming" as I have said at the beginning of
this chapter. Under the stress of trying to detach this
meaning from himself and put it into words, Ralegh
flings a succession of images at his thought-feeling. The
succession of allegorical figures in "Give me my scallop-
shell of quiet," for instance, is not descriptive. It reveals,
bit by bit, Ralegh in an intense moment of living experience. The increasing emphasis upon this way of regarding experience and the new words and images to convey
it did bring something "new" into Elizabethan poetry.

Ralegh's poems, as I have shown, often reflected this "newness."

In general, then, Ralegh's reaction to life is private, personal and subjective. Yet it is important because he had a large nature and was a part of large issues. If his poetry only half detached itself from him, this is for interesting reasons. First, and literally, it is because of the way he had to write it, in the times between important public actions. It is also because he saw life as a continuity, never resting in a position which could be described and concluded. He felt in the Elizabethan world a sense of alteration brought by time, fortune and death. He was suspicious of clear articulation; it would not be true. Life, changing as one wrote, could not be too clearly reported. A too clear definition, as of a completed fact, would be false to the altering thing he was writing about. Lastly, looking inward at himself with relentless observation, he saw a kind of thought-feeling which could not be caught and catalogued explicitly in words. He, therefore, recorded it indirectly, allusively, "conceitedly" and the result was a sheaf of poems saying "new" kinds of things about life in "new" ways.

A NOTE ON JOHN DONNE

John Donne was twenty years younger than Ralegh. He belonged to another generation. Yet he is separated from the Elizabethan poets by more than time. His poetry takes up into itself the conventions and gifts of his age. Yet it transmutes these qualities into something unique, different from anything in his contemporaries or followers. For this reason, he is difficult to study either as an Elizabethan or as a seventeenth century poet. Yet if he must belong to one age or the other, he belonged more closely to the seventeenth century. The only poems published in his life-time appeared in 1611, '12 and '13. His great career as Dean of St. Paul's was from 1621 to 1631. To be sure his love poetry, *The Elegies* and *The Songs and Sonnets* as well as some of *Satires* and *Letters* belong in part to the 1590's. Ben Jonson in his pontifical utterances to Drummond in 1618, maintained that Donne had "written all his best pieces ere he was twenty-five years old." This would mean before the year 1598. Jonson's dogmatic statements of course are a little ludicrous. Yet it is true that purely from the point of view of time, a part of Donne's best poetry belongs to the reign of Elizabeth.

In spirit, however, Donne is separated from the Elizabethan world. There are various reasons for this separation. First of all he is isolated by the quality of his personality. Furthermore he took pains to withhold his verse from the stream of popular publication. None of his poems strayed into the verse collections of the late Nineties and early 1600's, as did Ralegh's. In his letters in which he sometimes enclosed copies of his verses to his friends, he besought their secrecy and specified that the manuscript poems must not come to print. The friends who collected them were faithful to this request. Another thing which separated Donne from contemporary secular poetry was a persistent preoccupation from childhood with religion. This sensual, worldly and fashionable young man of the Nineties carried always with him a teasing bewilderment about religious beliefs. He had to cross the great chasm between Catholic inheritance and a Church of England career. While he was not a "religious" in the mystical sense of that word, yet religion, as a body of knowledge and tradition, seized upon his intelligence and perceptions and would not let them go free. Thus the Elizabethan ingredients were mixed in John Donne in proportions so different from their proportions in men like Ralegh or Shakespeare that the resulting personality is hardly contemporary, in the spiritual sense of that word.

Yet Donne, if one studies him retroactively, is wonderfully clarifying to Elizabethan issues in poetry. What was completed and distinguished in his work, though it took a new era to mature it, casts its light backwards upon poets like Ralegh. One finds in their poetry the tendencies which worked forward and received their apotheosis in Donne. Upon one phase of Ralegh's poetry, for example, that quality in it which in a certain sense deserves the adjective "new," Donne's poetry throws light. Ralegh's intellectual probing of his feelings for poetic material; his expression of that material in unconventional figures of speech; his writing for self-expression, not for a public; these qualities are paralleled by John Donne's much clearer and completer undertakings along the same lines.

To these qualities in Donne the words "conceit" and "metaphysical" have been applied. They have added a good deal of learned mystification to the critical estimate of his work. I shall not here go into a discussion of them in Donne. But I do believe that some plain daylight upon the meaning behind these two critical spectres may rob them of their mystery and aid their sane use for Elizabethan poetry in general. The Elizabethan term "conceit," so arrogantly appropriated to Donne by his later admirers, covered shades of meaning which made it appropriate to several Elizabethan poets.

What then lies behind the Elizabethan word "conceit," and its seventeenth century companion, "metaphysical"? "Conceit" meant first of all something that was the opposite of *action*. This is a negative definition. Positively it stood for those qualities in the realm of non-action which may be named *imagination* or *fancy*. As used by Dryden and all the troop of later critics, it has been refined upon, burdened with shades, until its meaning is hard to comprehend. To be sure, Donne's poetry was "conceited." All that this meant in his own day, however, was that his poetry was largely occupied with functions of the human being which are *not* action. Or, to put the point positively, that the material of his poetry is speculative, philosophical. It was with this essential quality in his mind that Dryden in the *Essay on Satire,* said that Donne "affects the metaphysic . . . and perplexes the minds of the fair sex with nice speculations of philosophy." To express in words this intangible material, a poet needs images, comparisons. Donne's daring creation of such images was so distinctive that the Elizabethan word "conceit" was coloured by the peculiarities of his practice. Thus "conceit," which meant originally any imaginative or fanciful method of conveying material drawn from the realm of speculation, became narrowed to mean that particular kind of imaginative comparison which Donne used.

By the last third of the eighteenth century Samuel Johnson undertook to analyse the flavour of a seventeenth century "metaphysical" poet. It happened to be Cowley, not Donne. But Donne came into the discussion. Johnson focused on the oddness of Donne's figures of comparison. The essential meaning of "conceit," its kinship with the idea in "metaphysical" seemed entirely to escape him. Yet even Johnson said: "Sometimes [the 'metaphysical' poets] struck out unexpected truth; if their conceits were far-fetched, they were often worth the carriage." Here Johnson, in spite of himself, gives penetrating praise to Donne for the very thing which made him distinguished. He did strike out "unexpected truths."

One sees, then, that Donne and other Elizabethans before him, notably Ralegh, worked the mine of the "conceit." They searched that part of man's life which is not *action* but which is *reflection, introspection*. The things which they discovered they expressed in poetry with the aid of *imaginative* or *fanciful* figures. Because of this fresh material and this fresh expression of it some of the English poetry at the end of the sixteenth century seemed "new." If the manner of conveying these "new" things seemed strange, even Johnson allows that "they were often worth the carriage."

Thus Donne articulates a new quality which was tentative and fugitive in Ralegh and some other Elizabethan poets. The Elizabethan term, "conceit," so often warped from its essential meaning, holds in itself the simple interpretation of this quality. It is a new or revived emphasis upon the thought and perception of individual man and an immediate and untrammelled use of figures to transfer this material to poetry.

CHAPTER VI

The Progress of Prose across the Century

What is prose? This innocent question is less capable of answer today that it ever has been. Where lie the boundaries between prose and poetry? To this question, too, only a rash fool would offer a categorical answer. The fact seems to be that even more than verse, prose is the very shadow of day-to-day existence. It alters like a weathercock. At the end of the same person's pen it comes out variously as his intent, his mood, the sunlight falling upon him or the stick blackening in the grate, warms or retards his blood. It alters as the readers for whom it is designed alter. A letter, an editorial, a play, a novel, a cookbook, an "article," all may be written in prose. It is, too, made more volatile by the fact that it is the twin of talk. Poetry, however various its faces, is a concentration of life, a distillation from existence. Prose may be these things, too. But prose includes everything that is not poetry. Its range is as various as life, its versatility as infinite as talk. Because talk is amorphous, the very breath of life, always going on, never isolated and imprisoned in bounds, the written twin of talk, prose, is amorphous, too. It is all things by turn, and nothing very long. As soon as limitations, rules for the game of prose are imposed, the effectiveness is likely to elude the mould of words which has been devised to capture it. The art of prose is very difficult.

It is for these reasons' that the writing of prose probably was a later acquirement of the human being than the writing of verse. It is hard for one to realise this to-day, when framing a telegram or writing a letter is the gift of a vast number of men. It may be retorted that the telegram or the letter is not notable prose. That is granted. The mere transference of life to paper, however, is an acquired art. Now if it is transferred in metrical form the artificiality of this form is admitted at the outset. The writer is free, within the pattern, to select and fill out the feeling and ideas. But prose is without a set pattern. If a man transfers life to paper in prose, he must make his own pattern. This is a more difficult and presumably a later accomplishment than writing in metrical form.

Whether this supposition that prose is a later development in literature than poetry is generally true, there can be no doubt that the writing of English prose was a difficult task at the beginning of the sixteenth century. There are many reasons for this. The first is that verse had almost superseded prose as a form for literature written in the vernacular during the high Middle Ages, and in the early renaissance on the Continent. In a rough and ready way literature was synonymous with poetry. This tradition died hard. As late as the end of the sixteenth century, literary critics like Webbe and Puttenham and

Sidney, tended to treat the subject of literature as if it involved only those things which were written in verse.

The things that were written increasingly in prose were more workaday in subject matter; chronicles, philosophical dialogues, historical records. To be sure fiction in the early renaissance was normally in prose, in the romances and Italian *novelle*. But fiction, outside of drama, was not recognised as a respectable member in the household of literature. Furthermore when a man addressed himself to prose in a book on conduct and education like Elyot's *The Governor* (1531), or in a dialogue on sports and the intellectual life like Ascham's *Toxophilus* (1543), he did not feel that he was practising the art of literature as he would have done if he had been writing in verse. In the broadest sense his purpose was informational, not artistic. He was making a useful book not a contribution to *belles lettres*. But the need for useful and informing books in an increasingly literate and democratic world was very strong. Therefore the business of learning to write effective prose was urgent.

Almost any writer at that time would have found Latin prose much easier than English. There are a score of well-known testimonies to this fact in the prefaces to early Tudor books in English prose. The ways of the Latin sentence had been familiar during the whole Middle Ages. Now the style of mediæval Latin prose was being checked and altered by the example of classical prose, chiefly Cicero's. Any educated person had a tolerable prose style in Latin. But Latin simply would not do any longer. By 1525 the New Testament was translated into German and into English. Tyndale's wish that the ploughboy should have the Bible to read in his own copy in his own tongue was realised. Thoughtful Englishmen like More and Berners and Elyot realised that the arrogance which separated the few literate from the mass of illiterate and which widened the separation by writing in Latin was at an end. The printing-press was both a cause and effect of these new ideas. It was the symbol of a new order, and it was already forty years old in England when Henry VIII came to the throne. Furthermore, the movement toward literature in the vernacular was growing all over Europe. There must be translations not only from Latin into English but from great books written in Italy, Spain and France. The growth of religious confusion, developing with the new freedom to think and challenge accepted ideas, made controversial pamphlets in the vernacular a vital force in the campaigns of Church *versus* Dissent. A reading public, capable of being influenced through the press, was already born. The importance of English prose, then, was established.

But how did one write English prose? This was not a stupid question. The formula was not ready at hand. A long period of imitation and adaptation from Latin, both mediæval and classical, from Italian, from French and Spanish set in. Fantasticality had free rein in many of the resulting concoctions. On the whole it is fair to say that the sixteenth century in England is a period of experiment in the forming of English prose style. It

may truly be said, too, that the final achievement belonged to the beginning of the next century. The Elizabethans endured a difficult period of trial and error, and
the seventeenth century profited by their experiment.
There were a few isolated achievements in prose in the
sixteenth where the man, the style and the matter fused
into artistic achievement, as in some of More, Hooker,
Andrewes, Ralegh and Donne. Of a different kind,
Tyndale's translation of the New Testament was notable
prose. As a whole, however, modern English prose was
gestating, not born, in the sixteenth century.

For this very reason, because the century is full of
blatant experiment, critics have been too categorical
about Elizabethan prose. They have divided the whole
output into rigid classes. There is the prose that follows
classical pattern and imposes upon an uninflected language like English, the word order which was only possible in a highly inflected language like Latin. There are
the English followers of the Spaniard, Guevara, with his
antitheses and balances. There are the special fads of
Lyly in his two novels on *Euphues*. There is Sidney's
prose pattern in the *Arcadia*. But the classification of
sixteenth century prose is not so simple as this. Prose
depends upon the mood and the moment and the readers
addressed. Within the English prose of More or Lyly
or Sidney there is diversity of style. Lyly's prose in his
plays is different from the prose of his novels. Sidney's
Defense is on an entirely different pattern from the
Arcadia. One must refuse the clarity of a chart for six-

teenth century prose and be content to listen now to this
and now to that particular person. The whole voice of
England increases in volume and effectiveness till it
achieves in Bacon and his seventeenth century successors
a clear, versatile medium for conveying the range of
human ideas and feelings.

The one constant force throughout the century's development of English prose, which rode out all tempests
and seasonal confusions, was the demand that prose
should *convey*. Religion needed its aid from the fourteenth century onward, from Wyclif and the Lollards
onward. One of the earliest practical demands upon
prose was made by religion. As the Church began to fail
in its unquestioned authority over all classes, a reform-
ing group of clergy "went the people" directly in English prose, in translations of the Bible, in oral sermons
and in books of instruction. The circumstances made the
prose effective. Its only virtue was to carry enlightenment and conviction. It was never an end in itself.
Wyclif exhorts his priests to use a direct and intelligible
style:

What else is it, I ask, but adulteration of the word of God
when the preacher wraps himself in cloaks and other mere-
tricious ornaments . . . employed for his own ostentatious
delight and to the destruction of the flowers and the fruit
of preaching, which is the honor of God and the conversion
of our fellow men.[1]

Sermones, IV, 267-268

[1] G. P. Krapp, *Rise of English Literary Prose,* Columbia, 1915,
p. 4.

Of course Wyclif is referring to oral prose in this
passage, but the principle was recalled again and again
after the introduction of printing. Religion was, in fact,
the disciplinary nurse of English prose. R. W. Chambers has recently argued for an unbroken tradition of
English prose from Alfred to Sir Thomas More, preserved in books of religious instruction and devotion.
He says that the fourteenth century ended with a prose
"as noble in its simple lucidity as any English prose ever
written." [2] While secular prose of the fifteenth century
went capering off into many flowery meads, Chambers
contends that religious prose continued its plain and
moving style. Thus, when More in the early sixteenth
century undertook a *Life of Richard III* in English, "he
had not to make an English prose. He found it ready
to hand; not in Chaucer's *Pardoner's Tale,* not even in
Mallory . . . but in the living tradition of the English
pulpit and in the large body of devotional vernacular
literature dating from the fourteenth and early fifteenth
centuries." Whether Chambers is right in tracing More's
style to so pure and simple a source, in isolating him so
completely from the contaminations of the worldly prose
of the fifteenth century, one cannot be sure. But in any
case the simple grandeur of English prose from the first,
when it was used for proselytising and religious instruction, is unquestioned.

For a host of reasons, then, historical and social, a

[2] In Nicholas Harpsfield, *Life and Death of Sir Thos. Moore,*
Ed. E. N. Hitchcock, Intro. by R. W. Chambers, "The Continuity of English Prose from Alfred to More," p. cxv and *passim.*

situation arose where, rightly or wrongly, people felt
that English prose must be built up. The natural procedure among scholars and educated people was to look
about in modern Europe, in ancient Rome, for successful
methods of constructing prose. Imitation, too quick
adaptation into English of methods not suited to the
genius of the English language, wholesale incorporation
of French and Latin words to make the English vocabulary richer, all these ways of undertaking new English
prose were followed. This method would have produced
nothing permanent if it had not been checked at every
turn by the practical test of effectiveness in conveying
ideas. It was a century full of changes socially, with an
increasing number of middle-class men eager for new
ideas. They were, in fact, forced to have new ideas if
they were to fight tradition and secure opportunity
within the social order for their own advancement. The
spread of ideas by prose was as necessary as bread. This
necessity subdued the vagaries of experiment.

The share of democracy in this making of English
prose is fascinating to watch. The condition of society
had everything to do with the forming of literature. It is
not too much to say that a class war was fought out in
the prose of the sixteenth century. When one compares
Tyndale's prose pamphlets which he wrote to persuade
the people of the need of the Bible in English, with the
answers which More, as the supporter of Henry VIII
and the Roman Church, made, one sees how the social
attitude of the author modifies the nature of his prose.

Tyndale's zeal had burned up those fanciful decorations, those thickets of learned allusion which delighted the self-conscious writers. But in More's replies these interests throve and blossomed. Consequently his pamphlets lacked the directness and driving force of Tyndale's. Right there in the controversy of More *versus* Tyndale, the distinction of aims created a distinction of style which was to last on into the next century. The spare and burning style of the dissenters was for all men and their common God. But in the writings of the Catholic Church or the English Church of Elizabeth the opulent, renaissance *décor* was never discarded.

We must not judge any Tudor prose, even the plainest, by our modern ideas of terseness and lucidity. The structure of the sentences, even among earnest writers who address wide audiences, was more elaborate than the structure of our modern English sentences. This, one must always keep in mind in judging Elizabethan sentences. For one thing, the sheer clumsiness of doing something new produced long, tumbling periods, full of afterthoughts. For another thing, the written sentence if it had an English tradition, had an oral tradition. When the power to read had been limited for centuries and was only beginning to be spread through the classes, the capacity to listen was much stronger in the common man than it is to-day. The radio and the movies are again building a world of listeners who get news, sermons, political propaganda, even short stories through the ear. Before these inventions, however, the capacity

to listen accurately and continuously had much declined
in the modern world.

But in the sixteenth century, people stood for hours
at Paul's Cross to hear sermons or messages from the
government. They stood or sat on uncomfortable
benches in the theatres to listen to plays. To aid listeners,
oral speech had evolved many useful tricks like rhyme,
repetition and alliteration. A pair of words beginning
with the same letter forced upon the listener the relation
between the ideas represented in these two words. Alliteration which had played an interesting rôle in Middle
English poetry, was utilised in renaissance prose from
the beginning. Skelton, writer to Henry VII, used alliteration as a structural device of his English prose
sentence. One does not have to look abroad to Spain or
backward to the Roman rhetoric of Quintilian or the
practice of Cicero to find these word patterns. They were
independently arrived at even in the mediæval world.
They sprang out of sheer necessity to capture emphasis
and enforce points through the ear rather than through
the eye. When one remembers this, one is less impatient
of these "frills."

Furthermore, after centuries when reading aloud was
the normal thing, the kinship between talk and printed
prose was much closer than it is today. The structure
of Elizabethan talk was certainly different from the
structure of modern talk. A good deal of Elizabethan
talk was, by and large, committed to print in the sayings
of statesmen and wits, in dispatches, in letters. All of

these show that Elizabethan conversation, like Elizabethan clothes, was elaborate. Talk was an art, to be
slowly built up. No long-distance operator constricted it
to the limit of three minutes. They spoke largely and
with leisure. They built up something graceful and pro-
portioned as they talked. Of course the fashionable fop
built up a structure of nonsense, empty of meaning, and
was roundly satirised for it. But if the meaning was
weighty or truly witty, it could support the towers and
minarets of words. Sidney's *Defense of Poesy* read
aloud brings back the leisurely conversation of Dyer,
Spenser and the rest, who met at Leicester (later Essex)
House. In sentences not much less considered than those
of the *Defense* they may have invoked the spirit of
poetry and speculated upon its glorious future in their
England. Even the popular preachers like Latimer in
the middle of the century and Henry Smith at the end,
could risk involutions of phrase and play on words. The
passion for punning, often so irritating to us, was partly
a useful device for focusing the attention of a listener.
He thought two ideas under approximately a single
sound. His mind was forced to move backward and forward between them, retaining them, possibly comparing
them. This need for an elaborate pattern in oral speech
was transferred to written prose.

Because of these essential differences in the method of
transmitting ideas and facts then and now, Elizabethan
prose is alien and unsympathetic to modern readers. It
lies like a great colossus across their way. It is fantastic

and long-winded and boring. Certainly these accusa-
tions are merited if one judges from our own point of
view. But if one is patient and curious enough to construct for oneself something approaching the Elizabethan point of view, the differences between their
method and ours are a matter of interest. Their prose
was, on the whole, artistically unsuccessful. But one
catches, through it, the tones of their voices and the
whimsies and absurdities that make them alive. One
gauges, too, through their sensitivity to their audience,
the ranges of society, from the courtier to the prentice.
In the development of prose one feels the parallel development of the citizen into a shaping force in the nation.
The courtier meanwhile shrinks back behind the walls of
his own class. While he preserves elegance for a time, he
preserves it at his peril and finally loses his force before
the march of modern life.

But let us listen to what they are saying. There are
two biographies in the first half of the century in which
the warmth of private feeling simplifies the early Tudor
prose. One is the life of Sir Thomas More written by his
son-in-law, William Roper. Upon a simple but observant
man, with no literary ambitions, More's everydayness,
lit by his spacious attitude toward life, made such an
impression, that the resulting biography is almost like a
transcription of life itself. The style seemed unimportant
to Roper. The resulting prose is very effective. George
Cavendish had an equal opportunity to observe More's
great contemporary, Wolsey, at first hand. Cavendish

was a gentleman in Wolsey's household and accompanied him on his travels and through his adversity and dying. He saw his faults, felt his greatness and the theatricality of his fall from power. After Wolsey's death Cavendish, in his retirement in Sussex, wrote his account of the Cardinal's life. He is imperious with his English, makes it hurry at his command, recording great scenes and trivialities as he summoned them before his memory. In those difficult months when Henry and Ann could not bear to sever connections with Wolsey, yet were being pressed by his enemies to desert him, Cavendish records how the King sent Sir John Russell with a loving message and a gift. Sir John and his troop arrived at midnight on a rainy night.

Then I [Cavendish] . . . brought Master Russell from thence to my lord, who had cast on his night-gown. And when Master Russell was come into his presence, he most humbly reverenced him upon his knee to whom my lord bowed down and took him up and bade him welcome. "Sir, quoth he, "the King commendeth him unto you"; and delivered him a great ring of gold with a Turkis [turquoise] for a token; "and willeth you to be of good cheer; who loveth you as well as ever he did, and is not a little disquieted for your troubles, whose mind is full of your remembrance. . . . And, sir, if it please your grace I have had this night the sorest journey for so little a way that ever I had to my remembrance."

Neither of these biographies is a first-rate piece of literature. Of biography as an art neither author had any conception. That great men's lives were the most speaking illustration of the joys and perils of behaving ethically and unethically, that the caprice of fortune, stepping in between a man and his deserts, might bring about an illogical ending, both Cavendish and Roper believed. For centuries the lives of princes had been the *exempla* of good and evil conduct. These men followed this traditional way of handling biography. But both Roper and Cavendish worshipped as a part of their personal experience the achievements of the men about whom they wrote. For this reason one finds the greatest quality of biography present in their books, the quality of vividness and convincingness. Again and again one catches the very tones of voice, the gestures, the undercurrent of feeling. For this homely service both Roper and Cavendish found English prose well domesticated. As they use it, it is never great or moving in itself but it is lucid and flexible, and, more important, sufficiently self-effacing to be a tool for conveying personality, conversation, and crucial moment. I believe that this docility of the words and structure to the idea exists only because the authors were so in earnest about their subject. Personal admiration and the desire to transmit to posterity these great men, forced the English sentences to be effective. Their prose is, therefore, for its time and compared with the prose of more frivolous undertakings, satisfactory.

There is in these books an added pleasure for the modern reader. It is one which has nothing to do with the books themselves but is the gift of time. In the settings, the look of the rooms, the cushions in the window's embrasure, the gold chain about the master cook's neck, the discomfort on a hot day of More's hair shirt, the cool green of the garden arbour, the boat disappearing around a bend of the Thames, in a thousand and one commonplace details, we are assured that a day four hundred years ago was very like a day now. It gives us a naïve pleasure, a kind of wonder at the power of books to preserve life. It is a pleasure which increases as those books and their life recede into the past. Modern readers would do well to recognize this pleasure and count upon it.

Another piece of biographical prose, much read even into the seventeenth century, was John Foxe's *Acts and Monuments of these Latter and Perilous Days*, popularly known as "Foxe's Book of Martyrs." Foxe was an ardent supporter of Henry's new English Church, so much so that he had to leave England during the Catholic reign of Mary. As a piece of propaganda, he undertook a gigantic history of the Church in terms of the staunch persons who had died for the Faith. The first edition was written in Latin, and printed at Strassburg in 1559. When Elizabeth restored the English Church, Foxe came back to England and printed an English version in London in 1563. It was the English edition of course which held the public for nearly a century. The book is dull in the earlier portions. Remote facts were not vivid in Foxe's mind. When, however, he comes to the figures who suffered martyrdom, on one side or the other, during his own life-time, his English prose becomes a lucid and effective instrument. The resulting sections are very readable. They present personalities, conversations, poignancy of incident, realistic detail. Foxe must have known many of the contemporary figures whose martyrdom he describes. The book was widely popular. The public is always to be counted upon for appreciation, if what one writes has the stamp of authentic life upon it, especially if it is that part of life where great issues are joined. Moreover it was sensational reading, and at the same time it was religious. The example of these intrepid sufferers would strengthen the ethical fibre and the religious emphasis in every reader's life. As a religious excuse for reading a sensational book, what could be better than this?

For the modern reader, the pleasure is not so much in how the victims adjusted the brands for their speedier burning as in the intimate everydayness of the speeches and in the lively prose which reproduces the scene. The emotional import of the book is not achieved through personal admiration for the characters, as it is in the biographies of Cavendish and Roper. It is, instead, cumulative. The holiness from a thousand separate deaths is offered up to the stability of religious faith. Thus no single passage in Foxe is so moving as many passages in the lives of More and Wolsey. Yet the sinewy English is completely adequate to the requirements. Listen to this description of the Lady Jane Grey's last moments before her beheading:

Then she stood up, and gave her maiden, Mistress Ellen, her gloves and handkerchief, and her book to Master Bruges. And then she untied her gown, and the hangman pressed upon her to help her off with it; but she, desiring him to let her alone, turned towards her two gentlewomen, who helped her off therewith, and also with her frows, paste and neckerchief, giving her a fair handkerchief to knit about her eyes.

There is nothing notable about this passage in itself. But it does show how easily in the early Sixties English prose could report a scene. The account of Ridley dividing the contents of his pockets among friends before his burning, reads:

He gave away besides divers other small things to gentlemen standing by, and divers of them pitifully weeping, as to Sir Henry Lea he gave a new groat; and to divers of my Lord William's gentlemen some napkins, some nutmegs, and rases of ginger; his dial, and such other things as he had about him, to everyone that stood next him. Some plucked the points of his hose. Happy was he that might get any rag of him.

This is effective reporting of a moving public scene. English prose has already ceased to be a problem when the user has good material and the will to present it.

Another instance of the practicability of English prose is shown in the books written by Roger Ascham. He was tutor to some of the greatest men and women of the middle-century including Elizabeth before she was Queen. He moved, with a freedom resulting from their indulgent familiarity, among the most thoughtful and influential people. They consulted him on the problem of educating their children. They allowed him to lead their thought in many lines.

Ascham printed in English as early as 1543, *Toxophilus,* a book on the sport of shooting. Indirectly it said a good deal about the conduct of life and the value of intellectual pursuits. The fact that he printed it in English shows how native prose was coming to the fore. In his Preface "To All Gentlemen and Yeomen of England" he discusses English *versus* Latin as a medium of expression:

> If any man would blame me . . . for writing it in the English tongue, this answer I might make him, that when the best of the realm think it honest for them to use, I, one of the meanest sort, ought not to suppose it vile for me to write.

Here is the argument of a staunch "little Englander." Furthermore, he realises that English will reach more people than Latin and he has things to say in this book which he wants many people to read. He cares more about conveying ideas than about a reputation for elegant writing.

> Though to have written it in another tongue had been both more profitable to my study, and also more honest for my name, yet I can think my labor well bestowed, if with a little hindrance of my profit and name . . . come any furtherance to the pleasure or commodity of the Gentlemen and

Yeomen of England, for whose sake I took this matter in hand.

The *Toxophilus* is in no sense a great book. From the point of view of English prose, however, it is a good book. Ascham's English is dexterous and lucid. Hear him describe a windy day in winter.

I rode in the highway betwixt Topcliff-upon-Swale and Boroughbridge, the way being somewhat trodden before by wayfaring men; the fields on both sides were plain and lay almost yard-deep with snow; the night afore had been a little frost, so that the snow was hard and crusted above; that morning the sun shone bright and clear, the wind was whistling aloft and sharp, according to the time of year; the snow in the highway lay loose and trodden with horses' feet: so as the wind blew, it took the loose snow with it, and made it to slide upon the snow in the field, which was hard and crusted by reason of the frost overnight, that thereby I might see very well the whole nature of the wind as it blew that day.

For observation of nature and conveying of that observation in English prose, Ascham is not far behind nor far different from Thoreau in many pages of his *Journals*. Ascham's English is as simple; it is more external, more barely descriptive of the things he observed with his own eyes. Nearly twenty years later when he undertook his more famous book, *The Schoolmaster,* it did not occur to him to apologise for writing in English.

The tendency toward conscious arrangements of words, schemes of balance, contrast and accumulation, was present throughout the century. One could not have read classical and mediæval Latin, or Continental prose without being aware of these things. The pressure of conviction operated on the religious and informative prose and made it simple. But in *belles lettres* this purpose was not present to chasten the style. On the contrary, the more decoration there was in the prose of the romances and short stories, the more entertaining the whole performance was. With the "settling in" for a long reign which came very soon after Elizabeth had demonstrated her powers as a ruler, the literature of entertainment, the writing by courtiers for courtiers increased. Fine writing and conscious sentence structure are found here and there in that early collection of tales out of Latin, Italian and French compiled by William Painter in his *Palace of Pleasure* (1566). Geoffrey Fenton, too, who was one of the literary men in Ireland when Spenser was there in the Eighties, used formal devices of style in his *Tragical Discourses,* translated from Bandello. In other words the elements which in a highly concentrated form made Lyly's *Euphues* the talk of fashionable London and the model for much intolerable imitation, had been practised sporadically for years before the appearance of Lyly's book.

But let us look at *Euphues.* It was written by a worldly young man about three years out of college. It purports to combine story and morality, and to depict through the affairs of young Euphues, the well-nurtured one, the way to grow up and the way not to grow up among the pitfalls of the fashionable renaissance world. But its real intent is to further the young author in the regard of the *haut monde*. He writes for a group who affect leisure and boredom. His prose style therefore must be built into as many ingenuities for their jaded attention as the pastry cook devised for their puddings and cakes. The *décor* was as captivating as the matter it concealed. To accomplish this effect, Lyly evolved very little that was new. Yet he achieved the impression of newness by such consistent use of stylistic devices. Every sentence was notable for its construction. The care exerted upon the method of telling caught the Court taste. Here at last, they thought, English was curled and turreted to equal the elaborations of ancient and Continental style.

His dedication "To the Gentlemen Readers" commends the volume as a trifle:

We commonly see the book that at Christmas lieth bound on the stationer's stall, at Easter to be broke up in the haberdasher's shop, which sith it is the order of proceeding, I am content this winter to have my doings read for a toy, that in summer they may be ready for trash.

With more of the same, he banters his book into fashionable attention. Two years later, after a great success, he wrote a sequel, *Euphues and His England*. This time he knew exactly where his most profitable readers lay. He added a prefatory address: "To the Ladies and Gentlewomen of England. John Lyly wisheth what they would." He claims that "Euphues would rather lie shut in a lady's casket than open in a scholar's study" and con-

tinues with the comment, "I am content that your dogs
lie in your laps, so Euphues may be in your hands, that
when you shall be weary in reading of the one you may
be ready to sport with the other." Even among his gentlemen readers, he does not ask for steady attention:

Lovers when they come into a garden, some gather net-
tles, some roses, one thyme, another sage, and everyone
that for his lady's favour that she favoureth. . . . If you
gentlemen do the like in reading, I shall be sure all my discourses shall be regarded, some for the smell, some for the
smart, all for a kind of loving smack.

It is one of the ironies of literary history that this collection of commonplaces purveyed so wittily and casually,
should have been seized upon grimly as a landmark in the
development of English prose style. In a sense, but a
very obvious sense, it was this. The extreme practice of
self-conscious sentence structure, the direct assault upon
the fashionable world, the superlative quality of Lyly's
performance in all its phases, make the book a clear instance of many tendencies going on at the time. Its very
extremes make it easy to analyse, easy to use as illustration. But as literature, as a vehicle saying anything profound or witty about Elizabethan life, *Euphues* cannot
make pretensions. It is easy to trace its word patterns, to
check its curious and bizarre rhetorical figures. A wise
man, reading with a rose behind his ear and nothing
pressing for attention, may catch the light aroma of this
trifle. But such a reader is rare. The style simply is not
serviceable. Even within Lyly's own practice the elabo-

rateness of the first part of *Euphues* breaks down in the second part. When he comes to use this style in the dialogue of his plays, he modifies it even more.

Sidney was frightened by the self-consciousness of this English prose pattern. To be sure, he was among the first to recognise the need in *belles lettres* for some deliberate prose pattern until the method became natural and the guiding reins could be removed. But he was frightened by the results as he saw them in Lyly. In his *Defense* or *Apology for Poetry* (both words were used in the publication of this essay) which he wrote about 1583, just when Lyly was at the height of his vogue, Sidney puts his finger upon the essential weakness of too mannered prose. Authors lay their figures on externally, he says, instead of making them come from the thought and feeling. Authors keep "paper-books of figures and phrases" for surface application. Sidney wishes that they would "devour them whole, and make them wholly theirs." In his *Defense,* his own prose style is effective. It is lofty, leisurely, decorated when the decoration makes the idea more telling. It is cogent, progressive and strong in its general argument.

Two years earlier in his *Arcadia* he had written differently. The *Arcadia* is elaborate and discursive by comparison with the *Defense.* Perhaps the two kinds of writing should not be compared. The *Arcadia* was called a poem, if a bad one, by Milton. It might be argued that in theme and purpose *Arcadia* is not utterly different, though the difference in degree is very great, from his

friend Spenser's *Faerie Queene*. The very apparent
differences in result are explained by the different atti-
tudes of the authors. Spenser was determined, unremit-
ting, bound to win as a poet, who himself saw his books
through the press. Sidney was successful without the aid
of publication. His *Arcadia* was a rough draft, not for
print but for that literary sister's interested eyes. It
came to her in loose sheets of paper written often "in
your presence." Even if one takes with a grain of salt
the preface "to my dear Lady and Sister," in which he
commends *Arcadia* for private consumption only, one
does know that to come into the public arena was not
Sidney's habit. Granted this difference in the two authors,
the differences in the achievement of *Arcadia* and *The
Faerie Queene* are easily explained. The similarity of
ideas in the two is, however, worth pondering, though
it must not be taken too seriously.

If Sidney's *Arcadia* belongs almost as much to poetry
as prose, it is obviously wrong to apply the canons of
prose to its style. Certainly the content is much nearer
to poetry than the content of *Euphues* which is always
either story or sermon. *Arcadia,* on the contrary, often
is the reflection of mood. One can see from certain
passages in the *Arcadia* that Hamlet's soliloquies and
Burton's *Anatomy of Melancholy* are on the way. This
sort of theme is suited to the Arcadian sentence. It calls
for elaboration, indirect method, as poetry does. Occasionally Sidney's meaning in the *Arcadia* is equal to these
elaborations. At these moments its style is successful.

Though he was no professional writer, Sidney felt enough vitality in his theme and enough challenging difficulty in its form of execution to revise the *Arcadia*. There is an "Old Arcadia" and a new. The new is the one we usually see and by comparison with the old, its style is more elaborate. This fact only confirms our contention that the *Arcadia,* in Sidney's own view, belonged nearer to poetry than to prose. If one grants this contention, one sees that the *Arcadia* is not a retrogression, not a falling off from the ease and effectiveness of Sidney's English in the *Defense.* His practice in the *Arcadia* was not contrary to his theory when he attacked the over-elaboration of contemporary prose. For him the *Arcadia* might not have been prose. At least he might have refused to include it in either category of prose or poetry. But even if one regards it as prose, the *Arcadia* is maligned. To be sure it is often unsuccessful in what it undertakes to do. Its obviously decorated passages are often ridiculous when they are separated from the text. They should not be so separated; for they need the *afflatus* of sequence which often lifts them and carries them towering and billowing before it. There are, too, many pieces of straight narrative in the *Arcadia* where the English style is economical. One can, therefore, reconcile Sidney's strictures on decorated prose with his style in the *Arcadia.* The *Defense* and the *Arcadia* illustrate the two directions in which English prose was likely to move in the decade after his death.

The "publicity" as we should say now of the two tales,

Euphues and *Arcadia,* had an effect upon the prose fiction of the next ten years. Their obvious qualities were imitated and parodied. Echoes of their peculiar rhythms turn up sporadically in unexpected and unsuitable places. The reading public was steadily increasing. It already embraced a group of middle-class people, shopkeepers and merchants of the city. Women, too, became readers. Not only Court ladies read but house maids and harlots seem to have aped the reading of "society." A cheap edition of *Arcadia* was published in Edinburgh in 1599 and *Euphues* had had thirteen or fourteen editions before 1640. Besides the wide reading of these originals, the book market was flooded with imitations. Louis Wright in his recent and important book, *Middle Class Culture in Elizabethan England,* lists an imposing number of titles belonging to this sort of book. He shows, too, that Englishmen who did not live in London, or visit there, could still buy books. The London publishers had a far wider public than has hitherto been supposed.

The popularity of romances among the middle classes was founded upon their wish to escape from the meagre respectability of their lives. The main episodes were highly coloured, amorous or villainous, based upon or imitated from the tales of the Continental world. When these stories were adapted or imitated in English, they all, including *Euphues,* saved face by making the naughty incidents a vehicle for teaching conduct. This metamorphosis of story, a form once so free, into English renaissance *exemplum,* shows one way in which the ren-

aissance is inferior to the high Middle Ages. The
growth of democracy was largely responsible for this
new emphasis. The defeat of feudalism, the rise of the
middle class brought, as it always brings, increased
respectability and smugness. Philistia and the bour-
geoisie, though unnamed, entered England in the sixteenth century and Puritanism on its worst side sancti-
fied these qualities. No one was quite free from it; not
Spenser, nor Sidney, nor Shakespeare, nor Ralegh.
With Bacon and Donne, the quality is hard to find,
largely because Donne fights still with the high banner
of mediæval thought above him and because Bacon has
looked in through the door of the clearer-thinking seventeenth century.

In the romances exclusively for the middle-class people, this moralising of story is prominent. Authors like
Samuel Forde and Henry Roberts were turning out romances which are not recorded in histories of literature,
save by such recent researchers in middle-class life as
Louis Wright. The popularity of a moral lesson in the
light tale for entertainment (or in *The Faerie Queene* for
that matter) arises from the social situation. The individual was now responsible for the control of his life.
When the feudal system and the Church failed, each man
was for himself. The prize of fortune or power lay
ahead if he could so conduct himself as to win it. This
thought raised the question, how then should he conduct
himself? To answer this, he must inform himself on all
possibilities, see how others behaved, what policies were

effective and what ones not. Conduct of life, therefore, not as a religious preoccupation but as a practical guide for getting on in the world, became an absorbing interest among all classes. This fact explains the vitality of the didactic tradition in a society obviously and unashamedly worldly. Yet it was fun to read the tales, too.

Bachelers and Maids with his [Johnson's] tales have compassed the Xmas fire-bloc till the curfew-bell rings the candle out; the old shepherd and the young plow boy after their day's labor have carolled out a tale of Tom Thumbe to make them merry with . . . I will . . . bring him again into the chimney corner where now you must imagine me to sit by a good fire, amongst a company of good fellows over a well spiced Wassail-bowl of Christmas ale telling these merry tales which hereafter follow.[1]

The discussion of didacticism in Elizabethan fiction and the reasons in society which lay behind it may seem beside the business of this chapter which is concerned with prose style, not with the material which it clothed. But it is, I think, true that the author's feeling that he must not only amuse but convey the moral implications of his story affected his prose style. It became simpler, easier to take in. Of course it did not cheat its public by doing away with those airs and graces of alliteration and balance which characterised "society" reading. The rhetorical figures, however, are much less intricate and the sentence structure is easy to follow.

[1] See Louis Wright, *Middle Class Culture in Elizabethan England,* p. 393, note.

Greene's career in prose is a case in point. His first ten years of prose work was chiefly in novels. His style climbs determinedly after the fashionable precedent of *Euphues* and *Arcadia,* each in its turn. But about 1590 he began to season his far-fetched fiction with fact, to borrow episodes from his own life and his sordid London world. At first he braided these in with fantasticalities from Italian and other foreign settings.

Gradually, as early as 1591, he forsook both the dedications to high courtly names and the decorations. He began to write directly about the abuses of London, how and why one must avoid them. It is doubtful whether he was any more sincere than in his earlier work. He simply discovered a new, popular vein for fiction. This new matter called for a new manner, something plainer, barer, more like language in real life. In his preface to *A Notable Discovery of Cosenage,* he says that a high style ill becomes a base subject and that he must fit the manner to the matter. The resulting prose is distinctly different from what he had been writing before. Take, for instance, his comment on the victim of card sharpers as he takes his sad, empty way home:

Perhaps the man is very simple and patient, and, whatsoever he thinks, for fear goes his way quiet with his loss, while the cony-catchers laugh and divide the spoil, and being out of the doors, poor man, goes to his lodging with a heavy heart, pensive and sorrowful.

In *A Groatsworth of Wit Bought with a Million of Repentance* his warning to his friends on the basis of the supposed misdoings in his own life, is rhetorical; it makes an emotional appeal. The structure of the sentences, however, is simple.

Remember, gentlemen, your lives are like so many lighted tapers, that are with care delivered to all of you to maintain; these with wind-puffed wrath may be extinguished, with drunkenness put out, with negligence let fall; for man's time is not of itself so short but it is more shortened by sin. The fire of my life is now at the last snuff and the want of wherewith to sustain it; there is no substance left for life to feed on.

The idea is carried by figures but they are simple figures, effectively used for the sentimental purpose which Greene had in mind. The disappointing thing about Greene's prose is that he paused upon the verge of a simpler and stronger narrative and expository style. Either his death or the essential frivolity of his point of view about writing kept him from creating a stable and well-knit style. When his prose moves, it moves through exhortation as if he transferred a personal interview to paper. But as a whole he did not achieve a firm prose style.

Just at the time of Greene's death in 1592, Thomas Nashe was voicing the university man's attitude in his *Pierce Penniless, His Supplication to the Devil*. Although he is speaking in behalf of poetry, he mentions prose and argues for decoration in it. He declares that Henry Smith, the popular preacher who died in 1591, was good in his prose sermons only because of the les-

sons he had learned from poetry. Nashe saw no art in
the undecorated prose of "your lay chronographers that
write of nothing but of mayors and sheriffs and the great
frost." A simple narrative style for plain events was a
necessity but Nashe could not imagine that it might become an art. Such writers "cannot sweeten a discourse
or wrest admiration from their reading." In those two
phrases to "sweeten" and to "wrest admiration," Nashe
voices the old joy in the arrangement of words as an
end in itself. Yet he, too, felt the pressure of newer
and simpler standards. In his *Unfortunate Traveller* in
1594, he saves his euphuistic style for the courtly lover,
Surrey, and satirises the rhetoric of public speeches in
the performance of the "bursten belly ink-horn orator"
who spoke before the Duke in Wittenberg. But when his
rascally hero, Jack, moves among camps and soldiers and
eats his food in inn kitchens, Nashe's prose is simple and
realistic.

The truth of the matter is that prose is moving slowly
forward. It will soon cease to be a preoccupation in and
for itself. In the interim of years between the great-
mannered *Euphues* and *Arcadia* and this new stage, men
like Greene and Nashe and Dekker stand like Januses
looking backward and forward, vacillating between
formalism and simplicity. No one of them was a writer
of the first rank. No one of them, consequently, felt the
necessity to seize prose by the throat and make it do his
urgent bidding. Dekker came nearest to it in some of his
stark pamphlets on the London plague and City nights.

But even he was a space writer. He "filled" his copy up. His effective prose is a matter of patches and, one is bound to feel, of happy chance. Tradesmen writers for tradesmen readers, of whom Deloney is the best known example, had to write simply for their public. Deloney believes, however, that the highly bred ladies in his stories must speak euphuistically:

Yes, quoth she, as welcome to me as a storm to a distressed mariner. I muse greatly that reason will not rule you nor words win you from your wilfulness.

Court fashions now slightly outmoded are still used by Deloney for his ladies. He does not know that fashion has changed. His commoners, however, are shrewish and jolly and coarse by turns in swift-moving and plain language.

During these last twenty years of Elizabeth's reign there was also the prose of great preachers. It was distinctly in a class by itself because it was orally delivered and to a public so present as to modify its structure in very special ways. In the personalities and congregations of two London divines whose lives overlapped, Henry Smith and Lancelot Andrewes, one sees how volatile and susceptible to special conditions prose may be. Smith, well trained but unorthodox, lecturing at St. Clement Danes in the City in the late Eighties, captured the attention of the citizens and middle-class people who went to hear him. His collected sermons, printed after his death, are in a simple, moving prose. They are at the opposite pole from the creations of Lancelot Andrewes, whose sermons were written and carefully revised for delivery to intellectual churchmen, capable of travelling with him the intricate paths of creeds and texts. The prose of these two men is essentially different because the men were different and the audiences to which they preached were different. Yet for each, one must conclude, the English sentence was by now versatile enough to receive the impress of his peculiar accent.

Donne again is different from either. As he did not begin his preaching till Elizabeth had been dead twelve years, he belongs in point of time with the seventeenth century. But the versatility, the freedom of wide experiment which belonged to the Elizabethan sentence, was useful to Donne. For this reason his sermons belong more to the Elizabethans than to the new seventeenth century style. Donne selecting his text, then choosing his headings and, as Walton tells us, committing "his meditations to his memory," went into the pulpit with only these headings before him. The resulting sermon was forged in the moment-to-moment contact between this "angel from a cloud" in the pulpit and the vibrations of feeling which arose from the dim audience below him. What he said there was sometimes taken down stenographically. Compared with the written version which he made from memory with the aid of his notes, it shows many differences. But whether speaking or writing, the adaptability of Elizabethan prose, its length or brevity, its starry complexity or daylight plainness, served him well. It was a basis upon which to construct his learning, his logic and his passionate immediacy. Because Elizabethan prose was never fenced off from poetry, it served particularly well the emotional need of preachers as different as Smith, Andrewes and Donne.

When Francis Bacon in 1605 surveyed the output in English history and found it undistinguished, there can be no question that his judgment was just. The chronicle with its patient jog from event to event was encyclopæ-dic, not critical. Remarkable men and the effect of their personality upon the events of their time, this would have been interesting. But the chronicles gave little of it. It was this kind of history to which Bacon addressed him-self when his enforced freedom from affairs allowed him to complete his *History of the Reign of Henry VII* in 1621. But Bacon was of the seventeenth century. In the sixteenth century except for the good early biographies by Cavendish, Roper and More, history was pedestrian, willing to be judged solely on scope and inclusiveness. Holinshed, if Shakespeare had not used him, would have been unimportant.

There is one fact about these chronicles and surveys, however, which gives them a place in the development of English prose. Their purpose is to convey and their prose is consequently simpler, more direct and colloquial, than the prose of "literature" in the same period. They were read constantly and their plain style furnished a healthy check on tendencies toward extravagance and decora-tion. The same thing is true of Stow's *Chronicle of*

London, printed in 1603, the year of Elizabeth's death. Stow was a London tailor whose taste and spare time revealed to him the history in the ancient walls and gates and oratories of the crabbed streets and lanes which he haunted. His prose is colloquial and natural, as he talked. It lacks exaltation and it is free from plodding. He loved London and loved to talk about its antiquities and curiosities. He doubtless had never heard that prose was an art about which one had theories. His practice of this art contributed something to the integrity and varied usefulness of the English sentence.

But Bacon's strictures about English historians are deserved, for none of these people had perspective. The philosophical implications of history were not within their view. The lives of bad kings might be handled as a warning to the wicked but such morality was explicit. A world like the Elizabethan, glancing boldly into the forbidden deeps of knowledge, discovering the stark roots of human life, needed a different sort of history. It needed a mirror where, in what was past, the interpretation of their present might be seen. There was just one person who wrote history this way, Ralegh. One must believe that he did so not of any set theory but because the great alembic of experience which he was, made him see life here in the present or there in the past as one. The pitiful and stupendous doings of man whether in London or Jerusalem, in Devonshire or the Garden of Eden, in his own Guiana or Cleopatra's Egypt, moved in him and made him vocal.

The resulting prose style of Ralegh's *History of the World,* written between 1607 and 1614, when the Elizabethan world was completed and behind him, is worth considering. For high matters and affairs in which the inference from the event is as important as the event, Ralegh needed a high style. The material called for long periods containing their feeling in mounting phrases till the essence broke forth in the last line; pairs of opposite words for sharply opposed ideas; quotations borne along and assimilated in the slow power of a lengthening sentence; and most characteristic of all, figurative and allusive ways of saying things that would not endure the frontal attack of literal expression. All these things were ready to his hand. The bizarrerie of much earlier prose, the consciousness of the architectural thrust in a sentence, and the refusal to isolate from prose the devices of poetry had contributed to the formation a rich style. It was capable of carrying with strength and light reverberation the burden of his thought and the caprices of his mood.

True it is, that among many other benefits, for which it [History] hath been honored; in this one it triumpheth over all human knowledge, that it hath given us life in our understanding, since the world itself had life and beginning, even to this day; yea it hath triumphed over time, which besides it nothing but eternity hath triumphed over; for it hath carried our knowledge over the vast and devouring space of many thousands of years, and given so fair and piercing eyes to our mind; that we plainly behold living now, as if we had lived then, that great world, *Magni Dei sapiens opus, the wise work* (saith Hermes) *of a great God,* as it was then, when but new in itself.

By 1590 English prose was ready for philosophical discussion in a simple form. Richard Hooker's *Laws of Ecclesiastical Polity* shows this. The English sentence was friendly to a quieter field than moving history or moving sermon. Hooker, living in the Master's House (burned in the Great Fire and replaced by the present Wren mansion) in the rear of the Middle Temple Church in London, found controversy within his own close. His assistant, Travers, in the afternoon service "spoke pure . . . Geneva" in antiphonal response to Hooker's "pure Canterbury in the morning." Their amicable disagreement on the government of the Church set Hooker thinking of the gigantic task of constructing the ecclesiastical universe. What were the immutable laws behind Church sovereignty? If he stood for them, he must know why. The urgency to design a cosmography of the Church led him to leave the Temple where his responsibilities were engrossing. In the quiet of small country livings he evolved a great book. It is full of ecclesiastical vistas. Columns of intricately cut argument support the dignity of Church law and policy. Five books of this undertaking appeared across the Nineties. After his death in 1600, the last three were edited or compiled afresh from his notes.

How serviceably the English sentence adapts itself to the exposition of the philosophical causes of Church government. The visual structure of the Latin sentence, its

balance and parallelism, were, of course, very real to
Hooker. They no doubt were an aid to the plain exposition of these abstruse matters. Hooker hoped that his
book would reach the laymen and, for that purpose, he
chose as direct and lucid a style as possible.

Dangerous it were for the feeble brain of man to wade
far into the doings of the Most High; whom though to know
be life, and joy to make mention of his name: yet our sound-
est knowledge is to know that we know him not as indeed
he is, neither can we know him; and our safest eloquence
concerning him is our silence; when we confess without
confession that his glory is inexplicable, his greatness above
our capacity and reach. He is above and we upon earth;
therefore it behooveth our words to be wary and few.

But

They err therefore who think that of the will of God to
do this or that there is no reason besides his will. Many
times no reason known to us; but that there is no reason
thereof I judge it most unreasonable to imagine. . . .

Thereupon Hooker sets off to explore the reasons. His
learning presupposes for its full effect a technical knowledge of the philosophy behind all law and sovereignty.
But the humility of this man before the task, the simple
greatness of the design which he unfolds, give even the
lay reader a sense of seeing original causes lying before
him, clear if not quite apprehended.

Men of action who wrote prose were likely to exercise
their imagination not in their style but in their behavior
in tight corners. This fact is well illustrated in the ac-

counts of voyages to new countries which Richard Hakluyt collected in his volume of 1589. Of course when men
like Ralegh or even Lodge went on a voyage, they had
the literary art not only to transfer the events to paper
but the feeling which accompanied the events. But they
were the exception. The majority of the accounts of
travel in Hakluyt are bald narrative, where the English
sentence is plain and useful but nothing more. "A Gentleman in the Voyage" of John Hawkins to the West
Indies in 1564-5 wrote an accurate but succinct account,
which is typical. There is no elaboration of his feelings
under difficulty:

Thus sailing forwards on their way with a prosperous
wind until the twenty-first of the same month, at that time
a great storm arose, the wind being at north-east, about nine
o'clock in the night, and continued so twenty-three hours
together; in which storm Master Hawkins lost the company
of the *John Baptist* aforesaid, and of his pinnaces called
the *Swallow,* his other three ships being sore beaten with
the storm.

The fame of Hakluyt's collection of these accounts
through three hundred and fifty years is a tribute to the
active imagination of the lay reader. It shows how a bare
report, even an understatement, of stirring events calls
the imagination of the reader to clothe the incidents with
the terror which must have surrounded them. The prose
of these "gentlemen in the voyage" is serviceable but it is
not notable.

The prose of Elizabethan plays is, of course, the reflection of talk. Every shadow of contemporary conversation, the serious speculations of young Hamlet and Horatio and Prince Hal, the ridiculous affectations of Armado and Sir Tophas, the plain country talk of Justice Shallow, when he forgets his official dignity, the wit of citizens, the bawdry of hostesses, the color of colloquialism and dialect, all are there. How close Elizabethan conversation was to prose, these speeches in the plays show. Thus daily talk acted upon and was acted upon by the manifold forms of prose that came from the press.

After a century of experiment pedantically imitative, or plain and submissive to the matter in hand, English prose was ready for the certainties and maturities of seventeenth century style. It is customary and right to laud the English of the King James Version of the Bible, completed in 1611. The shaping influence of its style upon later English literature is proved. But no band of translators and stylists, however distinguished, could have created the King James Version in vacuum. The long story of false starts and brave experiments, the steady desire to make English prose a dexterous tool, which was present throughout the whole sixteenth century, made possible the King James Version of the Bible. It presented a body of experiment which was ready to be crystallised into appropriate forms for the mood and intellect of succeeding ages.

CHAPTER VII

The Backdrop for Elizabethan Drama

Elizabethan drama is so remarkable that it is likely to make fools of the people who comment upon it. They peer and squint at this colossus, too large for their comprehension. Yet the tremendous vitality of it and the impression it gives of being sprung fullgrown from barren ground challenge the critic to provide explanation and pique that ruinous curiosity out of which literary historians are made. If they believe that a study of the drama that went before Shakespeare and Webster and Jonson will explain the work of these men, they are indeed foolish. But if they go humbly through the hundreds of indifferent plays which fed the daily appetite of the English public for a hundred and fifty years before the Elizabethan drama, they will discover some interesting things. They will come to feel what the public wanted and they will see why it gradually changed in its demands. They will believe that in the last analysis what the public wants in any age is the only unfailing canon of dramatic criticism.

But they will also see when they arrive at the work of the greatest playwrights, how genius outwits the tyrant public. It gives them precisely what they want but it is also untrammelled. It gives them what it wants to give, too. The conflict between tradition and original talent is resolved. A great play of Shakespeare, for instance, is a product of the dramatic history which lay behind it and a submission to contemporary public taste. But it is also what Shakespeare as an original artist is compelled to write. If the literary historian will remember this and will summon the predecessors of the great Elizabethan playwrights lightly, shrugging a shoulder at them for the poor relations that they are, mindful of the gulf between their tendency and the miraculous realisation of that tendency in the great dramatists, he will find dramatic history useful.

With this caution, it will be safe to set forth upon an exploration of the backgrounds behind Elizabethan drama. The study of mediæval-renaissance drama is a study in the taste of the people. Its beginnings in Miracle and Morality Plays were not devised for the nobility, the listeners to the spacious cycles of Charlemagne and Arthur and Alexander. They were for the rank and file, for that potential middle-class who stood gaping in the market-place to see their fellow guildsmen enact the scenes of Old and New Testament history or dramatic moments in the life of a saint, or the allegorical story of man's journey from birth to death.

The origins of this popular religious drama are worth considering for the light they throw upon it as an essential part of the people's life. The older theory of these origins is well known. Dramatic moments in the liturgy of the Church were gradually secularized in the market-place. There is also a new and different theory. It emphasises the dramatic quality of mediæval sermons and the transfer of this quality to the mediæval stage. Either one of these theories shows the natural and inevitable way in which drama evolved from basic circumstances in the daily life of the people.

The new theory of the obligations of popular drama to dramatic qualities in the mediæval sermon is worth looking at, as a concrete illustration of the way in which what was to be a literary genre centuries later, was originally a rough and ready response to contemporary conditions. One of the essentials of mediæval preaching was the interlarding of argument with dramatic accounts of scriptural story. G. R. Owst of Cambridge has recently paralleled, episode for episode, the dramatic rendition of great scenes like the Sacrifice of Isaac or Christ before Pilate, in the sermon and in the Miracle Plays. "Every variety of expression to be found in the plays," says Owst, "canonical and uncanonical, serious and humorous, satiric and tragic—is of the very stuff and essence of Mediæval English sermon." He goes on to show how common was the dramatic use of allegory and personification in the pulpit, the casting of a story into dialogue to bring far away, holy figures nearer.

The people in those days were constant listeners to sermons. Nothing is more logical therefore than to argue that these dramatic qualities of the sermons influenced the plays. Owst shows one more way in which religious story was presented to the people. He explains the use of dramatic devices, whether in the pulpit or in the market-place, to impress the imagination and memory. The dramatic liturgy of Christmas and Easter in the Church had been for the same purpose. It is not important therefore whether one derives secular mediæval drama from liturgy or pulpit or both. What is important for the history of later renaissance drama is that dramatic presentation had for centuries been regarded as the handmaiden of story. Drama was the great popular method of story-telling. Reading a book and looking at a stage were just two ways of receiving the story. There was small differentiation of method. Much narrative technique clung to stage shows; much dramatic vividness was utilised in narrative. This is the very key to understanding the tradition behind Elizabethan drama.

To reach the people, to stage religious story in terms that would affect them, was then the chief reason for mediæval drama. It was for the audience that the play was written and it was a popular audience. The same situation obtained in the gradually changing world of the renaissance. It was still a popular audience, unreflective, thick-skinned about its thrills and its humour. But it belonged to an expanding universe, a slowly secularized world in which the scheme of mediæval society was breaking down, and the common man no longer knew one place as irrevocably his. Individual ability and political opportunity when brought into happy conjunction might raise him out of one class into another. Social chaos, for so the renaissance must have seemed after the strong mediæval framework of life, worked its spectacular upward and downward curves and bore men up and down with it.

While anything as clearly defined as a middle class did not exist, this expansion of life for commoners made them demand new opportunities. Their education and their diversions in reading and seeing plays became important. Furthermore the relaxation of religious rules of conduct threw their ideas of behaviour into chaos. They were eager for new light on problems of conduct. All these new urgencies had their effect on the plays of the sixteenth century.

First let us consider the nature of the great bulk of renaissance story; for this story was transmitted to the public more easily by way of the stage than by way of the printed page. The reading public was slowly building itself up on increasing literacy. In volume, however, it was not to be compared with the theatre-going public. Renaissance story was largely popularised and vulgarised mediæval romance. It was contaminated by mixture with other kinds of stories, by mediæval *exempla* and *fabliaux,* by late Greek romances, by the Italian *novelle.* Geographical adventures, too, in strange lands filtered into this conglomeration. The result was an interesting body of narrative. Sixteenth century drama is largely an experiment in conveying this narrative to the public by way of the stage. It is necessary to see what the qualities of this story material were. For, though drama can refine away a good deal, the nature of plotting and characterisation in the original story has much to do with its dramatised version.

First, for the mediæval romance. In it the manipulation of plot and character was not "convincing" from the modern point of view. There was very little probability in the events that made up the plot. Motivation of character according to the inward springs of human behaviour, was practically unknown. Chaucer had created the psychological novel in his *Troilus and Cressida* and the short story in the *Canterbury Tales*. But Chaucer's discovery was not led up to or followed immediately by other experiments in the same kind. In general, mediæval fiction cannot be called a "criticism of life." It reproduces certain isolated elements of life; action, danger, moments of nobility and cowardice, humour, marvel. But the individual character with his complexities does not emerge. In the popular mediæval drama, the same thing is true. The moral effect of action upon the character is important in the play. But that moral effect is asserted by the lines of the play, not felt. In general it is fair to say that motivation and character analysis as the great Elizabethans understood it, and as we understand it, is *not* in mediæval fiction, dramatic or narrative.

Nor did they develop in the debased renaissance versions of these stories; nor in the new stock of story which the renaissance authors collected. They plundered Ovid and Oriental history. They adapted the late Greek romances with their Daphnes, Chloes, Clitophons and

Leucippes who were shipwrecked on Greek islands or
piped in Arcadian vales. But these stories contributed
nothing toward the realistic presentation of life in plot
and character.

When one comes to the Italian renaissance short story,
newly compiled partly out of mediæval remnants, partly
out of domestic intrigue as it existed in actual Italian
life, one looks at last for a view of life more nearly akin
to experience. The old world had gone; the new world
was here, being lived experimentally by the renaissance
man. Now surely the transmission of real life to fiction
would be effected; character and plot would become
more convincing. But as a matter of fact, story technique did not change. In the collections of Italian short
stories by Cinthio and Bandello which found their way
into England in the Sixties and were a storehouse for
Elizabethan drama, plot motivation and character analysis are still unimportant.

Why is this? One is tempted to argue, not without
support from the ethical backgrounds of the century,
that the average renaissance man has not yet evolved the
power to analyze character. Having relaxed their belief
in Christian ethics, men were in an interim, had not
evolved any other objective system of ethics. Even
Machiavelli's political ethics were pragmatic, a trial and
error system, not in any sense a completely articulated
plan. Perhaps life itself, to the renaissance man, was
only a series of unrelated moments. In each of these he
acted according to the expediency of the particular occa-

sion, by his wits and chance. Even Queen Elizabeth's reign must have looked to the average subject like a reign whose policy was to have no policy. If this was so in life, it was, of course, so in fiction. Having received from the Middle Ages a fiction with little motivation of events and character, they found nothing in their immediate experience to change or modify that tradition.

But in England the moral temper of the public somewhat altered the Continental condition. The interest in what makes a good life or what makes a happy life, was so strongly ingrained that early sixteenth century plays in England were bound to touch the problem of conduct. The dramatists had not yet learned how to imply their theories through realistic plotting and characterisation. But they had substitutes. Let us look then in early Tudor drama for substitutes for the realistic handling of plot and character, for other devices by which a play may carry with it a criticism of life.

At first the playwright, failing to make the story speak its moral through the action, told the story to illustrate the moral. This is illustrated in a representative group of early Tudor playwrights, men who felt the weight of tradition and the spur of experiment, who stood at the crossroads of mediæval and modern England. Consider Medwall and Rastell and Heywood. These men, with Sir Thomas More, were grouped around Cardinal Morton, Archbishop of Canterbury. Across their world the long pageant of the Church was still marching and the new humanistic and Continental ideas were bravely countermarching. Plays were a diversion of Cardinal Morton's household. The handling of plot and character and the way of making a criticism of life in these plays illustrate the borderline between mediæval and renaissance drama. Medwall's *Fulgens and Lucrece* (circ. 1490), for instance, and John Rastell's *Calisto and Melibœa* (circ. 1502) use plots drawn from the modern secular literature of the Continent. Yet they cannot endure the complete lack of ethical implication in these foreign stories. Both plays alter the originals so that the moral lesson is perfectly clear.

It seems as if in most mediæval and a good deal of early renaissance drama, the dramatist did not know how to make a criticism of life through plot and character. He did not have the skill to tell a particular story about particular people so that the man in the audience would be moved to say, "There, but for the grace of God, go I." Yet in the renaissance world it was necessary to establish the transfer from the characters on the stage to the spectators. It was important both for instructing and for establishing a vital contact between play and audience.

As the century came toward its end the playwright and the public cared less about the specific moral of the play. It was enough to create realistic plot and character and imply the comment on life. Yet the dramatist was often unsuccessful in doing this. Even Shakespeare sometimes failed. The dramatic method vacillated between an explicit statement of the moral behind the action and a realistic presentation of the action which implied the moral. Finally in a play like *Hamlet,* the traditional moralising and the new speaking of life itself in the lines, have become one. The external comment on Man has become the inmost revelation of a particular man's thought and feeling.

The slowness with which sixteenth century fiction, dramatic and non-dramatic, arrived at this result is important to realise. It explains the failure, from the modern point of view, of a good many things in the greatest Elizabethan plays. On the other hand, it makes their achievement in character depiction all the more remarkable.

The Italian *novelle,* on which so much Elizabethan drama was based, were as deficient as all the other stories in realistic plotting and characterisation. In Cinthio and Bandello, for instance, there is violence and licentiousness right out of society as it existed all around them. But there is very little good characterisation or plot structure. Diversion and terror are found in these stories and separate scenes of engrossing interest. But there is no sense of reality permeating the tale from beginning to end.

In England the popularity of these Italian short stories was great. Painter published, in three editions between 1566 and 1575, one hundred and one tales. A few were of his own devising, but most came from renaissance Italian sources. He wrote chiefly for a court audience, and with an eye on the moral problems which confronted

men in high public positions. When he comes to the
stories themselves, however, he is as awkward about conveying the moral as the writers of plays. He announces
the principle which the stories should convey in a separate preface, forgets it and proceeds to translate or
adapt the tale for itself. Apparently the readers were not
looking for serious comment on life after the prefatory
admonishment. No doubt they often skipped the ad-
monition and proceeded at once to the business in hand.

Yet the linking of story with lesson died hard. As late
as the middle Eighties a famous collection of tales prepared by Pettie, the *Petite Pallace,* used the story only as
a kind of moving belt on which to place soliloquies and
long speeches on character and conduct. It is a crude
interlarding of action with comment on action. Yet in
Pettie one begins to see how the external lesson of the
story would become at last the living interpretation of
story in terms of human experience.

The playwriting tradition thus far and the story tradition have had certain distinctive qualities. They present
a series of episodes. They lack the artistic unity which
might make these episodes a comment on life. They are
divorced from life, though often full of lifelike detail.
They lack the force of inward meaning. They compen-
sate for this by applying the meaning externally, either in
a preface or in an admonitory ending. But they lack the
power to combine event and the meaning of event in one
creative whole.

It is no wonder, then, that Seneca's artificial closet

plays, which were now being translated or acted in Latin in schools and colleges, were eagerly studied for their dramatic technique. They might possibly provide some method which was lacking in the native tradition. In the first place, physically, they look very different from the English plays. They are neatly constructed, arranged in five acts, with a small number of characters. The speeches are long and pompous, making trim parallelograms of print upon a page. There are blocks of line-for-line altercation, in which grief or anger or villainy never forget themselves so far as to break the symmetry of this stately tit for tat, which the rhetoricians called *Stichomythia* (a line to a speech). The courtiers, the Inns of Court men and university scholars took an interest in them but they were caviar to the general. Fashionable English plays were modelled on them. These English Senecan plays were, for instance, deemed suitable for performance at Gray's Inn when the young Queen in the Sixties came there to a Twelfth Night entertainment. This snobbishness which made them artificially popular with the few, brought their doom. For this was not an age of the few but an age for a great public, wanting honest entertainment and bound to get it. Yet during their brief vogue they had an influence on popular drama. They are, therefore, worth looking at.

The first interesting thing about these English plays which were supposed to be modelled on Seneca, is that even in them the force of the English dramatic tradition is strong. Take, for instance, *Gorboduc*. It was played first at the Inns of Court Christmas festivities in the winter of 1561-2, and then before the Queen at White-hall. Whether the dumb-shows in it were consciously borrowed from Italian *intermedii,* or devised by the noble gentlemen who wrote the play, Sackville and Norton, they certainly were not in imitation of Seneca. His plays have nothing of this kind. If they were devised in England, an historically minded person takes pleasure in seeing how directly they join on to previous English expression of ideas by allegory and symbolism. They have much in common with the Morality plays. Also their spectacular effect, to the accompaniment of music from instruments appropriate to the mood of the dumb-show, prefigures those masks which Ben Jonson, less than forty years after, would make famous.

For instance, before the second act of *Gorboduc* the dumb-show presents, to the music of cornets, a king on a throne. One courtier offers a transparent glass of wine and is refused. Another courtier offers a cup of gold which conceals by its opaqueness the poison within. The king chooses the second cup and dies. Thus flattery concealing poisonous counsel wins over clear, honest advice. The spectacle, the music, the pleasure of reading the riddle, all are similar to features found earlier and later on the English stage. They are not in the least Senecan, in the original sense of that adjective. The play concludes with a hundred-line speech summarizing the situation and pointing out its moral implication, just as English plays had been doing for hundreds of years. Convincing motivation of character and plot are as lacking here as in the other fiction of the period.

More than twenty years later, still under the auspices of the Inns of Court and for a royal performance, three gentlemen "reduced into tragical notes" another Senecan play, *The Misfortunes of Arthur*. The story deals with English history and the sources are the great storehouses of mediæval story, Geoffrey of Monmouth and Sir Thomas Mallory. The same kinds of things that were in *Gorboduc* are still here : the ethical tang, Fate and its consequences, dumb-show with its allegory and music. Here, too, are kings, playing for high stakes and losing, to the accompaniment of rhetoric. The plot and characters are simplified. The story is, in fact, chiefly useful as the occasion for a series of poetical speeches. The piece belongs almost as much to lyric as it does to drama. It is a series of declamations, accompanied by music and spectacle. But the soliloquies have something new. The reflections of Modred and Arthur on guilt and its psychological effect, the states of feeling it induces, are more realistic than the soliloquies in *Gorboduc*. One begins to see that the ability to transfer real personal feeling to paper is growing. One recalls, too, that the rhetorical soliloquies of the wicked Richard III are only six years off and that Shakespeare may have been in London when the *Misfortunes of Arthur* was performed.

Though Shakespeare might have heard about it or even read it, for it was both played and printed in the Eighties, he would not have seen the performance. That

is an important point. This sixteenth century revival of
Seneca by Court and University did not touch the popular
stage. It went on in its own separate channel across the
Nineties, still the property of the literary nobility, like
the Countess of Pembroke and Fulke Greville and Sir
William Alexander. If an important popular playwright
like Kyd tried his hand at a translation of a French
Senecan play like Garnier's *Cornélie,* he did this as a
literary man, not a playwright, to show his polite learning. The Kyd who made this translation is utterly
divorced from the great popular melodramatist of the
Eighties whose *Spanish Tragedy* and *Hamlet,* directly
and indirectly, froze the blood of London audiences for
the next twenty years.

In roundabout ways, however, these Senecan plays
had a good deal of effect upon the popular drama. Before
one can discuss their influence, one must distinguish the
different kinds of plays that were included under this
rough term "Senecan," and note the qualities of each
kind. Take the original Seneca. His plays were really
rhetorical poetry, for declamation, not acting. They were
the poetic rendering of great emotional moments rather
than plays. As far as realistic plot and character went,
they were as guiltless as English drama and story. They
carried their comment on life explicitly through eloquent
speeches.

The man who created these speeches was primarily a
philosopher and orator. With his rhetoric and his sen-
tentiousness, he cast a spell upon the renaissance play-

wrights. If instead of Seneca, they had encountered the plays of Euripides, they would, I think, have been too naïve to profit by his example. His mature gift for realistic character and plotting would have been beyond their powers to imitate. But Seneca's plays were all compact of morality and didacticism. They were purple patches of rhetorical comment upon a slight plot enacted by stock figures. In this respect, Seneca simply surpassed the native drama on its own ground. His rhetorical finish and perfection in a style which they already admired made Seneca easy to assimilate. His dramatic pattern appeared in Whitehall before the Queen, or on the boards of Henslowe's theatre, refurbished or metamorphosed by time and history.

Seneca slipped in without a violent wrenching of English tradition. Sackville and Gascoine and Hughes and Kyd did not fully realise the fact. That we do realise it, is one of the pleasures of historical retrospect. To them Seneca had the charm of daring and novelty. He came out of the antique world, long forbidden and full of stolen sweetness. His Medeas and Didos seemed at the opposite pole from the Magdalenes and Pilates and Judases, from Perseverance and Hick Scorner and Everyman. Certainly they were more sophisticated in their violence and more eloquent in their figurative expression. But they were not, as the Elizabethans thought, of an utterly different *genus*. Nor was the method of presenting them and their story essentially distinct from previous English dramatic usage.

Before passing beyond the original Senecan contribution to the Elizabethans, there are certain specific gifts within this general one of congeniality which may be mentioned. The "high astounding terms" of the great dramatists from Marlowe through Shakespeare, Webster, even on to Ford and Shirley, the tall talk which blows along so many of the scenes, is the very mark of their Elizabethanness. The dramatists might have achieved this out of their own tradition. It probably was a "literary" heightening of the endless thinking aloud which went on in actual life. But the reading and imitation of Seneca encouraged and gave method to this kind of speech. According to tradition the rhetorical speeches in Seneca's plays were declaimed at Nero's court. The Elizabethan acting tradition, too, in the hands of such men as Edward Alleyn or Hamlet's travelling player, was declamatory.

Seneca's ghost was an important gift to Elizabethan drama. It spoke from a different *milieu,* with a different set of values. It was an allegorical presentation of one's conscience. It was useful in making articulate for the audience intangible things like remorse and guilt, things which were wordless in the soul of the murderer. The dumb-show, too, though it was not found in Seneca, was useful for conveying intangible things. It did not so much furnish a synopsis of the coming act as it prefigured the mood of what was to come. That is, it carried, as the ghost did, the other side of real events, the overtones of event in terms of mood. Thus in *Gorboduc,* the dumb-show which precedes the murder, does not enact the murder but presents a troop of mourners passing thrice across the stage to the music of flutes. In other words, these spectacular devices of ghost and dumb-show convey to the eye and ear of the auditor the spiritual connotation of the actual persons and events. Later, they will turn up in the very greatest tragedies, where realistic presentation is only *one* of several levels for conveying the idea.

From all this it may be gathered that Seneca's gift of form, five acts, chorus and the like, is the least of his gifts. It is the easiest one to see and has therefore been over-emphasized. The Universities and Inns of Court imitated the formal Senecan outline meticulously. But in popular plays for the London stage, this formalism was very cavalierly handled. In the popular English authors at that time the sense of form as the classical world understood it, and as the renaissance French world understood it, simply did not exist. For a small space, the length of a sonnet or a piece of rhyme royal, or within the pattern of a euphuistic sentence, the Elizabethans were sensitive to form. Form on a great scale, however, they did not know. Their exuberance was nearer to chaos, unordered but sometimes beautiful.

It was, then, in influences not clear-cut and external but nebulous and easily fusing with native taste that Seneca permeated the Elizabethan stage. His gifts were doubly precious because they in no way shut the door upon development along native lines. For example, Seneca was quite guiltless of plot as the renaissance story-world understood plot; as a mesh of intrigue woven by a throng of people, restless and vociferous, each bent upon his own small game. The simple Senecan pattern of events left room to accept this superstructure of renaissance plot. Furthermore the Senecan soliloquy was quite different from the soliloquy which was to develop along native lines and flower in famous speeches like Hamlet's "To be or not to be." Seneca did not obstruct the English development. His gifts could be fused with contemporary method. They furnished a bright, sharp blue-print of lines along which to build.

The history of Senecan influence in Italian drama is very similar to its history in England. It is worth spending a moment upon, because it illustrates once more the peculiar renaissance combination of subservience to models and independence of them. Seneca's precedent lent valuable direction but did not dominate the Italian renaissance playwright's notion of a play. Take, for example, Cinthio, whose plays were as popular as his short stories. In 1541 he wrote a strictly Senecan tragedy, the *Orbecche,* from a story of Persian history. It was his first and last play "by the book"; for he had his eye always on the public not on the scholars and *littérateurs.* In five subsequent plays he gave this public what it wanted. His definition of what it wanted appeared in the Prologue to the *Atille* (1543):

It seems to me that many of you have frowned at the mere name of tragedy, as if you had nothing to see but tears.

But be content, for that which is to take place here to-day will have a happy ending . . . if you like you may call it tragicomedy . . . from the ending in which it has conformed to comedy—after sorrows, full of joy.

He reflects in another place in the same Prologue:

In nature everything is transformed; must not the rules of art also be adapted to the task of each epoch? The Romans did not imitate the Greeks completely and they did well.

Cinthio then cuts free from rules and writes by the pragmatical test of what the public wants. He uses Seneca but he uses him cavalierly. His tragedy (which he admits would be more accurately labelled tragicomedy) is so-called because the play contains thrilling and horrible scenes. It might end on one of these or, more popularly, it might close in happiness and peace after a progression of violent scenes. Even if the last episode was happy, the play, studded with these shining horrors, was considered a tragedy. He worked for an audience who cared nothing for the tragic climax based on psychological principles. Renaissance horror was an isolated thing, complete in itself.

Cinthio made another interesting alteration of the Senecan emphasis. His plays still dealt with important persons, royalty or famous heroes, but the plots were likely to be concerned with the private life rather than the public life of these personages. In making this alteration Cinthio expressed the changed social emphasis of the renaissance world. It existed in England and was

reflected in English drama as well as in Italian. The
chief phase of private life which was stressed was love.
This change from interest in the King as King to interest
in the King's *amours* was natural; for it was supported
by the conditions of contemporary life. In the renaissance world, public life was by turns strong or weak. It
was full of trial and error. It had no objective reality
as a system. In such a world the public responsibility
was always there but it did not command devotion. The
individual dreaded his public world, suspected it, tricked
it, or was tricked by it. His devotion, his emotional experience lay rather in private life. The effect of this
public chaos upon love, upon individual power, this was
what the renaissance Italian was interested in. This
accent in life was reflected in drama. It gave the formula
not only to Italian but to a great many Elizabethan plays.

These plays, furthermore, taking after life itself, were
full of characters and sub-plots. Compared with Seneca's characters and the formal renaissance imitations
of them, the size of the cast in these popular plays was
tremendous. Kyd's rendering, for instance, of Garnier's
formal French Senecan play, *Cornélie,* has seven characters besides messenger and chorus. But Kyd's popular Senecan play, *The Spanish Tragedy,* has twenty
characters. The crowds of people, the different stories
about different groups, the actual uncertainty sometimes
as to which is the main story; this confusion is common
in the popular drama. It imparts a peculiarly renaissance
flavour. Jostling, talking, gesticulating when there is

too much noise to make talking audible, loving, killing, succeeding and failing, the characters were flung into the expanding mould of the popular stage. The whole of private life, unselected, bearing upon its surface the flotsam and jetsam of myriad inconsequentials was there.

Because of this complex inheritance and this deliberate appeal to popular taste in the plays, the literary historian must not make too great a claim for influences. The influences were there, but they were seized cavalierly and mingled with things new and different. The one steady criterion of drama throughout this century is "what the public wants." The public wanted everything at once, tragical, comical, historical, pastoral. They did not understand plot motivation and character analysis as we know it and for the reasons already set forth in this chapter. They wanted dramatised tales of violence and intrigue, events dancing to the tune of Fate or Fortune or Providence. All must be seasoned with realistic touches out of life but need not reproduce life on its own inexorable terms.

A humorous sidelight on the whole affair is the way in which the playwrights protested that they knew the best ancient critical theory of drama in the Greeks, and considered what Horace and Seneca thought on the subject. When, however, it came to actual playwriting they either frankly abandoned theory for popularity, as Cinthio did, or they talked learnedly about criticism and made no application of it in their plays. The fact that the taste of a new world must be satisfied, some of them admitted, some of them denied. But that fact staunchly remained and created willy-nilly the new renaissance drama.

Lope de Vega faced this contradiction between dramatic theory and practice with frankness and cynical amusement. After experience with writing five hundred Spanish plays, he wrote in 1609 his *New Art of Writing Plays*. It is a remarkable document, summarising in its few pages the chief points of plays as they were, not as they should be. He who writes artistically "dies without fame or guerdon," Lope says. He goes on to outline what has brought fame to him in his plays. The list includes the points we have just been making for Italian and English drama; tragedy mixed with comedy and suspense. In one sentence he banishes the need for probability of event: "in defiance of art I dare lay down precepts . . . for sometimes that which is contrary to what is just, for that very reason, pleases the taste." One is reminded of the boggled-up plotting of many modern movies. He knows, too, that the audience wants every phase of the story put upon the stage. The more characters and intrigues the better; "for the wrath of a seated Spaniard is immoderate, when in two hours there is not presented to him everything from Genesis to the last Judgment." Most characteristically of all, he sees himself, as they all did, as a hack writer, purveyor to the public, not an artist aloof in his tower. He knows how many sheets of paper to the act, like any honest space-writer.

In England the most successful Elizabethan playwrights do not talk about their plays but write them. There is, however, a humorous and futile chorus of complaint by critics, Puritans and theorists. This adverse criticism is not only humorous but informing. It attacks just the conditions which we have outlined and defended. Whetstone furnishes an early example (1578) of this unfavourable criticism, though his practice in play-making did not follow his precept. He complains that "in three hours runs he through the world, marries, gets children, makes children men, men to conquer kingdoms, murder monsters, and bringeth gods from heaven and fetcheth devils from hell." Sidney follows (circ. 1581) with his complaint that the hero "is lost, groweth up a man, falls in love, and is ready to get another child, and all this in two hours' space." They are simply complaining that mediæval-renaissance fiction is not Greek drama, nor even Senecan. The complaining, of course, is entirely irrelevant. As late as 1612 Webster was protesting "Should a man present . . . the most contentious tragedy . . . observing all the critical laws . . . the breath that comes from the incapable multitude is able to poison it." In general, however, most of the great popular playwrights in England said nothing. Their success justifies their practice. They wrote for a new world with a new inheritance. The gifts from the past they took fearlessly and freely and used them as became their new world. Because of their courage and honesty, their closeness to things as they were, they created what is probably the greatest drama in the modern world.

CHAPTER VIII

Great Elizabethan Dramatists Who Created Their Plays against This Backdrop

Against this backdrop Elizabethan drama went forward ranting, stabbing, torturing, summoning ghosts and symbolic creatures to pass in procession across the stage. There were songs, dances, plays within the play. There were scenes on moonlit balconies, in the dark passages of a fortress, in the Duchess's chamber, in the throne room, in the plain air of the city square, in the madhouse, in the Cardinal's study. Sometimes the scene was swung halfway between earth and heaven in a no-man's-land where the character expressed that precipitation of thought and feeling which we call great poetry.

In the thirty years from 1585 to 1615, such a gamut of violence and tenderness, of balderdash and poetry was run as has not been equalled in any other thirty years of the modern world. The division between the wheat and the tares is not easy. The best plays, even Shakespeare's, are unsure in places, gathering into their capacious selves temporary things which have no validity in the perspective of time or art. This unevenness within a single play is hard to deal with. The critic would have an easier task if some plays were good and others were bad and there was an end of it. He would be better off if some successful playwright had only announced a formula, a pattern by which the dramatic product might be judged. But unhappily the critics announced their formulas and the playwrights wrote their plays in splendid isolation of one another.

It would be easier to value this output if there had been fewer influences upon the Elizabethan play. But it was the catch-all for every kind of dramatic fashion, ancient, mediæval and renaissance-Continental. It undertook to embrace the whole library of mediæval-renaissance story. This was an added difficulty; for drama depends upon qualities quite distinct from those of story. But more confusing than all the rest, are two facts. First, within those thirty years (1585 to 1615) Shakespeare's career began and ended. It makes a fair estimate of his contemporary dramatists almost impossible. With the apparent effortlessness of genius he played the game of Elizabethan playwriting with complete attention to the moment, to popular taste, to changing fashions. He wrote plays in the manner of Lyly and Marlowe and Kyd and Marston and Chapman and Jonson and Beaumont and Fletcher. He plundered the same sources, relied upon the same devices, compounded the same diverse elements. Yet his result is essentially unlike the drama of any of his contemporaries. It has that timelessness, that simple rightness, that inexplicable magic which contemporaries like Jonson realised. This fact blinds the critic's judgment of the Elizabethan dramatic output as a whole; he tends to put Shakespeare too high and his fellows too low, to lose the estimate of the time in his response to timelessness.

The other fact that confuses the critic is the element of change in the outlook upon life during these thirty years. England came to its maturity. It came to know the mutations of individual feeling. It became intrepidly agnostic about the moral framework of life. It bravely suspected the old formulas of cause and effect. It invited new chaos and was willing to bear it in order to arrive at the truth about man and society and life and death. It did that most difficult thing, to rest in solution, to sift each turn of circumstance for what it was worth, to put off conclusion from year to year. Yet along with this daring experiment in living, it kept old codes, old simplifications, and cherished them on equal footing with the new. The critic therefore must straddle two worlds; mediæval, one might almost say, and modern. He must be able to run backward and forward with assurance that the journey in each direction is equally valuable. He must never impose the standards of his own century. This is a very difficult task. But let us undertake it.

Literary historians are able by actual count to summon some thirteen hundred titles of plays (including fragments and translations) between 1559 when Elizabeth came to the throne and 1616 when Shakespeare died. Nearly twice as many plays probably existed between the accession of Elizabeth and the end of the old drama. The number actually surviving the rough weather of three centuries is about six hundred. In certain moods one feels that time has dealt kindly with the modern student of Elizabethan drama. It has reduced his field of observation to at least one-fourth of its original size. But even at this, the range and variation is bewildering. Yet with certain frank limitations of the field, it is possible to find a path through this forest.

In the present chapter, I shall exclude the work of Shakespeare except indirectly. I shall also exclude that topical comedy which clung to the very skirts of the particular moment for its point. Domestic tragedies, too, which were based on actual contemporary events, representing middle-class or provincial society as it then was, will be omitted here. These exclusions are not entirely logical. There is something to be said against making them. But there is, I believe, more to be said for making them. By simplifying the field, the way is open for a clear view of the outlines and proportions of this strange creature, Elizabethan drama. Both so-called tragedies and comedies will be included; for the distinction between tragedy and comedy is not clear-cut in the Elizabethan field. Plays which wear these labels of difference are discovered to be, in their essential Elizabethanness, of a single kind. For example, from the Elizabethan point of view, for the similarity of their ways of regarding life, Marlowe's *Tamburlaine* or *Faustus* and Jonson's *Volpone* are more at home within the confines of a single classification than they are under the separate headings of "Tragedy" for the first two and "Comedy" for the third.

What guides, then, are there for choosing one's way through this great wood of Elizabethan drama? First, one will have to remember the inheritances for both dramatist and audience from the plays and stories that preceded them. Diverse as the body of mediæval drama is, it would be fair to say that in all of it, life was formalised and standardised rather than individualised or represented realistically. In morality and miracle plays, interludes and masques, and even in the conventionalised horrors of Senecan drama, this was true. The facts were not represented as we ask them to be in a modern realistic play or novel.

If this is a characteristic of all literature, dramatic and non-dramatic, in the mediæval and early renaissance world, it means that the Elizabethan playwrights and audience were acclimated to a way of writing and reading about life which was different from ours. It was a way which has, in the main, been lost by ours. Generations of comment on life by parable and allegory had produced a world in which this double way of thinking, this seeing what was actually there and inferring from it what was potentially there, was natural. The symbolic transcription of life so that it conveyed a meaning on two levels, the literal and the allegorical, was perfectly familiar to the Elizabethans.

But this method of portraying life is unfamiliar to us, repellent and often boring. Its use, for instance, by that great, perhaps most representative Elizabethan poet, Spenser, is what places him beyond the reach of our merely modern appreciation. Spenser is caviar to the general, much more than Donne, or Shakespeare or Marlowe. Yet Spenser permeated the literary experiment of his day. The Elizabethan public were used to finding a conventional version of life in their literature. Our modern failure to follow them in this taste has done much to becloud our understanding of Elizabethan drama. We criticise adversely when we find plot "unconvincingly" handled or characterisation "badly" motivated. We say with a shrug of the shoulder, "nothing could make me believe that Tamburlaine loves Zenocrate or that Olivia's duke changes to love of Viola in a line, or that the wicked Pierre becomes a saint in a moment, or that the plotting Oliver suddenly loves his persecuted brother Orlando." We laugh at the naïveté of Elizabethan dramatic construction. How improbable that Lear on a caprice should so dote and divide his kingdom or that twins cast up in shipwreck on the coast of Bohemia should so lightly and improbably weave themselves into the life of the town.

Our strictures may be somewhat lightened by remembering that these Elizabethan plays are based on old stories where pages in disguise and love tests and sleeping potions were commonplace. But to transfer responsibility for the way of presenting life in Elizabethan drama to the shoulders of mediæval story is only to push the dilemma one step backward. It does not explain it.

The explanation lies in the fact that the standards of story-telling, mediæval or renaissance, were not ours. The broad distinction lies in the difference between a representational, individualised portrayal of life as we know it in modern plotting and characterisation, and the use of plot and character to present life in a formalised and symbolic pattern.

There is another element in the creation of Elizabethan plays which had a strong effect on the finished product. This, too, the modern reader must keep in mind. The Elizabethan playwright had a similar point of view to that of the modern writer of scenarios for the screen. His work would make money for him if it were well done. Being well done meant fitting the particular drama to the actors, the company's size, costumes, financial resources. It meant bearing in mind the successes of rival producers, defining as far as possible that volatile thing, public taste of the moment. The man who wrote the play was only one of several people who were equally concerned in it. He worked in collaboration, or he revamped a script already in the manuscript chest of the company. His work was conditioned by the resources at the disposal of the caster and the property man. He worked sometimes at breakneck speed. The writing of the script was simply one of the manifold activities out of which a play was created.

This meant that there was no great pride of authorship, no rarefied atmosphere in which from the public's point of view the author lived. The effect of this condition upon the author was both good and bad. It made for slovenliness, for hasty and often crude work. But on the good side, there were many counts. Such an attitude toward writing fostered experiment. Playwriting was lightly undertaken. The writer was not inhibited by "rules." He was not afraid of the dramatic reviewer. His momentary improvisation, therefore, might strike out a new line in stage effectiveness. There was spontaneity and easy invention. Happy collaboration often sprang out of a chance meeting in a tavern.

It is, of course, a commonplace of literary history that Shakespeare instead of relying on his plays for his literary reputation, undertook two long non-dramatic poems, *Venus and Adonis* and *Rape of Lucrece.* To these he put his name, went to the pains of a dedication and publication by a reliable printer. None of his plays, of course, were treated this way. Kyd, too, translated Garnier's academic French Senecan play, *Cornélie,* and took trouble over it as a serious "work." But his great popular successes like *The Spanish Tragedy,* which not only brought him money but in the perspective of centuries have brought him fame, were not considered as literary productions. They were just a part of the job of furnishing entertainment to the public. It was unique in the history of playwriting when Marston and more pompously Jonson collected their plays and saw them through the press. Their attitude was ridiculed and Jonson's "Works" were long a standing joke.

One begins to see then that because of the nature of

dramatic and narrative technique which lay in the centuries behind it, and because of the spirit in which the
playwrights undertook their work, the Elizabethan
drama requires a different set of standards for reading
and appreciation than those we have for contemporary
drama.

Let us look at some plays which illustrate what we
mean by this conventionalising of reality in plot and
character. Lyly's plays held the stage in the middle
Eighties at the beginning of the great period of Elizabethan drama. The way in which he became a playwright
is a specific illustration of that opportunism in undertaking plays which we have just discussed. He was a
successful novelist, member of Parliament, and secretary
to Lord Oxford when he suddenly found himself,
through the gift of that Lord, presented with a company of boy actors and a theatre. Overnight he must
change from novelist to playwright. He did this lightly,
amateurishly, successfully. *Endimion,* perhaps his best
play, was produced at Court in the winter of 1585-86.
What was it like? In the first place it was frankly an
allegory. In the list of characters appeared names from
Greek mythology, like Cynthia and Endimion. There
were names symbolising qualities, like Favilla and Scin-
tilla, meaning a pair of sparkling young ladies. The play
is the lightest kind of phantasy. Endimion, for changing
from love of Tellus to love of Cynthia, is through the
jealous Tellus' machinations put into an enchanted sleep
for forty years. It is a picturesque sleep upon a pretty

bank. The plot, if one may use so heavy a word, is the story of Endimion's release from this magic sleep. Cynthia's courtiers travel to remote lands in hope of finding a counter-spell to release him. One of them, Eumenides, reads a riddle at the bottom of a marble fountain. This riddle, interpreted by an old man who is conveniently at hand, leads to the happiness of every one and everything in the play.

The motivation of this fairy-tale is as light as gossamer and the sequence of events is strung on a fine thread of caprice. Tellus for her speech against Endimion is banished by Cynthia to "the castle in the desert, there to remain and weave . . . stories and poetries wherein were showed both examples and punishments of tattling tongues." But she "only embroidered the sweet face of Endimion." The play has a dumb-show. There are songs which are musical versions of the repartee they interrupt. Critics have emphasized the specific instances of characters and situation in *Endimion* which became stock qualities of many later comedies. There are the witty pages, the use of prose to reflect Court conversation. There is a silly titled braggart. In all these things, Lyly set a fashion for his followers. But in emphasizing these separate details, critics have, I think, neglected the significance of the design as a whole.

It is obvious that in this play Lyly had some courtly compliment to pay, some contemporary political innuendo to convey. First, he took the outline of the story from the Greek myth about Endimion and the moon. He borrowed the mood of mediæval wonder and romance. He listened to court talk until he could turn it into the embroidered prose of his speeches. Then he relied upon his audience to see two things at once, to look at the pageant, the literal outline of the story, and to look beneath it and discover public figures of the day playing for power and preferment, in a game where the stakes were life and death. Whether Cynthia represents Elizabeth, and Tellus, Mary of Scots (who was to be killed the very next year) and Endimion the future James I of England, we cannot be sure. Perhaps the Elizabethans were not sure either. But these figures stand to one another in some implied relationship of this sort. Lyly specifically refuses to say what the precise meaning of his pretty play is. He says in his prologue:

We hope in our time none will apply pastimes [i.e. interpret the play as referring to some specific event of the moment] because they are fancies.

In the same prologue he forestalls against placing the play in any of the well-known categories:

We present neither comedy, nor tragedy, nor story, nor anything but that whosoever heareth may say this: Why here is a tale of the Man in the Moon.

The truth of the matter is that Lyly's *Endimion* is a very obvious example of this drama on two levels, which was peculiarly Elizabethan. It has both a literal and symbolic meaning in its plot and characters. The implications of its plot hover lightly above some of the blackest situations of the English Court. Its simplified, two-dimensional characters move with a mechanical precision. They move as the carved figures move in patterned dance upon a music-box. Their speeches achieve the studied wit and innuendo at which real Court speeches aimed. Thus real life and convention are fused. This tale of The Man in the Moon has its roots in contemporary London. It transports reality into moonlight. It can count upon its audience to infer the bitter facts of the year 1585-6 from this riddle wrought in moonshine.

It is not so quixotic as it may seem to place Marlowe's *Tamburlaine* next to Lyly's *Endimion* in this study of Elizabethan methods of presenting life upon the stage. There are of course fundamental differences between these plays. They are as far apart as black and white; physically, in the opposition of mannered prose to blank verse, spiritually, in the opposition of the low plane of Court intrigue in *Endimion* to the high plane of universal human aspiration in *Tamburlaine*. One is ephemeral, the other moving and eternal. In the circumstances of their creation, too, they are opposed. *Endimion* was devised for a small, homogeneous Court group, whereas *Tamburlaine* represented the whole renaissance world neighing, snorting, rearing to be off in a race for omnipotence. These differences between the two plays are obvious. Yet because in their import and feeling they are so very different, their underlying similarity of method in transferring life to the stage is all the more striking.

Tamburlaine is the story of a Scythian shepherd who conquers Africa and Asia. For the material Marlowe consulted at least three different histories. He also studied the map of Africa. He felt the magic of geographical names but he also knew their accurate boundaries upon the pages of Ortelius's atlas. Not only in his historical and geographical facts was he tied to his own time, but in the spiritual meaning of the play. He hit upon a common, almost hackneyed theme then, human ambition. Tamburlaine starts as a shepherd. He knows the hills of Georgia and their thieves as the young Stalin knew them. He dreams and acts upon his dreams and is monotonously and unbelievably successful. In the public audiences at the Rose who saw this play, no one would fail to respond to a "success story" which embodied so obviously his own aspirations. To all classes of Elizabethan London, *Tamburlaine* was as sympathetic as Lyly's *Endimion* had been two years earlier to the limited circle of Elizabeth's Court. Of course, it deals with the aspirations of life, not its realities as *Endimion* does. Yet both *Endimion* and *Tamburlaine* belong to the same convention. In both, experience is conventionalised and heightened. Both are about life but they do not reproduce life as the courtier or the London citizen actually saw it or felt it. Both convey their reality indirectly.

If one does not believe this, a glance at the pages of *Tamburlaine* will convince him. The persons of the play are great abstractions, symbols of rich imposing coun-

THE BEAR GARDEN, THE ROSE AND THE GLOBE

This portion of an equestrian portrait of King James by Delaram shows the public theatres in the left foreground (the round and octagonal buildings). Opposite them on the north bank of the river is the City of London. London Bridge crosses the river at the right

tries for Tamburlaine to conquer. There is Mycetes, King of Persia, Bajazeth, Emperor of the Turks. Sometimes they are not given individual names. They appear simply as King of Arabia, King of Fez, King of Morocco, Soldan of Egypt, Governor of Damascus. They are useful symbolically; they are splendid obstacles for Tamburlaine to remove one by one from his victorious path. The play has no actual dumb-shows, but it constantly relies upon the pageantry and double-meaning which is the essence of dumb-show. At intervals, for instance, crowns are used to feature pictorially the meaning of a scene. They are taken from the head of his dead opponent and placed on Tamburlaine's head; hidden in the skirts of a scheming dissembler; served at a banquet instead of cakes where the stage direction reads "Enter a second course of crowns." Conquest is graphically represented by drawing onto the stage a king in a cage. He is taken out and made the footstool upon which Tamburlaine mounts to his throne. Colour is used symbolically. Tamburlaine appears at a triumphant banquet in scarlet and two scenes later, to represent his changed mood, "all in black and very melancholy." There are processions, alarums, drums, a graphic reflection of the warlike mood.

Thus the physical progress of conquest is symbolised by crude stage devices. The intangible import of the play, the intoxication of conquest, is also symbolised, not by stage devices but by the figures and movement of lyric poetry. Marlowe had read Spenser so closely that his images and rhythm sometimes verbally reproduce Spenser's. But whether he had read Spenser or not, Marlowe or any other playwright of this period, when he undertook a high theme, was bound to use the rhythm and figures of poetry as the only suitable medium. Just as the emotional import of mediæval religious life could be caught only by the symbolic ritual of the church, so the terrific impact of experience on the renaissance man could be conveyed only in the symbolic language of poetry; for poetry is, in a sense, a symbolic representation of the actual. In poetry the meaning of the actual is distilled. What Tamburlaine, for instance, would actually have felt though in silence, Marlowe can make him say in the golden far-flung images of poetry. In general, it is true, the things which are implicit in experience as they knew it, were made explicit in the poetry of Elizabethan dramatic speeches. The audience was the touchstone of its validity. It was an enthralled spectator at the poetical transposition of its own unuttered thought.

In this sense, then, the passages of lyric poetry in Elizabethan drama are a convention, a formalisation of actuality. Their success and their eternal validity give a final answer to the critic who cries for verisimilitude on the stage and when he does not find it, condemns the product as unreal, untrue to life. When Tamburlaine outlines to Techelles the scope of his intended conquest, he can do it only by comparison with the range of the winds and stars:

> As far as Boreas claps his brazen wings
> Or fair Bootes sends his cheerful light.

Zenocrate's beauty can be measured only by comparison with the lovely figures of Greek mythology or with beautiful places of the earth. Even when these are named, they are inadequate:

> Zenocrate, lovelier than the love of Jove
> Brighter than is the silver Rhodope,
> Fairer than whitest snow on Scythian hills.

Death with which he has had so much traffic, who has toiled invisibly in his cruel service, is caught and shown to the audience in a poetic figure:

> He now is seated on my horsemen's spears
> And on their points his fleshless body feeds.

After *Tamburlaine,* came *Faustus* and the *Jew of Malta.* The heroes of these plays are less symbolic, more flesh-and-blood creations. The Elizabethan world was changing almost overnight. These changes would destroy the old method of drama; or if they did not destroy it, they would modify it greatly. The conventionalised presentation of life on the stage would decrease. The resulting dramatic output would be greater in some ways but less great in others. When it tried to serve the two gods of conventional and realistic presentation in the same play, as it sometimes did, the resulting drama would be uneven and confused. But before coming to that stage in dramatic development, let us look at one more early play, Kyd's *Spanish Tragedy*. It probably appeared in 1586, between *Endimion* and *Tamburlaine*.

The Spanish Tragedy was one of the wonders of the Elizabethan stage. It was a byword for old-fashioned popularity as late as 1614 when Jonson took a fling at the "old Victorians" who for twenty-five or thirty years had loyally supported its crudities. Its author, Kyd, enjoyed great prominence, largely through the jealousy and abusiveness of the university playwrights, who envied his success but despised his popular methods. He read Seneca only in English they said, and that, too, at night when the meek tasks of his little day were over. So he looked to Nashe and Greene and the early group of M.A.'s who, proud in spirit and poor in purse, came from the Universities to London to live by their pens.

Despite the condescension of university-trained authors, Thomas Kyd was a man of parts. He translated French academic tragedy. He was secretary to Sir Thomas Puckering. In the course of this service, he had a connection with Marlowe. To be sure, he was not a poet, not an idealist, not interested in theory and speculation. His output in drama in the last five years of the Eighties is all the more interesting because of this strong practical disposition. He knew what the public wanted. He saw the clear lines along which popular entertainment succeeded. He put his observation into practice in at least two plays which are the very pillars of the Elizabethan dramatic house. One was *The Spanish Tragedy* which sixteen years later, in 1602, Ben Jonson was to bring up to date in a peculiarly interesting fashion. The other was a revenge play about Hamlet,[1] Prince of Denmark, now lost, which Shakespeare was to revive and make practically new in what was and is, perhaps, his most famous play. Thus Kyd, staunch and workmanlike, met the requirement for public dramatic entertainment in the late Eighties. He met it so successfully that the next younger group of playwrights, working for the much altered London of the next decade, through Shakespeare and Jonson, rejuvenated Kyd's two tragedies into great successes for their new London world.

What was *The Spanish Tragedy* like? It was a popularised form of the Senecan revenge play. There are ghosts, dumb-shows, murders. The setting is at the Spanish Court. The action depends upon war between Spain and Portugal. The ghost of a young Spaniard, killed in battle, returns to earth and selects an avenger who in turn is killed. Thereupon his father, Hieronimo, goes through the stages of grief, discovery of the murderer and a plan to kill him in revenge for the death of his son. The plot is built up on the grim formula "Blood is a beggar." The blood of each new victim begs for revenge, and the violence increases.

In spite of this crude plot, the play is arresting even from the modern point of view. The sources of this

---

[1] For the indebtedness of *Hamlet* to other plays, see J. Dover Wilson, *What Happens in Hamlet,* N. Y., 1935, p. 55. Also see J. Q. Adams, edition of *Hamlet,* Houghton Mifflin, 1929, on whole subject.

pleasure are interesting. In the first place, the play is a well-constructed pageant of violence. Now a pageant in itself gives a certain pleasure. To this is added, in the case of *The Spanish Tragedy,* the pleasure of solving the riddle of crime and deception. The spectator watches an intrigue of ambition, war, murder, and revenge. He foresees the chain of complications through which the figures will move, and then watches its progress. There is the pleasure of spectacle, too. The ghost of a personable young Spaniard comes from Hell accompanied by Revenge to watch the working out of retribution for his death. There are two dumb-shows, allegorizing in silence the course of things past and things to come. There are arresting scenes, too. "Belimperia at a window," looks down from her prison. Handkerchiefs, dipped in murdered blood, appear as stage properties. They are like rubrics beside the rhetoric on the page. The princely murderers are killed in earnest while they act death in a play before their royal father. The whole drama is a design of violence. It is true that if the illusion of life as one knows it had been more realistically produced, it might have added depth to *The Spanish Tragedy.* But for every bit of deepening the play would have sacrificed some of the bold beauty and balance of this simplified design.

The motivation of character is simplified, too. Belimperia is bereft by death of her lover, Andrea. In real life a girl would gradually forget one lover and take another. But Belimperia is merely the symbol of this change. Her part in the pageant is to take a new lover, Horatio, who shall be the avenger of her dead Andrea. She turns to him not realistically but as the sharp, quick symbol of slow change, and says:

> Yet what avails to wail Andrea's death,
> From whence Horatio proves my second love?
> Had he not loved Andrea as he did
> He could not sit in Bel-imperia's thoughts.

This abrupt procedure to the next stage of the plot is ludicrous if one thinks of it as occurring in a realistic play. In a pageant which represents the progress from murder to revenge, this abruptness is not only right but positively effective. One does not ask, "Could each detail in this play really happen as it is presented?" One has no right to ask that question. One only says, "Out of this simplified design of violence the quintessential feelings of tragedy emerge." The fact that one can says this shows that the pageant has conveyed its meaning.

There is in *The Spanish Tragedy* one private, personalised emotion, Hieronimo's grief for his murdered son. The way in which Kyd handles this is particularly interesting because it was this portion of the play only which Ben Jonson chose to elaborate and refine in his additions of 1602. Kyd handles the emotion of paternal grief in conventional rhetoric, yet it is effective in conveying real feeling. Its formality, its complete divorce from anything like what the father would actually say, is ad-

mitted. Yet the figures of speech, the roll of blank verse
carry feeling as music carries feeling. Hieronimo, the
father, says:

> Yet still tormented is my tortured soul
> With broken sighs, and restless passions
> That, winged, mount; and hovering in the air,
> Beat at the windows of the brightest heavens,
> Soliciting for justice and revenge.
> But they are placed in those empyreal heights
> Where, countermured with walls of diamond,
> I find the place impregnable; and they
> Resist my woes, and give my words no way.

When Jonson, sixteen years later, attempted to bring
the play up to date, he worked only on the subjective side,
the private emotions. Of his five additions, the four long
ones are either speeches by Hieronimo reflecting his
overwrought state or they are situations devised to wring
from him the last drop of grief. Much skill in depicting
a psychological situation lies behind these additions of
Jonson. For instance there is the speech of Hieronimo
when momentarily he disbelieves that his son is murdered. He finds an everyday, normal excuse for Horatio's absence.

Hier. He supped with us to-night, frolic and merry,
> And said he would go visit Balthasar
> At the duke's place: there the prince doth lodge.
> He had no custom to stay out so late:
> He may be in his chamber; some go see

> Jaques, run to the Duke of Castile's presently,
> And bid my son Horatio to come home:
> I and his mother have had strange dreams to-night.
> Do you hear me, Sir?

This lapse of Hieronimo for a moment into everyday speech and incident is lifelike as the audience understands that word.

In another addition the touch of reason and cool argument comes in where Hieronimo goes at night to the scene of the murder to live it over. The moon had not shown the night of the murder:

> Had the moon shown, in my boy's face there was a kind
>   of grace,
> That I know—nay, I do know—had the murderer seen him,
> His weapon would have fallen and cut the earth.

A trivial thing, whether the moon shone or not, is combined with a lightning flash of recollection, "in my boy's face there was a kind of grace." It is this sort of thing which marks Elizabethan tragedy at its best. Jonson's method here belongs at least sixteen years after Kyd's rhetorical lines which I have quoted earlier about grief mounting up and battering against the windows of heaven. By contrast with that it shows whither the drama was moving in its method of conveying life. Yet one should not say that the new way was preferred by the majority of the audience to the earlier method. We like it better because it fits more closely our ideal for portraying life in fiction. We have no warrant, however, for assuming that, as a whole, they liked it better. It was simply a new method, reflecting new emphases in life but not necessarily displacing the old.

This development in dramatic method from conventionalising life to presenting it realistically was of course unconscious. Furthermore the newer method did not really supersede the old. Yet one does find a change in emphasis both in life and in fiction as the sixteenth century ended and the seventeenth began. There was a deeper understanding of the roots of action, an increasing ability to describe them. Mediæval morality became slowly renaissance and moral philosophy. This moral philosophy was really an analysis of human conduct, in terms of physical and psychical conditions. Miss Lily Campbell has shown what a large number of sixteenth century books there were on this subject. The Elizabethans were interested in the springs of behaviour. For an outward domination of "shalt and shalt nots," they tended to substitute an inward study of the causes in body and mind which allowed passion to dominate reason.

The anatomies of melancholy were only one manifestation of this interest. If this was true in life, of course it was reflected in drama. The "humour" plays owe much to this way of thinking. Even Shakespeare's greatest tragedies can be shown to be in their problems of crime and sin, almost case histories of certain types of "infected" will, as described in contemporary books on this subject. The modern discoverers [1] of this fact have

---

[1] *The Enchanted Glass, The Elizabethan Mind in Literature,* Hardin Craig, Oxford Press, N. Y., 1936, contains valuable material on this subject.

put the readers of Elizabethan drama much in their debt. But they must be careful not to overemphasise the awareness among Elizabethans that this change was taking place. Such things are clear only after the lapse of centuries. Even though Shakespeare's great tragedies and Jonson's comedy can be made to look like case histories for the Elizabethan books on reason and will and "humorous" disorders, of course they were not consciously this. The only thing that the playwrights were conscious of was the immediate occasion, and the stage tradition. The fact that the old moral categories of conduct were giving way to new psychological categories for explaining behaviour, gradually affected the average man's way of estimating the conduct of his fellow. Even more indirectly it penetrated the handling of human conduct on the stage. The audience did not relinquish its taste for and its skill in responding to the older, conventionalised presentation of life. To be fair to things as they were, however, the modern reader must remember that after Kyd and the early Marlowe, playwrights used both the conventional and realistic methods of representing character and action, and often in the same play.

This combination of two ways of portraying life on the stage is the cause of the greatness and the defects of the best Elizabethan plays. The minute the playwright forsook convention and moved toward realistic representation of character and event, he found a large, unmanageable material on his hands. The whole period of Elizabethan and Jacobean drama up to the closing of the theatres in the mid-seventeenth century was not long enough to mature and master this new technique. Shakespeare came near mastering it in his greatest tragedies. But he was far from succeeding with it in the bulk of his plays. Marlowe's work, too, in those six years of amazing development which lay between the creation of *Tamburlaine* and his death in '93, shows this deepening and individualising of character and event. But as his technique for working realistically increased, he lost the unity and heroic outline of *Tamburlaine* and *Faustus*. His plays became uncertain in their effect, spotty, partaking at once of both conventional and realistic technique. One misses in *Edward II* the lost beauties of *Faustus*. Yet one must grant that *Edward II* presents a more intricate, life-like world than *Faustus*. Something is gained in dramatic technique for what has been lost. Marlowe had embarked on a great development which nowhere nearly came to port before his early death.

At this point, a modern critic with his own standards for realistic presentation of plot and character, must be careful. He must not overpraise the change and decry the older method. One must steadily question whether Marlowe would have known when he did come to that perfection of realistic presentation which we call "port." Shakespeare, apparently, did not know it. In the last part of his twenty odd years of playwriting he moved away from what we call deepest presentation of life. He turned back to a stylized combination of realism and convention in his last plays, the romances. Thus in some ways, the end of his career found him announcing the same standards for the stage which his earlier plays announced. These are anything but our modern standards or the standards of what we choose to call his greatest plays.

Let us proceed, then, in our scrutiny of particular plays; some adhering to the old method, some inclining to the new. In all of them we shall find a good deal of the old method intact, sometimes flowing along beside the new between the capacious banks of a single play. Take, for instance, Chapman's *Bussy d'Ambois*. It has an accurate historical basis in French Court intrigue. There was a d'Ambois who rose spectacularly and was murdered at the French Court in 1579. Chapman uses this historical material to present man's audacious struggle to surmount events and plant himself in power. There is scarcely a realistic line in the whole five acts. The play is a conventionalised outline of the way of ambition and lust.

Let us see how Chapman conveys this idea. Bussy enters "poor" and in a long soliloquy presents his bitter view of life. To him at this moment enters the French King's brother. If he can raise Bussy in favour, he can bind him to himself against the king and so win the throne. He describes Bussy as if he were the figure of Despair in a painted cloth:

> A man of spirit beyond the reach of fear
> Who (discontent with his neglected worth)
> Neglects the light and loves obscure abodes.

Even Bussy's position, prone upon the ground, is symbolic. Monsieur's (the King's brother's) first words to him are:

> Turned to earth, alive?
> Up man; the sun shines on thee.

To this Bussy as figuratively replies:

> Let it shine
> I am no mote to play in it as great men are.

Once he is at the French Court, his bravado and arrogance immediately lead him to a triple duel in which, that the moral may be clear, all are killed save Bussy. This is reported by a figure called Nuntius. One cannot forget for a moment during Nuntius' long account in blank verse that Chapman is in the midst of translating Homer. There is the same formal rhetoric, the same conscious elegance about the recital. It records the doings of men in some far-off golden world where living and dying and being brave come to the reader through musical words. Nuntius uses long Homeric similes. For example, this is how he describes the fall of Barrisar, one of the courtiers:

> Then as in Arden I have seen an oak
> Long shook with tempests, and his lofty top
> Bent to his root, which being at length made loose
> (Even groaning with his weight) he 'gan to nod
> This way and that, as loth his curled brows
> (Which he had oft wrapt in the sky with storms)
> Should stoop . . .

and so on for several lines. The gift which Chapman had
for heroic narrative in verse was almost equally useful
upon the stage. In fact one can call *Bussy d'Ambois* an
heroic tale almost as fairly as one can call it drama. The
story is told almost as much through rhetorical narrative
as through dramatic action and there is practically no
attempt to reproduce life with verisimilitude.

As a separate source of entertainment for the audience, Chapman offers conjuring in this play and spectacular scenes. Devils are raised at the propitious moment by the Friar. There is a torture scene, too, and a
letter written in the tortured lady's blood. On a quite
different level of entertainment, there is the pleasure of
occasional passages of poetry.

> . . . study
> The errant wilderness of a woman's face;
> Where men cannot get out, for all the comets
> That have been lighted at it.

In *Bussy d'Ambois* as a whole, Chapman, the con-
veyor of Homer to the Elizabethan reading public, is the
purveyor of heroic behaviour and high rhetoric to the
Elizabethan theatre-going public. His dramatic technique, by any modern standard, is negligible. Yet
through this pediment group, elevated above reality,
drained of colour and life, he says simply and in rolling
tones that men's hearts are great and life is perilous. This
is true and the audience responded to it. Thus the import
of the play comes through a stylized presentation which,

the longer we look at it, seems a mark of sophistication, rather than a proof of Elizabethan immaturity.

Just at the turn of the century, John Marston, scholar and wit, destined ultimately to bring his speculation and brooding within the restful confines of clerical life, wrote a play called *The Malcontent*. It is an interesting play. It illustrates how the method of *Bussy d'Ambois* can become flexible enough to take in the new psychological view of life. There is no known source for the plot but if Marston created it, he based it on an important aspect of life in that period. It reflects, one could not say reproduces, the lust and political ambition in the renaissance state. The lascivious Aurelia, heroine of the piece, is a Medici from Florence. A usurping duke is in power, a deposed duke is in disguise. The complications which follow make the play. Marston's renaissance mind has the usual preoccupations. It is well stored with classical lore. Ægisthus and Clytemnestra, Penelope and the suitors are ready in his mind for parallel illustration. The list of characters includes both names of human qualities in the mediæval fashion and names of real persons. The wronged Duke, who is all that is good, is named Altofront (high and open countenance). Disguised and bitter, he haunts his wicked brother's court under the name which typifies his prevailing mood, Malevole (the illwisher or the malcontent). The jealous old courtier is called Bilioso. The bawd is called just that, Maquerelle. The lying schemer is Mendoza. But along with these names which give the predominant moral quality of the character involved, there are the names of individuals, too, such as Pietro, Aurelia, Maria. The old and the new ways of regarding character thus meet and mingle unembarrassed by any sense of incongruity.

The characterisation and plotting are highly conventional. The characters are always "in character." The plotting is high-handed and unconvincing. Pietro just by putting on a beard and hermit's gown is disguised. He has an unreal, sudden conversion from wickedness. Moved by Malevole's cynical comment on life, he suddenly renounces his power and apologizes to the supposedly absent Altofront:

> I here renounce forever regency,
> O Altofront, I wrong thee to supplant thy right, etc.

Malevole then removes his disguise and shows himself to be indeed Altofront. He comments

> Who doubts of providence
> That sees this change? A hearty faith to all!

The end of the play is like the end of a morality play. The cast divides into groups and each character receives his appropriate reward. There is joy for Pietro and Aurelia, now virtuously reformed. There is a kick for Mendoza, consignment to the suburbs for the bawd. The duke, restored to his throne, takes Celso and the Captain to his breast for true friends, and Maria, his faithful wife, to his heart. There is a masque in which the arrangement of the dances is symbolic. The good characters, Pietro

and Aurelia, Malevole and Maria are united, while
Ferenze, the libertine, goes with Maquerelle, the bawd.

What is one to make of this strange play. It is unreal,
oversimplified. A clever series of plots first announced
by Mendoza and then performed, gives to the audience
the pleasure of foreknowledge. But such a pleasure is
purely intellectual. There is nothing to grip the emotions
in watching a foretold series of events unwind. Yet there
are other elements in the composition of *The Malcontent*
which do grip the emotions. The real moving power of
the play comes, I think, through comment on the plotting.
Take, for instance, the comment of Aurelia. She is
neither a flesh and blood woman, nor an abstraction.
Halfway between the two worlds of reality and symbolism, she comments on them both. Seeing Mercury enter
for the masque, she says,

Are you god of ghosts? I have a suit pending in hell
betwixt me and my conscience; I would fain have thee help
me to an advocate.

The figurative nature of this speech conveys the essence
of the real situation. Aurelia moves easily from one
world to another, seeing in her passage the truth which
encompasses them both. So Lady Macbeth, released by
the intensity of her horror from the usual ways of regarding life, sees, as from another world, the underlying
truth of things. So Lear, freed by madness, and Hamlet,
by disillusion and revulsion, see the meaning of things.
The same sort of revelation occurs in *The Malcontent*

when Malevole hears Ferenze stir as he lies wounded
after his flight from the Duchess's chamber. Malevole
says:

Hark! Lust cries for a surgeon. What news from Limbo?
How does the grand cuckold, Lucifer?

It is appropriate that such a play, hovering between
symbolic and realistic presentation, should depend a good
deal upon music for conveying or sharpening the mood.
Songs for the particular moment are interspersed. The
metre adapts itself, too. Blank verse alters into a canter
of rhymed couplets and changes back again to suit the
feeling. A group of parallel figures of speech may show
how the different characters see night and dawn, each
jaundiced by his private mood. For instance, Mendoza
(a villain) says:

> 'Tis now about the unmodest waist of night;
> The mother of moist dew with pallid light
> Spreads gloomy shades about the numbed earth.
> Sleep, sleep, while we contrive our mischief's birth.

Malevole (the hero) a few lines later says:

> The beauty of the day begins to rise
> From whose bright form night's heavy shadow flies.

Pietro (unhappy husband) says:

'Tis grown to youth of day: how shall we waste this light?
My heart's more heavy than a tyrant's crown.

This is mere rhetoric, not even notable rhetoric. Furthermore it is not in the least what these three men would actually say. But cumulatively these three comments on the time by three different characters catch for each the shadow of his mood and convey the inner feeling of the situation.

It would be wrong to say that such a frankly unreal play as this is not "a criticism of life." In spite of its simplifications, its artificial balance and unreal turns of plot, its type characters, it does succeed in giving one the feeling of reality about the essential responses to life.

In the year 1605, Ben Jonson, at the height of his reputation as a satiric dramatist, critic, and deviser of court masques, produced *Volpone* or *The Fox*. It is pertinent to this discussion of the conventionalised presentation of life upon the stage. In a very special sense, it illustrates the truth of my general argument; that the centre of life's meaning may be as powerfully, if not more powerfully conveyed by symbolic simplification as by realistic representation. This play is interesting, too, because in a sense its method is a continuance of the method in the old morality plays. It preaches a specific lesson.

Volpone is set in a very real Venice. Its street squares and courthouse are peopled with mountebanks, travellers and Venetian citizens. Courtesans in gondolas "swim" upon the canals. The interiors are real. The long gallery of Volpone's house has books at the far end to amuse the caller while he waits. The two English travellers, Sir Politic Would-be and his lady, are caricatures of particular foibles of the moment. Sir Politic is a pompous courtier, busy about nothing. His London news is a rehearsal of pointless trifles. His sense of affairs of state, espionage, intelligence, is a parody. His lady's parade of fashionable clothes and fashionable culture is built upon the frivolities of a particular moment in London. In these respects the play is just another one of the many satiric comedies which were being produced.

The names of the characters, too, as in many other comedies, are symbols of their dominant quality. Volpone, for instance, means the Fox. In this play he is the cunning grandee who with the aid of his parasite Mosca, The Flesh Fly, has accumulated a vast estate. He is visited, flattered and presented with gifts daily by a group of hangers-on, each of whom hopes to be named his heir. This heir-hunting was a vile phase of late Roman society. Jonson found the theme handled graphically in Petronius' *Satyricon*. He knew he could adapt it to early seventeenth century Italy. The unfolding of the play is an allegory. The cunning Fox is unsuccessfully tempted to ruin himself through a series of illustrative scenes. His tempters are the Crow, the Vulture and the Raven. At last he over-reaches himself, makes out his will to Mosca, goes forth in disguise to play a trick, and never returns to his fox's hole. Æsop could have managed the tale in his own way; so could the writer of a mediæval morality play.

But Jonson's way of handling this material is peculiarly Elizabethan. First of all he could rely upon his audience to accept two-dimensional characterization and ready-made scenes which were created to illustrate the moral. The audience would also accept without question a convention of disguise which if it were once measured by probability, would be ludicrous. At the end of the play, they would stand for a review of the characters, where each was revealed in his true colours and allotted punishment appropriate to his misdeed. Furthermore they would feel the significance of Volpone's household troop of oddities. The Dwarf, the Eunuch and the Hermaphrodite are symbols of the unnatural atmosphere in which the Fox lives. Their grotesqueness, expressed in rhyme and interspersed with songs, furnishes a dark accompaniment to the main theme. It is similar in purpose to the ugly antimasques which Jonson used for contrast in his famous court entertainment. The audience would catch the appropriate undertone to the main action which was lent by the references to strange medicines, brewed with witchery.

With an audience accustomed to such symbols, Jonson could do many things which would be lost to a modern audience. He conventionalised his episodes in order to show their meaning, until they are almost a mathematical demonstration of that meaning. For instance, Volpone pretends to be dead and Mosca pretends, as the happy heir to a vast fortune, to be sitting in his chamber making an inventory of his riches. The avaricious Crow, Vulture and Raven when they come to pay their daily call of flattery, will be greeted by the sight. Volpone in hiding will overhear and rejoice in their disappointment that they are not the heirs. "I'll get up," he says

Behind the curtain, on a stool and hearken;
Sometime peep over, see how they do look,
With what degree their blood doth leave their faces.
O, 'twill afford me a rare meal of laughter.

This scene is really a scientific demonstration of deception and greed. It is distorted from reality until it has become an allegory. Yet the whole plot of *Volpone* has the conviction of truth underlying it. To be sure the rhetoric in which various characters announce their reflections is unreal. Yet if deviltry could become articulate it would speak in just such rhetoric. Mosca's long soliloquy in the beginning of Act III is a case in point, as is Volpone's long mountebank speech in prose.

Volpone then is a sophisticated reminiscence of that earlier fiction which explained reality in terms of allegory and symbol. It bears upon its face the mark of long and high ancestry. But it bears, too, the features of its own world. It expresses life in its own day and hour, as it was breathed and lived. But it illustrates, as other Elizabethan plays illustrate, how effectively reality can be carried in a conventionalised design. By throwing probability and verisimilitude to the winds and by substituting an artificial design, the play presents in shrill, clear tones essential human feeling. *Volpone* is a demonstration of how the old method, made subtle by the new world, worked its effect.

In a different way the *Duchess of Malfi* by John Webster shows the same thing. Webster was immersed in Elizabethan stage practice. He worked with all sorts of playwrights at all sorts of plays, in the manner of an artisan, not an artist. Yet he created two great plays, *The White Devil* and *The Duchess of Malfi*. They are complete and fully conceived things. *The Duchess of Malfi* was written about 1614. Shakespeare's activity was over. The Jacobean world was already ten or eleven years underway. This play is a part of everything it has met in the Elizabethan dramatic world yet it is peculiarly itself. Let us see how and why.

The story comes from the commonest source for romantic tragedy, from Bandello's collection of *Novelle,* via the French Belleforest to Painter's English collection. The type of plot is familiar. It has a realistic background of corruption in high places in renaissance Italy. The Duke of Calabria and his brother, the Cardinal, have a lovely sister young and newly widowed. For purely practical reasons they wish to prevent her re-marriage. They set Bosola, an intelligent unmoral person over whom they have a hold, in her household to watch her. She, of course, does marry her steward, Antonio. But she does this secretly. From this point the hounds of espionage, discovery and cruel punishment are in full cry and leave her finally strangled to death. In the train of her death follow the madness and death by violence, poison, or accident of all the other chief actors in the play.

There is nothing new or notable about the outline of the story, but there is something notable about Webster's way of presenting it. His characters are not symbols. His plot is not conventionalised. In fact the play shows a good knowledge of individual states of mind. Yet along with this increase in realism, Webster still clings to spectacle, rhetorical figures and a kind of poetry which could not have existed in actual life. His method, all unconsciously, is a combination of preceding methods and the new discoveries in subjective analysis of motives and actions. The result is a piece of imaginative fiction which acts well.

But over and above these things, *The Duchess* probably owes its long dominance over the imagination of posterity to its passages of lyrical poetry. The plot moves adroitly from great moment to great moment. In the lulls between storms of violence, the beauty and rhythm of life are announced in passages of poetry. This is still often gnomic. But now instead of coming out of Seneca, the epigrams often come out of Elizabethan non-dramatic poetry. Webster admired Donne. He kept notebooks of favourite passages of poetry. He wove these so skillfully into the text of his play that only slowly his word-for-word indebtedness has been discovered. Webster explores in these poetic speeches the outermost verge of passion or despair. They are more effective than they would be as isolated lyrics. The actual drama which accompanies them heightens their power.

In general, I think it is fair and not only fair but neces-

sary to say, if Elizabethan drama is to be rightly understood, that from its earliest to its latest development, it
is the vehicle for the poetry of great moments. How that
vehicle is constructed, whether it ignores realistic plotting and character, or whether with increasing penetra-
tion it swings toward life-like presentation, is incidental.
The important thing is that the dramatist will in crucial
moments speak the meaning of the particular situation in
universal poetry. Hence, as T. S. Eliot rightly argues,
the greatest poetry will occur in scenes which are most
dramatic. Shakespeare's poetry and drama are "the full
expansion of one and the same activity." Seneca, on his
own plane, knew this. He alternated his tragic scenes
with moral pronouncement. The mediæval morality and
miracle writers, too, offered both drama and lesson from
drama. Their Elizabethan successors juggled the same
two balls. Sometimes they did it stiffly. But their agility
increased until the whirling figures in the air blurred and
blended into oneness. Then the design of the whole and
the separate moments of specific poetic comment combined to make the single glory of a great play.

Elizabethan drama is as interesting in its decadence
as in its strongest period. Frequently it parodies itself.
Occasionally it rouses itself into accents of strength and
beauty. Middleton's *Changeling* (circ. 1623) is a fair
example. The ghost of didacticism still hovers over it.
Middleton got his plot from a book printed in 1621 with
the title of *Triumph of God's Revenge against Murder*.
There is very little of God's revenge, however, or of any

other tribunal of justice in Middleton's play. It presents a world of confused standards. Crime exists for its own sake. In the great plays crime committed for ambitious ends gives spaciousness and dignity. But in this play lust is the only object. The distortion of real life is still here but it is a meaningless distortion. The play announces no general truth. The familiar dramatic devices are used, too. Time is telescoped; an hour passes in eleven lines while Beatrice comments on the time spent by her substitute in her husband's bed. A dumb-show is used but without attention to its artistic possibilities. It merely saves Middleton the labour of plotting a necessary incident in the body of his play. The ghost has become a signal only for terror in the minds of two guilty lovers. When it enters De Flores says:

> Ha! What art thou that tak'st away the light
> Betwixt that star and me? I dread thee not.

He "rationalises" in the next line:

> 'Twas but a mist of conscience; all's clear again.

There are no great passages of poetry because the underlying design is too insignificant to call forth great poetry. Many Elizabethan plays are like Middleton's *Changeling*. They cannot be put in a neat pigeonhole at the end of the period and labelled "The Decadence." It is true, though, that there are more of this sort toward the end of the period. Life grew more intricate and old lines of thinking lost their sharpness. Something newer and truer was developing. But this new thing, curiously, did not find its complete expression in drama again. Perhaps it has not found it even after the passage of more than three centuries.

In general, the picture of Elizabethan drama grows confused and congested as it reaches its height and moves toward decline. But the great plays of crime and satire remain. They stand badly in need of interpretation according to their own standards not ours, as I hope this chapter has shown.

CHAPTER IX

Shakespeare for Moderns

Unhappily Shakespeare often connotes to the modern reader a large "practical" volume in small type, containing an overwhelming body of printed words arranged two columns to the page, cluttered with technical notes in even smaller type. Or the name calls up a single play embedded in "apparatus" so that the introduction, notes and glossary muffle up the play, reduce it to relative unimportance. Teaching does take Shakespeare hard. There is so much about him that is unintelligible to modern eyes and ears without glossaries, footnotes and historical apparatus, that the instructor or the school editor may be forgiven if not excused. He is so eager to initiate the lay reader, to pull down the barriers so that he may step through into the past and feel and hear what these people are saying and doing. He knows, too, that their problems are so like our own that they furnish a perspective upon our own thinking and feeling.

It would, perhaps, be a corrective for all this if the modern reader would visualise the plays in the two written forms in which they existed in Shakespeare's own life-time, when they were not "masterpieces" to be studied. They were just the written record of an entertainment, an afternoon at the theatre. They were the property of a group of actors who, translating the written words into speech and action, enticed audiences, played with their eye on filling the house, on taking in as much money as possible and keeping the public eager for the next production.

The text of the play from which they worked was a very casual-looking document. It was very often the author's own manuscript, written out on long single sheets measuring about 10½ by 7 inches, with wide margins at left and right for the names of characters and stage directions. On the right the space might be utilized by the theatrical producer for note of properties, entrances, times for ringing bells or making sounds of thunder. Down the centre of these long narrow pages went a parallelogram of blank-verse lines, interspersed with prose speeches, in the author's handwriting. Often the manuscript plays which still exist show his false starts, crossings out, occasionally his rewriting of a line which went badly the first time he tried it. Sometimes an adjective is crossed out and another substituted above, between the lines. A good phrase which will fit better near the climax of the speech has a pen through it and turns up a few lines later in a more effective setting. The author's imagination is always on the theatre; occasionally he lets himself see how a scene will be produced as

A tempestuous noise of thunder and lightning heard

or

Enter Mariners wet

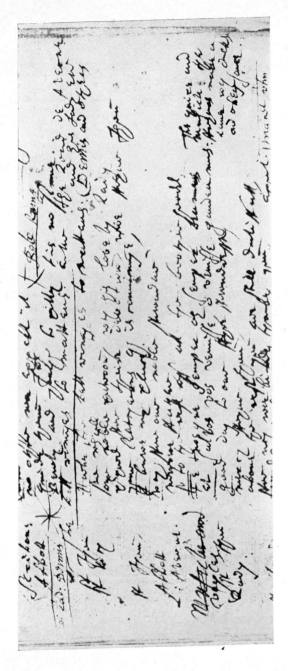

A PAGE FROM THOMAS HEYWOOD'S PLAY, "THE CAPTIVES" (1624) IN THE DRAMATIST'S OWN HANDWRITING

The author's manuscript was apparently used as prompt-copy for the production of the play in the theatre.. It bears the stage-producer's marginal notes on properties, exits and entries. Shakespeare's plays must have resembled this manuscript in their first form

Scriuen: no other wee expect it

Abbott, guide them In,   X Bell Rung

o: Lad:Dennis * Beuty and youthe to pitty tis no sinne.
The bell ringes to mattens. enter the Lord de Averne
and his lady &c
(Dennis and others

ff Ihon   Harke the bell ringes to mattens:
ff Rich   see uthall
our noble patroon, with his lovely lady
p'paid ffor their devotion, now ffryar Ihon
your letcherous ey is cominge,

ff Ihon,   I haue my place.
Abbott   may ffor our noble ffounder
L:Averne.   make the ffirst off all the brotherhood.
goe to the ffirst off all the brotherhood.
Te turque tempe oh semper beamus
et Salue vos venisse, o venisse gaudeamus:

Musicke and   good day to our ffrye ffoundress,
voyces   mercy ffryar Ihon,
ff Ihon   above the rest you are still dutifull, ff
Lady.   ffor uch wee kindly thanke you, exit

the quire and   878
musick: the
ffryars make a
Lowe with ducks
and obeysance.

Manet Iohn

A TRANSCRIPT OF THE ABOVE PAGE MADE BY E. C. DUNN

This is part of a transcript of the whole play, *The Captives*, which is being made by E. C. Dunn and which will be published by the Malone Society (ed. W. W. Greg) at the Oxford Press

or

He holds her by the hand silent

This is how the original written record of an Elizabethan play looked. Often the author's own draft was sent to the company, who regarded it as stuff for playing. They cut out minor parts, if the company was too small to accommodate the "list of characters." The actor of a particular part might find a speech too long to risk on the audience. A scene might be too slow, or the play as a whole too bulky to fit comfortably into the inside of a summer afternoon in London. Accordingly it was cut. An actor could write a speech for himself or have it written for him and inserted. This shows that the players knew that a play was a thing of fragments, of telling moments, dragging its slow length through time only by the aid of a succession of moving episodes.

That is how an Elizabethan play looked in its first appearance on paper. The second way in which Shakespeare and the Elizabethan public read it was as a little paper-covered pamphlet. Sometimes the paper for this cover was light blue, and while we cannot argue from the frivolity of the color to the trivial way in which the play was printed, we do know from other evidence that the publication was lightly undertaken and the book lightly purchased. The appearance of a play in quarto (for so the paper-covered edition was called) often coincided with the months when London was full of countrymen up in town for the term of court, or business men on brief visits to London. They not only saw as many plays as were then being performed but bought for sixpence copies of others no longer on the boards but likely to prove pleasant light reading in the interstices of a few busy days. These books were sold on all the most frequented news stands:

in Paul's Church Yard at the Sign of the Angel
(*Richard III*)
at his shop near the exchange (*Romeo and Juliet*)
at the Sign of the White Hart in Fleet Street
(*Midsummer Night's Dream*)
at the Spread Eagle in Paul's Churchyard, over against the
great North Door (*Troilus and Cressida*)
at the Sign of the Pide Bull near St. Austine Gate (*Lear*)

The description of them which was made to catch the prospective buyer was, happily, printed on the title page, instead of on the paper jacket, as the modern "blurb" is. We can still know through this what features the publisher thought would most easily recommend them to the reading public. One reason for buying, the publisher apparently thought, was that the plays had been popular and so the reader was assured that he had purchased something which everybody had approved. *Romeo and Juliet* was advertised as "often (with great applause) played publicly." *Hamlet* had been frequently acted not only "in the city of London" but "also in the two Universities of Cambridge and Oxford and elsewhere." Another desire of the reader, the printers seemed to think, was for a complicated plot and a good sensational story. The *Merchant of Venice* was advertised for the "extreme cruelty of Shylock towards the said merchant, in cutting a just pound of flesh; and the obtaining of Portia by the choice of three chests." *Richard III* promised meat for strong stomachs and a whole biography into the bargain: "treacherous plots . . . the pitiful murder of his innocent nephews . . . the whole course of his detested life and most deserved death." The advertisements for comedies often feature special funny men and isolated vaudeville events. *The Merry Wives of Windsor,* for instance, declares on the quarto title page that it contains "sundry variable and pleasing humours . . . with the swaggering vein of ancient Pistol and Corporal Nym."

From the form in which these cheap versions of some of Shakespeare's plays (just under half of them) appeared in his life-time, the features in them which were advertised, the times in the year at which they were printed, one gets a fair idea of their place in the contemporary world. They were light literature, something for distraction and entertainment, not at all in the field of serious artistic effort. They sprang from the roots of essential human experience and blossomed in the plain air of a hard-living, ambitious world, where every person, in every social circumstance, had a right to entertainment. The advertisements are vulgar in the best sense of the word; they are for any and all. It is not unfair to say that the present fertility of output in the movies has strong similarity with the fecundity of Elizabethan drama. The plays were as diverse in quality, many were relatively as bad, a few were very much greater. But all those and these had and have the saving essence of being written with the emphasis of contemporary life and for a contemporary public, with its social and intellectual differences, its common humanness.

What can be done by way of matching common features of Elizabethan drama with phases of modern popular drama, on stage and screen? First there are those simple things in the construction which are likely to be mentioned by the sophisticated critic with condescension because they are "naïve." Consider, for instance, the long parade of scenes, covering half the known globe, careering through ten years of time, like *The Two Parts of Henry IV*, or *Antony and Cleopatra*, or *The Winter's Tale*. Beginning, specifically, with Dryden in the seventeenth century, writers on the art of drama condemned panorama. They laughed at it because it embraced the earth and wandered from one continent to another. To be sure it wandered with unequal success, sometimes coming to a pause with a good scene, sometimes with an indifferent one, but there was usually enough drive in the play to send it lumbering forward with its everlengthening chain of places and moments.

There are many reasons, æsthetic and artistic, why this panoramic drama ought not to be good. But it *was* good, for the actual pleasure which it gave the Elizabethans and which it gives us in such moving pictures as *Cavalcade*. The succession of changing scenes and years

stirs the imagination by releasing one from the limitations of time and space. It offers variety of atmosphere,
enchantment of distance, sets the humdrum world by the
ears and goes gaily off according to its own laws. Then,
too, those changing lands and remote places had their
foundation then as now in fact. Correspondingly,
though with very different tempo from ours, the Elizabethans went everywhere and jumbled occident and
orient, sea and land, civilization and savagery together.
There was, too, a physical scope in these great backdrops
of the world, to match the vaulting ambitions and aspirations of the heroes who strutted and declaimed before
them. This panoramic quality in drama is, of course,
always accompanied by a breakdown in convincingness.
It is effective only if the auditor accompanies it with a
willing belief in the improbable. The Elizabethans were
willing to lend this belief and so are we. Nowadays this
quality is particularly characteristic of the movies, and
in this respect screen plays seem to score over the legitimate stage. The movie audience finds in the expansion
of space and time one of its peculiar satisfactions. Often
the legitimate stage seems wanting because this source of
entertainment is not there.

Another simple taste of Elizabethan drama, and of
Shakespeare in particular, is the intense interest in story
for its own sake. A throng of characters, each shouting
his own story and every word of it too, jostle one another
within the bulging confines of an Elizabethan play. In
most plays the separate stories have something to do

with one another, but not always. There are many irrelevancies, many flourishes of event and dialogue which contribute nothing to the main emphasis. Yet they are lovingly worked out like gargoyles on a mediæval cathedral. They sprang from sheer exuberance in the dramatist and were noted with appreciation by the auditors. The Elizabethans had a Gargantuan appetite for events in themselves. The more there were, the more of this good thing, life, was crowded into the show, the more their insatiable curiosity about existence was stimulated and fed.

"Story" was the simple element out of which all Elizabethan drama was made. The labels, comedy and tragedy, were trustingly taken over by the Elizabethans from a world where the tradition of the stage was different. They used these tags with assurance and felt that they lent dignity and height to the new Elizabethan drama. But Elizabethan drama was quite different from the plays which the world had called "tragedy" and "comedy" in ancient Greece and Rome. The thing which caused this difference is interesting.

Just about the time of Elizabeth, the old-fashioned vehicles for story-telling were being pushed into the background. Willy-nilly the whole library of narrative was tumbled out of its natural home between the covers of romance, tale, ballad, novella, and thrust upon the stage. More and more people *saw* stories as well as read them. For the dramatization of this story material the old classifications of "tragedy" and "comedy" were inadequate. How does the story end? This is what the Elizabethan at the play was asking, precisely as if he had been listening to some one reading aloud from a great volume. This was a question which the playwright, too, asked himself. He could, almost at will, or at the demand of his public, make the story turn out happily or unhappily. *The Merchant of Venice* ends happily, for instance, and is classified with the comedies, but it would not have been difficult to head it for disaster. In portions of *Much Ado About Nothing* the story seems destined for unhappiness. *Measure for Measure* might with a twist have become a companion piece to *Hamlet*. *Othello* might have been cast in the mould of romantic comedy. *The Winter's Tale* would have compressed exquisitely into tragedy. To say this is not to be capricious, but honest; for every story has two possibilities of outcome, happy and unhappy. This is especially true in periods of the world's history when the taste for story is stronger than the taste for subtlety of character. The Elizabethan Age, Shakespeare's life-time, inherited a stronger predilection for story than for character. How this emphasis changed during Shakespeare's career and how his artistry changed with it, is another matter.

The happy ending was more frequent in Shakespeare's plays than the unhappy. To achieve this happy ending was not difficult, provided his audience was not too sensitive about consistency of character and motivation of action. Now, as we have said, the Elizabethan audience was not primarily character-conscious. So long as all the people in the story were neatly rounded off, the lovers symmetrically paired, the innocent restored to their dues, the intricate plot tidily completed, they did not mind if the characters were pushed about a good deal, changed their natures in a single line for the sake of a happy ending.

Our sophisticated modern world is at the opposite pole in its dramatic interest. It's not what happens but *how one feels* about the happening, how one reacts to events, that they watch for. They decry the string-pulling and manipulation of characters for the sake of events in Shakespeare's plays. This modern point of view and the point of view of the Elizabethans are precisely opposite. This particular modern group, however, which includes the people who are conscious about art, is relatively small. The average modern public still prefers a happy ending, and is still fairly naïve about character portrayal. They should not be reproached for it. It is a sign not of decadence but of virility. They like a story where men wrench events to their desired ends, probably or improbably. Dreaming of happiness and success and failing to secure them in life, they must find them in the fiction they read or the drama they see. They are still too strong, too literal and close to life to be aware of standards for dramatic construction. In fact, the chief reason for the misunderstanding and distortion of Shakespeare in our modern world is that the people who should read it, the general public, cannot. They have unhappily no opportunity of learning how to overcome certain superficial oddities which Shakespeare's language and method have in their eyes. For this reason a great literature which should be popular in the best sense of that word is left for the practice of wit and sensitivity by a small minority of readers who often apply to it too fine responses.

Events are often the only handle by which men can talk about their own lives or understand the dramatic presentation of life. What happened after that, and after that? they ask. How did you act in this event or that, bravely or with cowardice? How did your reaction to your enemy, your rival, to a villain, show itself in the circumstances in which you each expressed yourselves? In answer to these questions arose the special kind of story pattern which is called intrigue. It was very popular on the Elizabethan stage. It is also frequent on the modern popular stage and screen. In fact, it persists wherever and whenever people are *doing* instead of *thinking*. How Iago weaves his web, the stages by which Malvolio is trapped into a crowning folly, how Orlando is reinstated, how Macbeth builds himself up on a scaffolding of murders, how Claudius almost rids the world of Hamlet, how Bolingbroke practises political chicanery upon Richard II, or Richmond topples the structure of Richard III's crime, all these pieces of intrigue form a special kind of story within story which has a fascination for the auditor. Of course, the presence of intrigue in real life makes the bridge between the auditor's experience and what is going on upon the stage. But the intrigue which he only partly sees in actual experience, is unrolled and sifted to its last secret upon the stage. The circumstances which produced intrigue in the Elizabethan times had outward differences from ours. There was a different kind of chicanery because there was a different political structure, a different foreign diplomacy and a different intricacy in trade. There was one great source of intrigue which is not present to the modern world, the intrigue by which the Roman Church and the English Church manœuvred and crossed swords with each other, like fencers in a badly lighted room. It had its reflections in government and private circles, in London, in remote English villages, and on the Continent. But this last sort of intrigue only rarely got into the plays because even to refer to it was perilous. Our modern intrigue falls roughly into categories parallel to Elizabethan intrigue but it takes different outward forms. There are the duels of Big Business, the intricacies of bootleggers and gangsters, and the machinations of political grafters. All these materials are used over and over on the modern stage and screen.

Violence was frequently an end in itself, and made a sure appeal to the audience. It is, of course, in both eras a reflection of the violence in real life. Crime and war then and now are important. They have done and are doing something to the imagination and sensations of the people. They are, as stage devices, useful, inflaming the sluggish imagination and the low-keyed nervous system, so that the tired man of dulled or average perceptions is able to receive sensation. In this fact, we and the

Elizabethans stand very near to one another. We are widely contrasted with the Greek theatrical audience at the greatest period of Greek drama. At that time physical violence on the stage was not practised, lest the auditors in revulsion from physical horror should lose the cumulative effect of more delicate values. But we must remember that by the Greek public was meant a highly selected group of Athenians from which had been excluded most persons of the sort who make an Elizabethan or a modern audience.

This Elizabethan or modern violence seems not overdrawn and theatrical because it had and has a basis in everyday experience. They saw hangings, beheadings, torturings, maimings every day in London. And we, if we do not see, at least read in the daily press, of shootings, bombings, hold-ups, punishments in the electric chair, scientific devices for opening secret doors, for locating criminals in remote places. The objects of desire then and now produced violence, for they were intensely coveted by men strong enough to risk anything to secure them. To triumph in the world, gain power, authority, wealth, was and is important. To triumph in love was so urgent that it often furnished added force to the passion for success. By worldly success, love might be secured or held. As the Elizabethans grew up (and they did grow up astonishingly fast while Shakespeare was writing plays for them) violence grew interesting not so much as an end in itself but for its psychological effects upon the perpetrators. It is violence from this angle, which one finds in Shakespeare's greatest tragedies. Even there, however, it is a special development from the cruder violence of bloody stories.

Romantic love, then and now, was a sure winner on the stage, and there were and are the same two ways of handling it. It can, in the first and commonest form, be merely pretty. It can be handled simply, not too deeply, allowing chance for sentimental unreality—and we have it today in light opera (which is not essentially parallel but is useful to think about in connection with such plays as *Midsummer Night's Dream, As You Like It, Two Gentlemen of Verona*) and in movies of the checked-sunbonnet, rustic well-sweep variety. In its second and profounder handling, it becomes psychological, presents a study of the progress and passion of love. Shakespeare handled this variously and movingly in such plays as *Romeo and Juliet, Othello* and *Antony and Cleopatra.* Both treatments were and are available on the boards and the theatre-goer either "goes in for it seriously," or listens to pretty airs and soft lights, according to his mood.

The comedy of Shakespeare's plays is, on the whole, the hardest thing for a modern to understand. In its lighter, more obvious forms, it was built upon the caricature of superficial follies in the Elizabethan world. There were visual follies in clothes, manners, ways of talking. There were patent absurdities, the pretenses of plain people to be aristocratic, of ignorant people to be cultured, of indigent people to appear wealthy. The comic distortion of these follies is funny only if one knows the real world from which they are taken. So that in this realm, the average modern has to be told first by the antiquarian how the fools of Elizabeth's London looked and acted, and then has to look into the plays for the distortion of these fools.

The process is laborious. It does not interest the general modern reader and he is quite willing to let Elizabethan fun be a kind of fooling to which he has lost the key. If he is liberal he will grant that it might be amusing if one had time to go into it. If he is engrossed in his present, seeking entertainment from his own world, he will call it jargon and turn over the pages rapidly. This fact is, of course, a commonplace. The comedy of manners and of type inheres in the ephemeral side of any period. It is built upon what is peculiar and temporary, and passes away with the particular society that gave it birth. But the essence of comedy, what Bergson called *pure comedy,* is in Shakespeare too. When we are once given the clue to Malvolio's comic deformity of mind and temperament, we can detect essential comedy in him by the universal tests for comedy. On the whole, however, and contrary to a good deal of hastily conceived opinion, Elizabethan comedy and even Shakespeare's comedy does not reach across three hundred and fifty years to our world.

The chief points of similarity made thus far between the taste of Shakespeare's audience and the modern audience are matters of entertainment. But there was then and there is now in any theatrical performance the possibility of some quality greater and more lasting than the moments of entertainment. If one gets entertainment for the time being, the average theatre-goer is forced to be satisfied. His mind has been removed for a few hours from the immediate problems of his own life. Occasionally, however, he has experienced something more. He has seen, through the play before him, into the very workings of life, understood how and why things are, felt the naked reality of existence. His entertainment has become enlightenment in those problems of living which form the significant islands in his voyage of existence. He has seen a presentation of life more real than any he can see in his daily experience, more lucid and essential. He has received a great deal more than his money's worth.

Among Shakespeare's plays, there are a number that gave the audience this precious gift which it had not asked for. This enlightenment which made his great plays great, lies chiefly in the realm of character. The Elizabethan world, especially in the last years of the old Queen's reign, became increasingly aware of the intricacies that make up character. This is not the place to discuss the ways in which mediæval physiology deepened and blended with a scientific study of mood, temperament, psychological cast of mind as conditioned by physical make-up, influenced by diet, environment, inheritance. For a long time the renaissance took Man on faith. His scope was boundless, his achievement would be perfect. At the end of the sixteenth century, however, they began to see that the achievement wasn't perfect. This glorious animal, Man, was frequently unable to achieve his aspirations, could not always make his energies flow in the direction of his aims. Greatness was honeycombed with folly, capable of disintegrating under the influence of vice and petty caprice. The scientific studies of psychology, of which Burton's *Anatomy of Melancholy,* begun in the last years of Elizabeth's reign, is the best known, were case books for dealing with these soul diseases.

The portrayal of Man upon the stage reflected this contemporary point of view. Right in the midst of Shakespeare's career as a playwright, the portrayal of character in the drama altered and deepened. The man who wrote *Richard III* in 1593-4, with its external conception of motive and character, in ten years or less was writing *Hamlet,* which for the portrayal of a complicated individual is hardly matched in our world. Within ten years, one of the most popular melodramas, Kyd's *Spanish Tragedy,* all blood and thunder and action and rant, had to be supplemented by passages of character analysis and reflection before it could be risked upon the stage. And this stage, too, was playing for the same public which had applauded its external horrors ten years before.

Thus, psychologically, the Elizabethans grew up over night and Shakespeare grew up with them. There was still demand for the more naïve type of play, and Shakespeare continued to produce that sort, right up to the end of his career. But interspersed among these entertainments appeared the great plays which were built upon a deepened sense of character. They said universal things about life. This fact raised them above entertainment and placed them in the company of those apocalyptic creations by which the meaning of man's life is revealed.

The place where this deepened sense of life could be most naturally shown was in tragedy. In *Hamlet, Macbeth, Othello, Lear, Antony and Cleopatra,* which appear at intervals from 1600 to 1608, one finds this new and deeper emphasis. In the great tragedies, Shakespeare used external violence as the starting point for exploration inward, for a study of the disintegration of character through crime, for the effect of violent acts upon the imagination. Hence it happens that the original *Hamlet,* composed ten or eleven years before Shakespeare took hold of it, is a melodrama of murder and violence. But Shakespeare in his *Hamlet* produces a play where the first deliberate murder occurs before the play opens and the second deliberate murder in the very last scene. All that lies between is, roughly speaking, mental *reaction* to violent action.

It is interesting to remember that the late renaissance is the first period since Periclean Athens to handle tragedy with this emphasis. Although they were unaware of the precedent, their discovery of the same formula proves, more than all the researches among the classical books which they admired, their essential kinship with the core of Greek thinking, their essential separation from the mediæval world. This mellowing of earlier intrigue plots into psychological tragedies suggests a vast range of thinking about the terms classical and romantic, mediæval and renaissance, for the person who is historically minded.

In connection with this essential change of emphasis, there is an interesting minor change. The soliloquy, in Shakespeare's greatest tragedies, is one of his most useful devices for showing the soul of his hero, its turmoil and confusion. It is, of course, even in its most successful instances, a convention. Persons in perplexity think to themselves. They may mutter a few audible words, but they are not so movingly and coherently articulate as Hamlet is in his great soliloquies. They do not let the world overhear them as he does. But the Elizabethans were friendly to this convention (which was so essential if the internal drama, the drama of reaction to action was to be conveyed to the audience) for two special reasons. In the first place, they liked declamation upon the stage. The great actor suddenly became the orator and stalked out to the front of the projecting platform to bellow forth his rhetoric-studded lines. Consequently, when the rant turned into subjective lyric poetry, like Hamlet's "To be or not to be," the actor's precedent for stalking forward, breaking the continuity of playing, seizing the stage and declaiming, was already accepted and liked. For this reason, the Elizabethan actor must have found these soliloquies much less awkward to deliver than the modern actor does.

There was another reason why the Elizabethans accepted their psychological comment in the form of purple
patches upon the action of the play. In many of the
novels and long prose tales which they were so fond of,
the narrative and dialogue would at intervals be inter-
rupted while the character spoke his or her mind in a
prose passage, separated from the main stream of the
story by a caption such as "Rosalind's Meditation." The
business of these meditations was to present in the character's own words, his dilemmas and debates with himself. Many a person sitting in the audience for *Hamlet*
and listening to those lyrical interruptions of the play had
learned as a reader to enjoy the same sort of interruption
in the Elizabethan novel. Thus two earlier conventions,
one of prose narrative and one of the stage, underwent a
brilliant metamorphosis and, with other ingredients
added, became a chief treasure of the Shakespearean
tragedies.

A parallel need for a convention of self-expression,
like the soliloquy, is present in modern drama. It is awkwardly met by Shaw, who, in his intent to deliver an
ultimatum upon some problem, disentangles his dustman
from his place in the play, places him upon a chair and
finds time for his harangue, while the plot stops in mid-
career and waits for him to finish. O'Neil carries the
necessity for inward revelation of character still further
by constructing his whole play on two levels, what the
character feels and what he says at any given moment.
He indicates the differences by differences in voice, if the

play is acted, or by difference of the size of type, if the play is printed.

This matching of common features in Shakespeare's plays with phases of modern popular drama on stage and screen, has distinct value. In the first place it reduces the elements of dramatic entertainment to their simplest form. When the incidental differences between two ages are swept away, one sees what is permanently effective. One sees, too, by this standard of measuring that Shakespeare's plays belong not primarily in literature but in life, that their ultimate values are simple and obvious. The fact that Shakespeare in meeting these plain require-ments has often bestowed upon them the magic of poetry and the flash of revelation is so much gain. It is not, how-ever, the essential thing to look for in reading him. The first thing to look for is the common denominator be-tween his success as an entertainer, the reasons in com-mon nature that underlie it, and the success of modern popular entertainment. Then the modern reader, look-ing back from here to there, from now to then, ap-proaches Shakespeare honestly and lets his entertain-ment work its sure effect.

It is easy enough for us to say, "We are simple and honest. We do take Shakespeare first of all as a purveyor of entertainment." Yet the weight of time, the centuries of praise, the reiteration of the word "classic" make it difficult to have a natural attitude toward his work. Vir-ginia Woolf has diagnosed the difficulty when she says that Shakespeare is "flyblown." When we are well, she

says, "his fame intimidates and bores and all the views
of all the critics dull in us that thunderclap of conviction. . . . Illness in its kingly sublimity sweeps all that
aside and leaves nothing but Shakespeare and oneself.
What with his overweening power and our overweening
arrogance, the barriers go down, the knots run smooth,
the brain rings and resounds with *Lear* and *Macbeth,* and
even Coleridge himself squeaks like a distant mouse." It
is not that one wishes the modern reader of Shakespeare
a fit of illness. But, well and in our right minds, we must
not allow the overlay of reverence to suffocate us.

CHAPTER X

Elizabethan Literature as its Own Public Saw It

How valuable, how really honest and representative
of the world of books and readers as they actually were,
is a twentieth century study of sixteenth century English
literature? That there were prose and poetry, plays and
novels, satire and sentiment, one has tangible proof in
the surviving volumes. But how correct is the emphasis
which we place on those volumes after the lapse of three
and a half centuries? When we have remarked the
changes in the style of prose, in the content and metre of
poetry, when we have seen stage plays develop from a
form naïve and stereotyped into a framework for the
pulsing of life itself, how far have we proceeded either
in an understanding of the people for whom these things
were written or in accounting for the changes and developments in the books themselves? How much more truly
can we explain their new emphases and new focuses as
the decades of that far-away century passed? At best we
cannot be sure that we have come very far. The books
that survive, large in number and bewilderingly various
in type, are only a small part of what was actually written and published. While in several instances we are sure
that the best has survived as the result of real excellence

and the wish to preserve that excellence, yet just as much more which we now possess is indifferent in quality and preserved purely by accident.

The ways, for instance, in which some of the most precious Shakespeare volumes have survived, show how haphazard and wanton has been the accident of their preservation. The first printed quarto of any of Shakespeare's plays, the *Titus Andronicus* of 1594, "a neat little pamphlet in a blue wrapper," must have lain in piles upon the open-air bookstalls "at the little North door of Paul's, at the Sign of the Gun" in the year when Shakespeare was only thirty and had his reputation still to make. Yet not a copy of that issue was available from the end of the seventeenth century till 1904 when, in Mr. Folger's words, "a Swedish gentleman whose ancestors were Scotch brought [a copy, the only existing copy] to the library at Lund, Sweden." Lying now in its bright blue wrapper in a glass case in the Folger Library in Washington, this paper-covered pamphlet is as fresh as when the London sun of three hundred and forty years ago shone down upon it.

Some Scotchman in London for a term of court, or stopping on his way home from a trip to Italy, may have picked it up. Here, he would feel, was something choice. For him it would be intrinsically different from any other copy of the same issue which he might procure by post in his far-away Scotland. At any rate, the volume for some reason had a special significance. It went over seas to Scandinavia. It lay safe from the ravages of dust and

sunlight in some old dark cupboard till the wealth of
caprice and accident which it accumulated in three centuries was worth thousands of twentieth century Ameri-
can dollars. The precious "Vincent First Folio" with a
contemporary presentation inscription from its printer,
Jaggard, to Vincent, the herald, turned up in 1907 in a
pile of old books in the coach-house of an English country estate. After such accidents of loss and re-discovery
one cannot be sure that Elizabethan literature as it sur-
vives to us is completely representative of that world of
books.

What of the people who wrote the books and the people who read them? How shall we guess even roughly
what aims the authors had before them and what success
they received at the hands of readers or the ears of listeners? For this query we are better prepared. For the
answer is not much harder for Elizabethan literature
than for recent literature. How do we know today, for
instance, what so recent an author as Kipling intended or
how his books struck his public? Old conversations can
be reported, old reviews of his books when they were
new can be re-read. But the quintessential truth will
almost certainly elude the searcher.

It is this fact that has, I think, discredited the usefulness of historical criticism in the minds of many people
in the modern world. The pieces of evidence, they say,
which survive either from Kipling or Shakespeare are so
incomplete. The essential things about them are too
nebulous for any evidence to catch. The far-reaching

and multitudinous reasons, for example, why empire and war seemed glorious to civilized peoples when Kipling wrote of these things, are already incomprehensible. The reconstructions of Kipling's emphases and Kipling's world which were made at his death cannot be entirely true or accurate. Time is indeed a "ceaseless lackey to eternity," but a lackey. The word implies that time follows the eternal thing at a little distance and behind, seeing and judging the acts of its master without the eyes of an equal. There is a good deal to discourage one from the effort to reconstruct the literature of the past as it was in that past. If it has something eternal in it, people say, we shall find it without the aid of historical critics. Whatever reconstructions of bygone taste and literary purpose these critics try to make, we shall not believe them because the task is hopeless.

But I do not believe that the task is hopeless. When all allowance is made for the accidental nature of our evidence and for our mistakes in generalizing from that evidence, there is an essential core of reality in the very phrase "Elizabethan literature." It has a positive quality which sets it off from mediæval or commonwealth or restoration or eighteenth century literature. Some peculiar way of trimming the scales, of estimating the value of those elements which make up our common humanity existed then. We call it by the word, Elizabethan. Its main lines are discoverable. Let us attempt, then, to name those lines.

Outside of the books themselves, there are certain

other kinds of evidence which illuminate this question, "What was Elizabethan literature like?" There is, for instance, some statistical evidence, if one may use a precise word for a very inexact set of records, about editions, titles and sale of books. From these records one can make certain deductions about the demands of the reading public. Closely related to this kind of evidence are a fairly large number of comments on the theatrical audience, what kinds of people attended the theatre, what they liked or disliked in the performances. Thus the taste of the public can be checked, to a certain extent, by evidence outside of the literature itself.

The reverse side of the coin, what the authors and publishers conceived as the public taste and how they strove to meet it, can also be reconstructed. The book advertising of the sixteenth century was not in periodicals and book reviews as it is today but in prefatory epistles attached to the books and thereby preserved. In these the author and sometimes the publisher presented "to the great variety of readers" those angles of the book which they thought would commend it, and commend it strongly enough to extract money from the reader's pocket. In these epistles, therefore, we can still see what the producer of the book considered its strongest and most popular points. Furthermore in the machinery which the government, both national and local, set up to control publication, to exclude from the printed page and the stage certain topics, one sees that the force of the reading public was to be reckoned with. As that public was handled it would either support the government and internal harmony or it would menace the established order. Thus from contemporary evidence about the reading and theatre-going public, from the nature of book advertising and the regulations of the government on publication and censorship, one can arrive at a top view of the state of English literature in the Elizabethan Age. If honestly compiled, this top view should furnish an interesting check on the critical estimate which is based on the books themselves.

The Elizabethan public, as is indicated in the range of phrases by which they were addressed in dedicatory epistles, comprised every class. First was the Court. Then came the citizens, a group which would ultimately become the "middle class." There were, too, the servants of these two classes and also the workers. The workers were apprenticed to this or that trade. They grew up in it. A worker might emerge into a proprietorship; more likely he would continue as a worker. The Court and its offshoots, the Universities and the Inns of Court, might be supposed to represent the sophisticated group of readers. There are many dedications addressed to this group: "To the Gentlemen Readers," "To the Gentlemen Scholars of both Universities." But the cleavage of classes was not distinct in the author's mind. He had, no doubt, learned by observation that there were dullards and boors with Court titles and many penetrating wits among citizenry and commoners. Greene made a fine show of dedicating many of his works to the Court. But his actual public lay wherever adventure, sentimentality and a dash of pastoral tradition could catch an ear. One dedication quite frankly embraces the public of all classes: "To the Young Gentlemen, Merchants, Apprentices, Farmers and Plain Countrymen." Toward the end of the century romance writers from among the workers themselves like Thomas Deloney would dedicate a book exclusively to their own class. "To all Cloth Workers in England" the dedication of Deloney's *Jack of Newbury* reads. By 1623, when the first complete collected edition of Shakespeare's plays was printed, the public who were invited to read and buy included all "from the most able to him that can but spell."

The evidence from these dedications about the elements which made up the Elizabethan reading public is good so far as it goes, but it does not go very far. It is chiefly valuable for showing that the taste of different conditions of men and the effect of this taste upon books was frankly recognized. But the sincerity of the address must often be questioned. Not only the "Dapper Monsieur pages of the Court" who are addressed in his Dedication read Nashe's picaresque novel, *Jack Wilton*. How he "that can but spell" could summon the necessary funds for that expensive 1623 folio of Shakespeare's plays is difficult to imagine. Of course the truth of the matter is that books and the men who read them will not stay in categories. Such books as Sidney's *Arcadia* and Lyly's *Euphues*, both of which were written and specifically dedicated to Court readers, were frequently reprinted in cheap editions and "must have been bought by many a well-to-do tradesman." [1] What one gathers, then, from these prefatory letters is that a reading public, various in taste and interest, was growing up and that the variety of its standards influenced the men who were writing.

It is perhaps fair to say in general that the outstanding thing which marks the development of all types of literature in the sixteenth century English world was a movement from what was external, explicit, objectively true to what was not content with this outside view of men or action. This newer type of literature saw something behind the external view of life, something more intricate, varying subtly with each character, each plot, each lyrical manifestation of love or sorrow. Quite naturally the portion of the reading public which most quickly responded to this deeper and more individual view of life was the Court. But other readers, too, responded to it. If they did not belong to this class by birth, at least by education and environment they had come to live by its standards. Spenser, Sidney, Marlowe, Shakespeare, Ralegh, Donne increasingly leavened the literary conventions and inheritances which they used with something personal and immediate. This thing was so close to man as he lived in contrast to man as he had been handled in literature, that it warms us today without benefit of erudition.

---

[1] For new evidence on the reading of Court literature by workers see Louis Wright, *Middle Class Culture in Elizabethan Literature,* Chapel Hill, 1935, *passim.*

Nashe and Greene and their friends would have written more in this vein if they could have afforded it. But they wrote for money and hence for the largest number of readers. Now the bulk of the reading public lay outside the Court, and, if one dares to generalise, had other tastes. They wanted action, adventure, happiness and misery wholesale. They craved fantasticality to relieve their humdrum. They liked their books to portray life painted in high and simple colours. They preferred a poster of life instead of a living portrait. Greene and Nashe and the whole troop of story-writers whose names do not even get into histories of Elizabethan literature, met this need. *The Short Title Catalogue of Books to 1640* gives an idea of their output. Louis B. Wright working over this "middle-class" literature has dared to say: "this huge outpouring of books could not have been printed if there had not been an enormous demand from the generality of citizens. The publishers of Elizabethan England could no more live by the custom of learned and aristocratic readers alone than our modern followers of their trade." This means that the bulk of books and readers was from the modern literary historian's point of view mediocre. The things that were most promising, the things that we read and re-read for their beauty, represent the taste of the minority. Reflective literature was fostered by this minority of readers. But for the bulk of readers action and adventure, simple joy and sorrow were all.

There was, however, a pervading element in all Elizabethan living and thinking, an element belonging to all classes and reflected in all kinds of books, which must be taken account of here. The period was transitional in more than the superficial sense of that word. The Elizabethan world had not fully come of age or, to put it differently, its diverse elements were not yet fused, had not come to easy terms with one another. There was an unreconciled opposition at the heart of that time. This opposition took a variety of forms. It caused Spenser, for instance, to swing from earthly to heavenly love, from pagan to Christian values, from romance to realism and back again without ever coming to grips with the opposing factors. He did not try to see whether they might not be two sides of the same things, two aspects of a single humanity. The love poetry of the period, too, alternated between sensuality and spirituality, between conventional description and description of specific feelings. The romances and fiction in general, including the drama, were never perfectly certain whether they were for amusement, for diversion in the finest sense of that word, or whether they needed to insert proverbial quips here and there, and discuss particular issues for their moral bearings.

Swung between one great system of thought in the Middle Ages and another just beginning, the Elizabethan felt life with extraordinary rightness. But if he was asked intellectually to analyse his feeling, to define it, he fell back upon tags of old or new. He presented nothing of his own which was articulate and well-rounded. It is this confusion, this necessary interim between two great ages, which lies behind the greatness and weakness of Elizabethan thought as a whole. When it is intuitive and immediate, it is often great. When it tries to make an intellectual and articulate approach to the meaning of life, it stumbles. It is Bacon's triumph over this difficulty which makes him belong essentially with the next age. Ralegh and Shakespeare may have striven toward an articulate view of life. Happily for us, however, they did not find it so strong as their intuitive and immediate approach. Because of this fact they belong essentially to the Elizabethan world. A reader of Elizabethan books cannot afford to forget for a moment this unreconciled opposition which was at the bottom of both life and literature then. The fact goes a long way toward explaining the first- and third-rate lines that house together in a single sonnet; the excellence and claptrap that combine in a play by Marlowe; the convention and revolt that fight it out through the pages of Shakespeare's .First Folio.

The Elizabethans were, for instance, equally interested in literature handled as art and in literature handled for its moral lesson. They still had a sincere interest in morality, in actual rules of conduct, in ethics on its practical side. This interest was forced upon men and women of all classes by the world they lived in. The accepted standards of conduct, religious and secular, of the preceding age had been weakened or actually taken away. In their place nothing clearly and explicitly new had been presented. The individual of whatever class, cut off from a regular code of behaviour much as he has been in our own day, simply had to make for himself a working set of rules for the guidance of life. Even in a novel he wanted discussion of morals in order that he might have some light on his own problem of getting through life. Spenser knew this when he wrote *The Faerie Queene*. It is many other things beside a moral poem on conduct, but it is that, too. Greene, writing sentimental trash for whoever would read, could reckon on interest in morality. The modern reader rebels against this explicit morality. Yet the reason for it is clear and lies deep in the conditions of Elizabethan life.

The audience at the public theatre was really a special division of the reading public. In descriptions of the London theatres by travellers, and especially in the satiric pictures of fashion and folly that frequented the playhouses, one finds what kinds of people went there and what their reaction was to the art of fiction in drama. The audience was very representative. It had people from every class. It included both men and women and there was always a noisy contingent of boy apprentices. In fact attending the public theatre was not a matter of class. It is true that the chief restrictions imposed upon performances came from a group in the citizen class, from the mayor and corporation of the City of London. It is also true that Puritan opposition to the theatre existed chiefly in the citizen class. Yet it will not do to count out citizens from a typical audience at a public theatre. They were there in large numbers. Beaumont and Fletcher's citizen grocer and his wife in *The Knight of the Burning Pestle* are only one of the many cases in point.

More important than any division of taste on class lines in a theatre audience, is the question of how they responded to what they saw. It may seem ridiculous to argue that what they saw when the plays were acted before them, was something very different from what we see when we read these plays. Yet from their own comments, from the method of acting and from their taste in non-dramatic literature, one is warranted in assuming that to Elizabethan eyes and ears an Elizabethan play was very different from what it appears to be today. To people like Essex or Donne or Ralegh or Hamlet if he had gone to the play it undoubtedly was very much the same. The intellectual vanguard of the Court world, the people who wrote and read the new poetry and satire would miss none of the individualisation, none of the reflective poetry of Shakespeare's best plays. But these people would be a minority in a public theatre. By and large the Elizabethan plays outside of Shakespeare and even a good deal of Shakespeare still presented plotting and characterisation which were naïve and external. Dramatists still relied on type character and melodramatic situation or clownish moment. We have no warrant that the Elizabethan theatre public placed these things so far below Shakespeare's greatest character delineation and plotting as we do.

In fact, the more one looks at the Elizabethan stage as a whole the more one inclines to believe that Shakespeare, being for all time, has kept faith with literary taste far beyond his own time, but has also kept faith with his own age. The beauties which so ravish us certainly were not, for the great majority of his audience, the chief pleasures of his plays. The crudities which we condone were surely not crudities in their eyes. They came to the theatre with a different requirement for fiction and a different ideal of characterisation. C. J. Sisson was right when he maintained in 1924 in a brilliant study of Elizabethan public taste that Shakespeare's sense of plot and character was the exception not the rule in dramatic production. Karl Young and E. E. Stoll have done much for the correct study of Shakespeare by emphasising this fact.

On the other hand, the contemporary play-goer found things in the Elizabethan plays which the modern reader misses or from which he fails to get pleasure. We have no such ear as the Elizabethan for listening to poetry or prose, no such quickness for perceiving double meaning. As for the moralising, the epigrammatic couplets or wise saws out of Seneca, those are things which no longer touch us. Yet they were intensely interesting to the Elizabethan audience. That audience had, too, a gift for seeing the characters and situations not only for what they obviously represented but for what they symbolised. This faculty came from a long training in discovering both a literal and an allegorical meaning in biblical and secular literature. It is a faculty in which the modern reader is utterly deficient. Partly because of this capacity to slide back and forth between two levels of value in a single play, I believe the Elizabethan accepted a different idea of plot motivation from ours. As long as the events were removed from reality, they might happen unrealistically, provided they made the plot pleasant and intricate. When, however, these events moved nearer to the circumstances of contemporary life, as they might in the same play, then they must take place as they probably would in the Elizabethan's own world. The incongruity between using the technique of fairy-tale plotting and the technique of realistic plotting all in one play, did not disturb them as it does us.

Another strong light upon Elizabethan literature is cast by the kinds of things which the government felt necessary to censor in books and plays. The central government fought to maintain internal peace in England while the country was coming to maturity and growing into one of the first-rate powers of renaissance Europe. Nothing small or large which menaced this internal equilibrium was beneath their attention. There was a strict control of printing-presses, a limited list of approved publishers and a censorship of the contents of books and plays. The carrying out of this control was thorough and rigorous. Playwrights were thrown into prison, books were banned, whole editions were bought up and burned.

This government supervision through the nature of the things it censored, throws light on the literature. In general its objections were to specific details: to oaths rather than to the discussion of religious principles; to the caricature of persons prominent in Court or Church. The play of *Sir Thomas More*, for example, was sent back by the censor with many minute changes required. The censor's objection was not to the discussion of a social idea running through the play. He minded the presentation on the stage of a riot against Lombard and French aliens in London. It was feared that the scene might by its concrete example foment the actual troubles between imported and native labour. This labour situation was particularly acute in London in 1586, 1592-3 and 1595, in any of which years the play may have been written. There is about such censorship as this an air of small-town personal politics, a rather picayune snatching at trifles. It was not founded upon broad constructive principles.

But, one may say, this is always the story of censorship in whatever country or century it may occur. One grants that. Yet the existence of this literal kind of surveillance over literature in that age is significant of a great lack in the age. I have said above that the Elizabethan Age was not completely mature. In social theory, it was well behind the Continent. It left to the seventeenth century in England a tremendous burden of social thinking. What Elizabeth and her advisers had to secure was a period of *status quo* in government and religion while the country caught up to itself in power, in education, in financial security. During this period there was plenty of speculation about man on earth, what he was and how he came to be that way. But about man as a political being,[1] in the theoretical sense of that word, the Elizabethan thinking was naïve. It was expressed poetically as in Ralegh's *History of the World* or practically in the manifold niggling restrictions of practical censorship.

The nature of literary censorship, therefore, emphasises a condition of Elizabethan literature; namely that it is lacking in anything approaching the great literature of propaganda. It left the underlying theory of social England alone, as Shaw or Ibsen or Wells or our most recent proletarian writers do not let their social world alone. To be sure it ridiculed with wit and acumen those absurd types of Puritan or fop or pedant which the system produced. But the ridicule of social types is very different from exposing the fundamental flaws in the social system which makes them. With or without the restrictions against presenting English politics or English religion on the stage, one doubts very much whether Shakespeare would have written differently, whether his plays would have had more to say about social theory. Probably he did not have an articulated social theory. The principles underlying the nature of society are strongly implied, of course, in both *Lear* and *Troilus and Cressida*. But they are only implied. Character, what man makes of himself in this world, is, of course, a sub-

---

[1] For two important new discussions of the backgrounds of Elizabethan social thinking, see J. B. Black, *The Reign of Elizabeth* in The Oxford History of England Series, Oxford, 1936, Chapters VI through VIII; and Hardin Craig, *The Enchanted Glass,* Oxford Press (N. Y.) 1936, *passim.*

ject for endless speculation in his plays. That particular phase of man, however, which presents him in relation to a definite society, as a political being, is relatively unexplored.

From the kinds of people who read or heard Elizabethan literature in its day, from their reaction to it, from the aims of the authors who wrote it, and from the censors who attempted to control it, what general impression does one receive? I think one feels first that it was a literature in the making, putting out experiments in various directions. On the whole it was a literature of promise not of achievement. The accident of a genius born and functioning in any age, as Shakespeare functioned in the Elizabethan Age, must not blind one to the nature of the period as a whole. There are great moments in the literature of many Elizabethan authors. But even Marlowe is promising rather than maturely great, completely realised. As a whole the period reflects an uncertain and changing world. If one does not like beginnings, promise, experiment, if one does not find the business of emergence as fascinating as fulfillment, then one will not like Elizabethan literature. While literature is always emerging and every age is in process of becoming another, this is particularly true of the Elizabethan Age. There is more of the literature of ultimate achievement in the seventeenth or eighteenth or early nineteenth centuries in England.

There were many reasons which made Elizabethan literature uneven. There was pressure from a great variety of public groups, differing in taste and demand. There was uncertainty about standards. There was a wish to include in one's method everything that was good in the past. Yet authors wished to contribute something new, something immediately and authentically drawn from experience. It was a wish too complicated to be successfully fulfilled. Elizabethan literature is a great prelude. It stands on the verge of achievement.

It is one of the romantic features of English literary history that the achievement which was potential in Elizabethan literature was not only never attained but could never be attained. Elizabethan ideas were submerged in the seventeenth century and cut off forever. The slow evolution of a mediæval into a modern world, which the sixteenth century so gallantly undertook, was destroyed by the seventeenth century. The new scientific world which had existed already on the Continent during the sixteenth century and to which Elizabethan England turned a deaf ear, caught the new England of the seventeenth century and claimed it for its own. This new seventeenth century England was a beautiful thing but a thing considerably different from the sixteenth. The valiant compromise which the sixteenth century began would never be completed now. In the late eighteenth century Warton and Wordsworth and in the early nineteenth Keats began again to turn the pages of Spenser. Samuel Johnson in 1765 found magnificently right things to say about the dramatic art of Shakespeare. He was followed in the early nineteenth century by Coleridge, Lamb and Hazlitt, that trio romantically enamoured of Shakespeare's genius. With them the prestige of the sixteenth century was restored. But such strong and different ideas had grown up in the two centuries that intervened, that these men's praise was greater than their understanding. They looked backward from another and alien world. No matter how great its idolatry, its spiritual kinship with the Elizabethans, it was bound to falter in its interpretation. The later nineteenth and early twentieth centuries have not failed in their homage. Yet the Elizabethan Age in literature still stands, for all our praise, a period eloquent in a promise which has never been fulfilled.

READING LIST

This is not an exhaustive bibliography on the subject nor is it a complete list of the books consulted by the author for the present volume. It is intended as a practical guide for the general reader who wishes to follow further the subjects discussed in these chapters.

CHAPTER I. BACKGROUND: VALUES OF LIFE IN SIXTEENTH CENTURY ENGLAND

Allen, J. W., *A History of Political Thought in the Sixteenth Century,* London, 1928.
Interesting and authoritative approach to some essential problems of society.

Black, J. B., *The Reign of Elizabeth* in The Oxford History of England Series, Oxford, 1936.
Chapters VII, VIII and IX contain important and interesting new material on the state of political, economic and scientific thinking in the Elizabethan world.

Burckhardt, J., *The Civilization of the Renaissance in Italy,* tr. S. G. C. Middlemore, with 243 illus., New York, n.d.
A classic on Renaissance Italy toward which the Elizabethan mind was frequently turned.

Byrne, M. St. C., *Elizabethan Life in Town and Country,* London, 1925.
A vivid reconstruction of many phases of Elizabethan life based on unusual original sources.

Craig, Hardin, *The Enchanted Glass, The Elizabethan Mind,* Oxford Press (N. Y.), 1936.

The first attempt to collect in one volume the position of Elizabethan thought on all important social and individual questions.

Garvin, K., ed., *The Great Tudors,* New York, 1935.

Forty-two studies by as many authorities on great figures, political and literary, of the sixteenth century. Important and interesting.

Greenlaw, Edwin, *The Province of Literary History,* Baltimore, 1931.

Chapter II "Transcript of Life" contains valuable material on the Elizabethan idea of history and the past and the peculiar province of poetry. Important and not to be found elsewhere.

Grierson, H. J. C., *Cross Currents in English Literature of the XVIIth Century,* London, 1929.

An authoritative book on ideas and values which lay behind the renaissance world.

Hall, Hubert S., *Society in the Elizabethan Age,* London, 1901.

Harrison, G. B., *Elizabethan Journals* (1591-1603), 3 vols., London, 1928-33.

"A record of those things most talked of" during the last twelve years of Elizabeth's reign. Compiled from pamphlets and records of all sorts. An illumination of everyday life. Important.

Harrison, G. B., *The Letters of Queen Elizabeth,* London, 1935.

Important new collection by an authority.

Innes, A. D., "England under the Tudors" (Oman's *History of England,* Vol. IV), New York, 1905.

Neale, J. E., *Queen Elizabeth,* New York, 1934.

A new authoritative and interesting life.

Pollard, A. F., *Henry VIII,* New York, 1930.

Pollard, A. F., "History of England from the Accession of Edward VI to the Death of Elizabeth" (Vol. VI of Hunt and Poole's *Political History of England*), London, 1910.

Potter, G. R., *Elizabethan Verse and Prose* (non-dramatic), New York, 1928.
A good anthology of sixteenth century literature.

Raleigh, Sir Walter, ed., *Shakespeare's England*, 2 vols., 1916.
In thirty chapters authorities in each field cover the various phases of Elizabethan life. Fully illustrated and indexed. Special bibliographies. The authority on this subject.

Saintsbury, G., *A History of Elizabethan Literature*, London, 1903.

Schelling, F. E., *English Literature during the Lifetime of Shakespeare*, New York, 1910.

Taylor, H. O., *Thought and Expression in the Sixteenth Century*, 2 vols., New York, 1920.
Interesting book for intellectual background of the century.

Woolf, Virginia, *Orlando*, New York, 1928.
A fanciful biography which in its opening sections gives an interesting conception of Elizabethan life.

CHAPTER II. THE PROGRESS OF POETRY ACROSS THE CENTURY

Arber, E., ed., *Tottel's Miscellany, Songs and Sonnets* (Arber's English Reprints), 1921.
A reprint of a mid-sixteenth-century collection of early Tudor poetry by Wyatt, Surrey and others. Very interesting.

Berdan, J. M., *Early Tudor Poetry*, New York, 1920.
Ideas, setting and the poetry itself interpreted.

Tillyard, E. M. W., *The Poetry of Sir Thomas Wyatt*, London, 1929.
A selection of Wyatt's poems and a critical study.

CHAPTER III. THE POETRY OF THE NINETIES

Ault, Norman, *Elizabethan Lyrics*, New York, 1925.
A valuable collection of the lighter Elizabethan lyrics and songs.

Brett, Cyril, ed., *Drayton's Minor Poems,* Oxford, 1907.

Bush, Douglas, *Mythology and the Renaissance Tradition in English Poetry,* Minnesota Press, 1932.
An important and spirited approach to some phases of Elizabethan poetry.

Chambers, E. K., *The Oxford Book of Sixteenth Century Verse,* Oxford, 1932.

Hebel, J. W. and Hudson, H. H., ed., *Poetry of the English Renaissance,* 1509-1660, New York, 1929.
A useful selection from the poetry of the period, well printed with interesting notes and appendices. Very desirable.

Sprague, A. C., *Samuel Daniel, Poems and a Defence of Ryme,* Cambridge (Mass.), 1930.

CHAPTER IV. SPENSER

de Selincourt, E., ed., *Poetical Works of Spenser,* Oxford, 1916.
Definitive edition of Spenser's poems with long, critical introduction.

Jones, H. S. V., *A Spenser Handbook,* New York, 1930.
A valuable history and interpretation of Spenser.

van Winkle, Cortlandt, ed., *Spenser's Epithalamion,* New York, 1926.

CHAPTER V. RALEGH AND THE "NEW" POETRY

Edwards, E., *The Life of Sir Walter Ralegh,* 2 vols., London, 1868.
A great deal of original material. Useful.

Grierson, H. J. C., ed., *The Poems of John Donne,* 2 vols., Oxford, 1912.
The definitive edition of Donne's poetry with a volume of comment and a critical essay.

Latham, A. M. C., ed., *The Poems of Sir Walter Ralegh,* Boston, 1929.
All of Ralegh's poems with an account of their preservation in manuscript, their printing, and a valuable critical essay.

Spencer, T., ed., *A Garland for John Donne,* Cambridge (Mass.), 1931.
Essays by several hands presenting Donne from several angles. Stimulating.

CHAPTER VI. THE PROGRESS OF PROSE ACROSS THE CENTURY

Chambers, R. W., "The continuity of English Prose from Alfred to More" in N. Harpefield's *Life and Death of Sir. Thos. More,* ed., E. V. Hitchcock, London, 1932.
Very important study establishing continuity of English prose from late middle ages to renaissance. New evidence.

Hadow, G. E., ed., *Sir Walter Raleigh, Selections from his History of the World, his Letters, etc.,* Oxford, 1926.
A charming book containing some of Ralegh's most famous prose.

Krapp, G. P., *The Rise of English Literary Prose,* New York, 1915.
Invaluable study of development of English prose.

Matthiessen, F. O., *Translation an Elizabethan Art,* Cambridge (Mass.), 1931.
A study both of the material and method of Elizabethan translation. Illuminates the whole Elizabethan point of view.

CHAPTER VII. THE BACKDROP FOR ELIZABETHAN DRAMA

Baker, E. A., *History of the English Novel,* London, 1924, vol. II.
Important comment on narrative fiction in the Elizabethan Age.

Chambers, E. K., *The Mediæval Stage,* 2 vols., Oxford, 1903.

Kastner, L. E., and Charlton, H. B., ed., *Poetical Works of William Alexander,* Scottish Test Society, 1921.
Very interesting discussion of the influence of Seneca on Elizabethan drama.

Lucas, F. L., *Seneca and Elizabethan Tragedy,* Cambridge (England), 1922.
Spirited and provocative.

Owst, G. R., *Literature and the Pulpit in Mediæval England,* Cambridge (England), 1933.
Important new evidence for the influence of the mediæval sermon on renaissance drama.

Pollard, A. W., *English Miracle Plays, Moralities and Interludes,* Oxford, 1909.
Valuable introduction.

Reed, A. W., *Early Tudor Drama,* London, 1926.
Important study of drama in the circle of Sir Thomas More and the early Tudors.

Withington, R., *English Pageantry, An Historical Outline,* 2 vols., Harvard, 1918.
Important book on a phase of drama too little studied.

Wright, L. B., *Middle Class Culture in Elizabethan England,* North Carolina Press, 1935.
Important new material on the Elizabethan reading public. Bearing upon drama.

CHAPTER VIII. GREAT ELIZABETHAN DRAMATISTS WHO CREATED THEIR PLAYS AGAINST THIS BACKDROP

Bradbrook, M. C., *Elizabethan Stage Conditions,* Cambridge (England), 1932.

Bradbrook, M. C., *Themes and Conventions of Elizabethan Tragedy,* Cambridge (England), 1935.
A new approach to the effect of acted drama. Very suggestive.

Chambers, E. K., *The Elizabethan Stage,* 4 vols., Oxford, 1923.

The definitive detailed survey of the Elizabethan theatre.

Dunn, E. C., ed., *Eight Famous Elizabethan Plays,* New York (Modern Library), 1932.

Eliot, T. S., *Selected Essays* (1917-32), New York, 1932.

Illuminating essays from a particular modern point of view on some Elizabethan dramatists.

Ellis, Fermor, U. M., *The Jacobean Drama, an Interpretation,* London, 1936.

An important new interpretation of both dramatic structure and content of the great plays after 1600. Provocative and essentially valuable.

Neilson, W. A., *Chief Elizabethan Dramatists, excluding Shakespeare,* Boston, 1911.

Schelling, F. E., *Elizabethan Playwrights,* New York, 1928.

A valuable critical survey of the whole field.

Sisson, C. J., *Le Goût Public et le théâtre élisabéthain,* Dijon, 1922.

Sprightly and original study from new material, of the Elizabethan theatre audience.

Sisson, C. J., *Lost Plays of Shakespeare's Age,* Cambridge (England) and Macmillan (N. Y.), 1936.

Important discoveries of the way in which contemporary events, London trials, etc., were used as the basis of plays.

Spencer, Theodore, *Death and Elizabethan Tragedy,* Harvard, 1936.

Interesting comment on changing ideas of death and its handling in Elizabethan tragedy. One facet of a general change in the emphasis of renaissance thought.

CHAPTER IX. SHAKESPEARE FOR MODERNS

Adams, J. Q., *A Life of William Shakespeare,* Boston, 1923.

The definitive life of Shakespeare. Full and interesting.

Baldwin, T. W., *William Shakespeare Adapts a Hanging*, Princeton, 1931.

An interesting argument for the reproduction of a contemporary event in a play by Shakespeare.

Bartlett, H. C., *Mr. William Shakespeare, Original and Early Editions of his Quartos and Folios, his Source Books and those containing Contemporary Notices*, New Haven, 1923.

Contemporary books, with important quotations and interesting description.

Boas, F. S., *Shakespeare and the Universities*, New York, 1923.

Possible contemporary performances of Shakespeare at Oxford and Cambridge. Interesting sidelight.

Brooke, C. F. Tucker, *Shakespeare of Stratford*, a handbook, in Yale Shakespeare Series, 1926.

Good arrangement of material, charts, and essay on "Shakespeare of Stratford."

Campbell, L. B., *Shakespeare's Tragic Heroes*, Cambridge (England), 1930.

Elizabethan theories of behaviour and ideas of morality which are reflected in Shakespeare's treatment of the tragic hero. Provocative.

Chambers, E. K., *William Shakespeare*, 2 vols., Oxford, 1930.

A full and complete record up to the latest material, on every phase of Shakespearean study. With a critical estimate. The definitive volume in this field.

Ebisch, W. and Schücking, L. L., *A Shakespeare Bibliography*, Oxford, 1931.

A volume of classified bibliography. Useful.

Harrison, G. B. and Granville-Barker, H., ed., *A Companion to Shakespeare Studies*, New York, 1934.

A valuable survey of the various angles of Shakespearean study by authorities. With reading lists.

Hotson, L., *Shakespeare versus Shallow,* Boston, 1931.
Evidence for the adaptation of some contemporary events and persons in Shakespeare's plays.

Mackail, J. W., *The Approach to Shakespeare,* Oxford, 1930.
A modern literary approach to Shakespeare by a distinguished English critic.

Neilson, W. A., *The Complete Dramatic and Poetic Works of Shakespeare,* Boston, 1906 (one volume).
Dr. Neilson's own text.

Neilson, W. A., and Thorndike, A. H., *The Facts About Shakespeare,* New York, 1931.
Various phases of study in authoritative and compact form.

Neilson, W. A., and Thorndike, A. H., *The Tudor Shakespeare,* 40 vols., New York, 1911-13.

Nicoll, Allardyce, *Studies in Shakespeare,* London, 1927.
Provocative modern approach.

Parrott, T. M., *William Shakespeare, A Handbook,* Scribners, 1934.
A new and delightful book, authoritative and entertaining, on Shakespeare's life, times and work.

Plimpton, George A., *The Education of Shakespeare,* Oxford, 1933.
Shakespeare's schoolbooks beautifully illustrated from the author's own collection.

Raleigh, Sir Walter, *Shakespeare,* London, 1926.
An interpretation of Shakespeare by the late Sir Walter Raleigh of Oxford. Stimulating and important.

Smith, Logan Pearsall, *On Reading Shakespeare,* New York, 1933.
Witty and stimulating approach for the layman by a distinguished writer of prose.

Sprague, A. C., *Shakespeare and the Audience,* Cambridge (Mass.), 1935.
An arresting reconstruction of what the Elizabethan audience saw and heard and its psychology of attention.

Spurgeon, C. F. E., *Shakespeare's Imagery and What It Tells Us,* Cambridge (England), 1935.

A new and original method for testing the contents of an author's mind and imagination. Important.

Stoll, E. E., *Art and Artifice in Shakespeare,* Cambridge (England), 1933.

A modern scholar presents some new critical approaches to some of Shakespeare's plays.

Wilson, J. Dover, *The Essential Shakespeare,* New York, 1932.

A daring reconstruction of Shakespeare's life by an authority.

Wilson, J. Dover and Quiller-Couch, Sir A., *The New Cambridge Shakespeare* (a volume to a play), Cambridge (England), 1921 seq. (In progress.)

An edition incorporating the newest theories about Elizabethan play-manuscripts in theatre and printing-house, with important and revolutionary critical angles.

CHAPTER X. ELIZABETHAN LITERATURE AS ITS OWN PUBLIC SAW IT

Gebert, C., ed., *An Anthology of Elizabethan Dedications and Prefaces,* Philadelphia, 1933.

Through this collection, one gathers the point of view of the Elizabethan reading public.

Smith, G. Gregory, ed., *Elizabethan Critical Essays,* 2 vols., Oxford, 1904.

Important contemporary essays on the theory and practice of prose and poetry.

INDEX

INDEX

The author wishes to call attention to the analytic index under the following subjects:

Drama, Elizabethan
Literary Taste, Elizabethan
Poetry, Elizabethan
Prose, Elizabethan
Sonnet, Elizabethan

323